Endorsements for *Journey Through Ten Thousand Veils*

"*Journey Through Ten Thousand Veils* contains Maryam Kabeer Faye's autobiographical account of her life long search to become closer to God, ultimately via Sufism, in Islam, and what a journey it is! The memoir is all the more impressive, because the author is a historical person in her own right. This book will be highly valuable to any seekers of God, as Faye examines all of the multiple dimensions of a quest. It is also a treasure as a record of a precious and significant part of American Muslim History."

—Khalid Yahya Blankinship,
Head of Graduate Studies, Department of
Religion, Temple University, Phila, PA

"This is Islamic Sufism from the inside; powerful, authentic, and inspiring. Read this book and believe."

—Marcia Hermansen
Director, Islamic World Studies Program,
Loyola University Chicago

"This book will no doubt be an inspiration to many readers. It will lead many to join her on this blessed pilgrimage."

—Mahmoud Ayoub
Professor Emeritus Temple University,
Professor of Islamic Studies & Christian-
Muslim Relations, Hartford Seminary

"Maryam opens spiritual doorways for readers of many religions and cultures, through which they will be able to recognize the profound and wonderful importance of their lives at this very moment and thereby enter the timeless reality of the spiritual path."

—Alan Godlas
Professor of Islamic Studies Department
of Religion, University of Georgia

"Faye's journey with her son to Medina and Mecca, and their visit to the Ka'bah, is probably the most exaltedly symphonic and overwhelming, of her pivotal experiences in the book, as she journeys in her relentless search for transformative liberation and the Truth of Certainty."

—Daniel Abdal-Hayy Moore
Poet, The Ecstatic Exchange

"Maryam Kabeer Faye lifts the veils to expose the spiritual bond between God, humans, and all lives. She shows her reader that life can be lived, should be lived, by seeking nearness to God."

—Aisha Michelle Byng, Ph.D.,
Department of Sociology,
Temple University, Philadelphia

In the Name of God
the Merciful
the Compassionate,
My Dear Sister Denise,
It is a blessing
and a joy to meet you

JOURNEY THROUGH TEN THOUSAND VEILS

The Alchemy of Transformation on the Sufi Path

on the sacred journey,
to celebrate the Divine
Unity and unite in the
light — May the

Maryam Kabeer Faye mission
of the Unity Church
be victorious and may
we all be servants
& instruments of

NEW JERSEY • LONDON • FRANKFURT • CAIRO

this beautiful truth

www.
Kashmir
dream.com

TUGHRA
BOOKS
New Jersey

Abundant
Blessings
+ Peace

Sheikha Maryam
215 605 3944

unite in the
light.org

Published by Tughra Books
335 Clifton Avenue, Clifton
New Jersey 07011, USA

www.tughrabooks.com

Library of Congress Cataloging-in-Publication Data
Faye, Maryam Kabeer.
  Journey through ten thousand veils : the alchemy of transformation on the Sufi path / Maryam Kabeer Faye.
    p. cm.
  ISBN 978-1-59784-135-1 (pbk.)
  1. Faye, Maryam Kabeer. 2. Sufis--Biography. 3. Sufism. I. Title.
  BP80.F413A3 2009
  297.4092--dc22
  [B]
                                                              2008054953

Printed by
Çağlayan A.Ş., Izmir - Turkey

On the road that leads to the Beloved
Every stone is made of gold.
Every step we take brings knowledge to us.
Even what appears to be a mistake, or an error,
Can bring us closer to purity and truth.
Every good intention, thought and action
Guides the soul toward the Goal.
Every true word that is heard,
Every understanding received,
Every challenge met,
Every station, by God's Grace, attained
Leads the traveler
Through the labyrinth
Of steps and tests
Surely, to the One
Who has left, at every turn in the Road,
Signs of His Existence,
Clear signs showing the Way
That leads to Him.

Not only do our successes show us the way,
But even more deeply, our apparent failures
Those moments in our journey
When we are most deeply humbled
And realize our limitations,
Realizing that every step we take
Is not due to our own power or will,
But occurs by the Grace of God.

The journey that leads to the Beloved
Is guided by His Love.

The traveler is like a leaf
Blown in the wind of the Divine Will.
I was blown from one place to the next
Then, carried to another place, and on and on.

Thus was I guided, without doubt,
And witnessed on every mountain path
And in every valley, in every city, on every street,
The signs that He unveiled before my eyes,
Signs of His Love, His Power, and His Truth,
The signposts clearly delineating His path,
That the Beloved enabled me to see.

I was guided in my journey
To see and love deeply
Lands and people of great beauty
That, no longer exist,
Lands and people that can never be found again
In this world,
But are alive in my heart.
They are alive within me,
And it is my loving duty
To bear witness
To their life and legacy.

By the Grace of God, the Most Merciful,
I was guided through the countries
To appreciate all the details of the life there
That I could see,
Before the devastating flood covered the land.

In this very lifetime
I have witnessed
The vast transformations
Of the earth, the nations, the peoples,
Powerful natural disasters,
As well as wars and oppressions,
All of which elicit
The deepest prayer, supplication, and compassion.

I met, on the journey, the ancient ones.
And received the gifts that they placed in my hands
Before they left this world, and went on their way.

What remains of all the places and the people,
That we have met along the way,
After the form of the flower has wilted
And disappeared, back into the earth,
Is the essence of the fragrance,
The essence of the truth that they imparted to us
In the precious time allotted
Before they left this world,
Leaving us to carry on the work and the journey.

And the underlying truth revealed
Through all that we are witnessing and learning
Is, as the Holy Qur'an tells us,
(As difficult as it is for us,
*   ultimately, to grasp)*

"And everything perishes
But the face of your Lord." (The Holy Qur'an, Rahman 55:26–27)

I pose the question to myself:
How can a creature that will perish
Comprehend this truth?

In every land through which I traveled
In my search,
I found the pieces of a puzzle,
Pieces of beautiful, colored glass.
Piece by piece, every piece found its place
In the stained glass window—my life
Until, the picture began to be complete.
And then, suddenly the Divine Light,
Nur Muhammadiyyah,
Came shining through,
Illuminating the total picture,
Causing my soul to proclaim,
"What a wonder!
So that is what it was all about!"

I followed the map
Only God gave me,
And was led from one situation and station
To the next,
From one Teacher to the next,
Everywhere, in every land and in every state,
In every holy place and gathering,
Collecting clues and messages,
Following the guidance
As it was given.

Thus, step- by- step
Through the stages of awakening,
The stages of acceptance, understanding, and healing,
I followed the light of guidance
To its Source and End.

I came to see
That, behind every veil,
Is the One, who sees all,
And behind every occurrence
Is the Hand that moves all,
And not a leaf falls,
But He knows it
And He wills it.

What makes every detail
Of this story sacred and significant,
Is that He willed it.
These are the messages, the gifts
That the Creator, Most Kind, gave to me
As He drew me
Through the veils of karmic bondage
Into the light, the liberation,
Of submission and divine peace.

Along the way,
I came to see
That it is not my business
To judge the people

That I happened to meet along the way,
They are all instruments of my awakening,
Just as I, am an instrument of theirs.

We see, as we continue to travel
In the way of God,
That there are no accidents
Or mistakes.
Every stone that we walk on,
Every piece of ground that we cover
Is a part of the Way, itself.
And every stage,
Every new level of awareness
Is a preparation for the one, which will follow it.

To reach each new step,
We must let go of the one that went before it.
The past is gone.
We must let it go.
The person that we thought we were
Is like water in the river that has passed by.
What is awaiting us, at every stage of the journey,
Is an unlimited new dimension of awareness,
That we cannot attain, except by letting go
Of at least some of the false concepts and patterns
That we had been dragging along with us
And, are now, ready to release.

Sometimes the veils are washed away
In the rain of Divine Mercy,
And sometimes, they are burned away
In the fire of Divine Love.

Moment by Moment,
Stage by stage,
The divine alchemy,
If we are willing and able to go through
The complete process,
Is powerful and intense.
Sometimes we wish we could get out of that fire,

And just go for a pleasant walk in the park.
But we are like fetuses in the divine womb
And we cannot come out of the fire
Until, we are gold.

Just as the baby becomes perfectly formed
In the womb
And then, exactly at the right moment, emerges—
What an amazing divine process!
Like this, does our soul—the purified life
Emerge from the crucible
Radiant with the light of God,
Its own true nature.

Such is the nature of the profound process
Of transformation, and once we have begun,
we must go all the way through
That deep tunnel,
Like the birth canal.
We cannot turn back.

As difficult as it seems to be
To carry on, from time to time,
What an amazing journey it is -
The journey of unveiling,
The journey of the opening of our inner eye!
What I saw, in the beginning,
Through a glass, darkly,
Is becoming,
Through the process of unveiling,
Brilliantly clear.

In truth, what I saw was always perfectly clear.
It was I who was obscured
And could see it only through
The densities of veils.
But the truth within me
Was magnetically drawn to the truth
In whatever form it was hidden.

Every where I traveled, I searched for the treasures—
The Divine Attributes and Messages,
And found them in every land
Manifesting in different people and places,
More, or less clearly.

Wherever I saw them,
Sometimes, even, hidden in the dust,
I recognized their great value
And collected them into my heart,
Saying, "This is what I was looking for!"

And, thus, through traveling for the sake of God,
Has the heart of the seeker for truth
Been restructured in the form of truth
For as we gather the treasures of Divine Knowledge
Into our heart, in truth, we become united with
That, for which we have been seeking.

I sought my Beloved
Everywhere that He led me,
And there was not a moment in the journey
Of my seeking Him
That He was not with me.
No doubt, I felt it,
And my heart was warmed and enflamed
By His nearness,
And yet, I had to continue to travel,
For years and years,
Penetrating the veils.

As close as He was,
I could not find Him and know Him,
Until, I came to know myself.

But, what is this knowing?
Knowing myself in Him
Is to be the drop
That disappears in the Ocean.

CONTENTS

1

Impressions Which Formed Me

Southern California, 1946–62

"Each second we live is a new and unique moment of the universe,
a moment that never was before and will never be again.
And what do we teach our children in school?
We teach them that two and two make four,
And, that Paris is the capital of France.
When will we also teach them what they are?
You should say to each of them:
Do you know what you are?
You are unique.
In all the world, there is no other child exactly like you.
In the millions of years that have passed
There has never been a child like you.
And look at your body—what a wonder it is!
Your legs, your arms, your cunning fingers, the way you move!
You may be a Shakespeare, a Michelangelo, a Beethoven.
You have the capacity for anything.
Yes, you are a marvel."

Pablo Casals

I was born as a mystery within mystery, descending to this earth and manifesting here for a reason known only to the One who created me and sent me here. The mystery of where I came from and why, exactly, I came here is a divine mystery. This is a mystery that all created beings share.

We, as souls, emanating from the light of our Creator, have the capacity for anything, only because He has the capacity to do everything, and He created us for a reason. As much as Shakespeare and Michelangelo and Beethoven had a reason and purpose, a mission to fulfill, a unique song to sing, so do each of us.

We came to this limited world, from the unlimited realm of souls where we existed within the Divine Presence, with precise tasks to fulfill, tests to pass through, and lessons to be learned.

From the vast sphere, that unlimited world, my soul was sent to incarnate in Hollywood, California, in 1946. And, although I happened to land there, for a reason, yet was my soul deeply connected to many other parts of the world I would have to discover. My mission in coming here has been an endless process of discovery.

As, step- by- step, I learned to walk and, word- by-word, I learned to talk, and, sight- by-sight, I learned to see, I was amazed by the marvels unfolding around me. And the greatest wonder that I came to discover was the knowledge that was within me, the secrets that I brought with me when I was sent to incarnate on this earth.

Everything that unfolded was a dance, an interaction between the inner world and the outer world. Where did the reality truly exist? This book is the legend of the journey of the soul in quest of the realization of its true nature and return to its Divine Source.

But the soul is implanted in a body, which walks and talks, sees and feels. While the body and personality were growing up as a young girl in Hollywood, California, the light of the powerful soul was hidden, within that child, unseen by the people around her, but guiding and inspiring her steps.

I grew up in a liberal Jewish family. Throughout my childhood, I spent a lot of time in Jewish community centers and camps that were held in eucalyptus groves and other natural settings. The image that I remember most was the assembling of the "circle," the joining of hands, the sense of invocation and belonging.

Within the power of the circle, which was formed for invocation and thanksgiving, I found that the sense of creative potential was unlimited. I knew, even then, that a *circle* had the power to accomplish what no individual could do, and that is why I felt empowered and inspired in the circle, turning to the Source in thanksgiving and in wonder, sensing the potential of all that was to unfold.

These joyous, energized, and liberating experiences in camp were a foretaste of the joy of Sufi fellowship that would later bloom from the seed planted within the circle itself, the seed of the divine assembly, awakening within the soul.... ancient memories.

Even when I was a baby in the crib, my mother noted that she often found me in a state of great contentment. She did not understand the source of the joy that enveloped me. When I consider now the way in which my life has unfolded, I believe that even then I was aware that I was surrounded by the light of the Divine and the souls of the illuminated ones, some of whom I would later meet and travel with on the spiritual journey.

In contrast to the joy and peace that surrounded me in the crib was the stress of the situation in the relationship of my parents. I never really understood what was going on, but it seemed there was ongoing conflict between them, and eventually, they split apart. When I was seven years old, they divorced. As they separated and went their own ways, in a certain way, the stress was relieved. As this occurred, I began to understand each of my parents better and what principle each represented, what part each played in the saga of my life.

I have come to understand that in the continuously woven tapestry of our life's journey, not one thread is without its purpose. Every part of the vast picture is delineated through contrasts. As in stained glass, without the dark leaded lines defining the light portions, there would be no picture, no story revealed. Every aspect of my relationship with my parents was like this. I see now there were no mistakes and that every part of the unfolding, whether apparently positive or negative, had to take place to create the conditions necessary to catapult the seeker within me into the quest.

Every liability is also an asset. Reflecting upon our childhood, my brothers and I recollect that we were left to our own devices a lot. Especially after my mother married my stepfather, she became so absorbed in her relationship with him that she did not have the time or energy to be really involved with my development.

But very early on she said to me, "I have found what is true for me. You must find what is true for you." This was a principle that she maintained strongly to the end of her life. Rather than forcing her ideas or way of thinking upon me, she wanted me to understand this one single idea—that I must discover the truth for myself.

Both my parents insisted upon this. Sincerely, they gave me the gift of freedom, which allowed me to journey very far, unfettered by their demands or expectations. Although often we may not have understood each other, and often I felt like a stranger in a strange world, I am indebted to them for this one great gift— the unconditional freedom to discover the truth for myself. That was a gift more valuable in the long run than understanding, acceptance, or any kind of appreciation or praise.

When my parents were still together, we lived on Valley Heart Drive in a donut-shaped, redwood house with large glass windows. In the center of the house, was a large grassy garden where we ran freely, along with our pet rabbit. But, then, the heart split in two. Soon after, my mother remarried and my brothers and I moved with her to a street called Lemona.

We lived a block away from the school that I went to. I still remember my first day at school, Kester Avenue Elementary. I was sitting on the black asphalt, children running, shouting, laughing, and balls flying all around me. Sitting as though invisible in the midst of this swirl of activity, not knowing anyone and not known by anyone, I entered into a kind of mystical experience of being selfless, independent, and free.

It was a foretaste of states to come, though certainly I had never heard the word "mystical," and did not know, in that mysterious moment, where "I" had gone. After a short while, I made many friends and became integrated with the life there. But the most vivid memory I have of all of my experiences at school was that first one.

One block away, I lived in the house of my mother and stepfather. It was their exclusive palace, in which I felt I did not really belong. I had a small room near the front door. My mother painted it pink, which was her favorite color, but which I found suffocating. In this small, oppressive pink room, I, who loved turquoise, felt compelled to continuously create art. That was the first crucible in which I began to realize the vision and purpose of my life.

Love came to me in the form of a huge, grey, fluffy cat I called Tiny Lou who was always with me, and in the form of Papa, my mother's father, with whom I was deeply connected. I sat at his feet for hours as he played the mandolin. We were bonded like this in silence, music and gentle peace. Eventually, Papa was afflicted by a serious stroke, was partially paralyzed, and could barely speak.

Still a young girl, I spent hours reading to him and drawing, playing games designed to help him learn to speak again. He never really did regain his speech, and I felt his sadness and frustration. Nevertheless, the love, which we shared, was a language beyond words. In this way, I learned in my earliest years about the love, which transcends sadness, illness, and disability. That was the realm in which Papa and I truly existed, the realm in which we were united.

At the same time, I had to adapt to the world created by my mother and stepfather. My mother and her husband lived as Queen and King in the palace belonging exclusively to them. I was a very marginal figure in their realm, wondering what I was really doing there. They expanded their bedroom with glass doors overlooking the garden. I, very tentatively, observed their world, how they played their parts with glory and mutual adulation, knowing that I had really no role to perform in their play. I had simply been dropped there as a visitor or observer for a period of time.

While I lived in the house as an exile, on the other side of the sliding glass doors was the backyard, the garden of my liberation. We had a large swimming pool, almost the shape of the state of California, surrounded by trees bearing fruits of all kinds—apricots, peaches, guavas, and avocadoes. I found my true self in this garden, radiantly free and contented, eating the delicious fruit provided so abundantly by the generous Source.

There were two *chaises lounges* in the garden. Very often, I would invite a friend as a guest for the night. We would swim in the illuminated pool, eat from platters of fruit and other food, and then sleep in the garden, refreshed, and with great joy. It was a vision and real experience of freedom, purity, and sharing, a foretaste of communion with companions in paradise.

> *And give glad tidings, unto those who believe and do good works, that theirs are gardens under which rivers flow. As often as they are regaled with food of the fruit thereof, they say, this is what was given us aforetime, and it is given to them in resemblance. Thereof, there are pure companions. There, forever, they abide.*
>
> The Holy Qur'an 2:25

For the rest of my life, I have dreamt again and again of bodies of illuminated water and gardens. In waking life too, I am always drawn to such places. All of this, we know, is for a reason. It is a metaphor, a sign, an invitation to return to a place we have been before and can, by the grace of God, attain again.

There was one picture that I painted again and again at that time. It was of a child with arms raised up into the sky. In the sky was a huge eye from which tears or drops of rain were falling. This water was falling into the child's hands and around her, causing flowers and plants to rise up all around her. Although no one around me was acknowledging the existence, the reality of God, the Divine Source, the signs of His Presence and the descent of His Mercy were revealing themselves within me.

While our family was not at all religious, understandings and moral values were nevertheless shared that were important to me. Almost every weekend, my brothers and I went traveling with my father. Usually, we went to Palm Springs where my father's parents had a hotel. I loved those desert journeys. I felt that I could relax completely and would be carried along, through no effort of my own, to our lovely destination.

My father, Lennie, sang all the way through the desert. Many of the songs were filled with messages relevant to the essence of my life as it unfolded. Those songs were so important to me that I have remembered them all my life. It was in this way that my belief system about the family of man evolved during my formative years, reinforcing the knowledge that I brought with me when I came into this world.

Again and again, as we traveled, he sang songs like these:

"If we could consider each other
A neighbor, a friend, or a brother,
It could be a wonderful, wonderful world
It could be a wonderful world,
O yes! It could be a wonderful world!
If each little kid could have fresh milk each day,
If each working man had enough time to play,
If each homeless soul had a good place to stay,
It could be a wonderful world,
O yes! It could be a wonderful world!
If there were no poor and the rich were content,
If strangers were welcome wherever they went,
If each of us knew what true brotherhood meant,
It could be a wonderful world,
O yes! It could be a wonderful world!"

I still remember the deep sense of peace and security I felt as I cuddled up in the back seat with my blanket, being carried gently through the night, desert winds blowing in the window, and these beautiful songs of brotherhood blowing through my consciousness, forming attitudes and understanding even as I slept. These trips also engendered in me the life-long love of travel.

Then, my father married Sophie, and we all traveled together. We often went to Family Camp in the mountains, where Lennie and Sophie were in charge of arts and crafts. That was a heavenly combination for me—art, nature, and family altogether. When I became the editor of one of the camp papers, I developed my love and capacity for creative writing. This was an activity that I enjoyed very much and that I would use later in life.

For the first years of her life with my father, Sophie was continuously creating mosaics, and for the next half she was constantly engaged in the creation of stained-glass windows. Wherever she lived, the house became an ever-unfolding work of art. She would begin the mosaic at one end of a room and continue until the whole room was a mosaic. Now, at age eighty-seven, her house of many windows is a museum of stained glass, which, to this day, she does not cease to create.

The atmosphere of creativity that filled the house, allowed me to be the budding artist that I was, not hidden away in my bedroom but right in the middle of the living room. I remember, for example, greatly enjoying sculpting a bust of Albert Einstein in the living room. This was exactly the kind of thing you would expect to be happening in Lennie and Sophie's living room.

Lennie and Sophie moved freely from place to place. Wherever they were, their house was always filled with people, from different countries, different walks of life. The guests would drop in, visit for a while, and often stay for unlimited periods of time. This atmosphere, this style of living was very invigorating and liberating for me. I came to understand that *our* family included everyone.

Anyone who came to the door from any corner of the world could come in and immediately be a part of our family. Since then, I have traveled around the world so many times I cannot count them and found in every journey my family everywhere. From the time I came to own a house, it has always been an open house, a refuge for wayfarers on the path, like all the blessed oases around the world where I was so graciously received.

As the spark of the creative spirit was ignited within me, and beginning to blaze, impelled to express it, I was drawn to the medium of theatre. I began acting at the age of five and continued to be involved in theatre until the age of twenty-three, when I went to India, and, as an actor, then moved onto the stage of the world.

When I was twelve, I heard that a theatre company called the Alley Theatre in the San Fernando Valley was auditioning for actors. I went to audition. I held the scripts in my hands like sacred hieroglyphs. I read them like a blind person reading Braille who then could begin to see. I understood—"I will follow the script and it will show me how to open my heart and be free."

Thus, I came from my mother's home, where I felt like I had no part to play, to the stage, where I could play any part I liked. I played a weaver in *The Emperor's New Clothes,* the Gypsy Shoemaker *in The Red Shoes,* the White Rabbit in *Alice in Wonderland,* and the Wicked Witch of the West in *The Wizard of Oz.* The script for me was a sacred key, which opened the door of intimate communion.

All at once, I was able to communicate with everyone. Although I did not know their names, I found the capacity within myself to touch the people in the audience, to share intimately with them. This was one important step in the journey of self-discovery. It was the understanding and experience of sharing generously from the wealth that my heart had inwardly received.

To confirm that, in fact, this was a sacred moment in my development, I received a gift from the Assistant Director of the theatre company, which was of great significance to me. It was a pastel drawing of an ancient man holding a staff and lantern, with his long beard blowing in the wind. Written upon it was: *"Seek, and the truth shall make you free."*

In truth, I was living, within myself, in an entirely different world than the world of late-fifties San Fernando Valley that I was temporarily visiting. When I saw the image of the ancient seeker, I knew that it was *me*, and I began to follow that deep instinct like a magnet.

Throughout my childhood, I was aware of the existence of subtle realms, realities, and beings other than those of the apparent world in which I was living. I saw in one of many dreams that I was standing in the middle of a circle of seven ancient men who were blowing upon me, blessing and initiating me. This dream revealed the truth that I would meet such beings of light, who would initiate and lead me with the light of guidance.

Even at this time, the *spirit of guidance* was manifesting in the outer world, just as it was within, and various people appeared as beacons in my life, exemplifying the message my father was singing about, the message of universal love, justice, unity, and peace, which was already, truly, singing in my heart.

One of these people was Sophie's father, Abe Wieselman. Abe was an extraordinary being who had a great influence on my formative years. He was inspired to go from country to country, especially to those countries where conflict and suffering prevailed. He was somehow able to meet with heads of state, such as Ben Gurion, saying that he was an Ambassador of Peace. He was an ambassador not sent by any governmental agency but by *peace* itself.

And wherever he went, with buoyant spirits, he delivered messages such as the following great poem.

For me, no poem written by a human being expresses more simply and more purely the true purpose and high noble goals, which we were created as human beings to fulfill.

And it was a great blessing for me that early in my life, I heard words such as these uttered, which significantly contributed to the development of my character and vision quest.

> "I want to be the One
>
> I want to be the Proclaimer
> That the world has finally
> Concluded a true and noble peace.
>
> I want to see ample food for everyone
> On earth who is hungry.
>
> I want to be the healer for everyone
> On earth who is ill and ailing.
>
> I want to be the smile on the face
> Of everyone on earth.

I want to be the eyes for all the blind on earth.
I want to be friend to all the homeless
On earth.

I want to be joy in the heart
Of everyone on earth.

I want to be a home for every wanderer
On the face of the earth.

I want to be a song in the heart of everyone
To sing.

I want to extend my utmost gratitude to
Mother Earth for providing us
With food and sustenance of life.

I want to be the lantern beacon that brings
Light and enlightenment
To every human on earth.

I want to be free like a bird
To fly without fear
Throughout the heavens and earth.

And it is my fervent hope
That all peoples and all nations on earth
Shall live as one nation, one people
In eternal peace."

Toward the end of his life, Abe made a practice of visiting retirement homes in hopes of inspiring his fellow elders to live their life to the fullest. He was reading the poem and had just uttered the line, "*I want to be a smile on the face of everyone on earth*," when he died. For evermore, when I think of him, I know that he is smiling within me, smiling with joy, understanding, and compassion for all lives. It was a great blessing for me that early in my life, I heard words such as his, which significantly contributed to the development of my character and my quest.

Another wonderful example of the noble human spirit, who was shining through his words and deeds for us all at this time, was

Dr. Martin Luther King. I was blessed to meet him and hear him speak in person at a local school gym. I felt the courageous truthfulness and purposeful clarity of his being and his mission and was always deeply affected by what he said and what he did.

Throughout my teens, I was passionately dedicated to the cause of racial equality and actively involved in CORE, the Congress of Racial Equality. Brought up as I was, from the time when I first began to think, to believe vigorously in equality and justice for all members of the family of man, when I came to realize the conditions prevailing for African Americans in the South, my heart was enflamed by longing for these grave injustices to be rectified and for the equality inherently due to all beings to be established in this world.

The ever-expanding Civil Rights Movement, in which people of all races and walks of life, joined hands and hearts in the courageous, loving call for justice and equality for all, was manifesting what I most deeply felt.

I was greatly inspired and encouraged by the power of the human spirit that was expressing itself during this era, the impassioned eloquent speeches of Dr. King which moved so many people to join together and walk together for freedom and peace, as well as by the song rising up in the hearts of so many of the great singers and social commentators of this time, such as Pete Seeger, Joan Baez, and Bob Dylan, that so passionately affirmed the rights of human beings to live in equality and peace. It was a period when the heart of the people was singing strongly, even in the face of the unfathomable darkness of bigotry and oppression, and it was not weakened but strengthened by the encounter.

Now, almost fifty years later, in 2008, while I was visiting Sophie, she played for me a documentary of the wonderful folk singer and activist, Pete Seeger. When I saw this film, suddenly, I remembered secret dimensions of my life and how my heart was originally opened, here in this world.

Finally, in the midst of this unfolding social movement, I understood what I was doing here and felt that I actually belonged in this world (albeit just for a time). I felt the kindred spirits and that we were all inherently dedicated to common high ideals.

In the documentary are scenes of countless thousands of people assembling in our nation's capital, not obstructing justice or threatening violence, but singing with unbounded love.

What strength for the country, I thought, that so many of its citizens were inspired to unite, surrounding the White House, somehow embracing that heart of our country and our people with the very spirit of liberty and justice that the founding fathers willed, under God, for this land.

When I saw in the film all the countless beings joining hands to surround the capital, I remembered the impact of those moments upon my evolving life; that was indeed one of the great signs in my youth that God was alive and ruling His universe with His Grace and Love.

These were the values that were nurtured and respected by my family. And they were also the very qualities that I later came to realize were most perfectly manifested in the prophets and messengers, peace be upon them, sent to this earth by a Lord Most Merciful who specifically requested and commanded that human beings treat each other with such love, justice, and respect.

When I saw people gathering together to affirm these human values, I knew that inherently they were not so much *protesting* injustice, as *affirming* noble divine qualities and God-given rights.

By the Grace of the One Who is the Giver of all goodness, on November 4, 2008, a few weeks before this book is to be released, there is still time to include in it the news that the dream of Dr. King—the song of all of us who have been singing for justice and equality, with hands and hearts joined, surrounding the heart of our nation and world—has manifested in reality. I do not speak about the political implications or consequences of this profound occurrence in our history, but about the fulfillment of the dream that all human beings have equal rights to attain the highest goals. This is a victory not for one person, but for humanity.

And, indeed, watching the response to the election results on television, it appeared that the whole world was celebrating. What were so many people sincerely celebrating.... the end of the racial divide, the opportunity for all to advance together. In the context of centuries of horrendous racism and apartheid, this was a victorious step for humanity on the journey towards justice and truth. May the One Most Merciful, Most Wise and Just, leads us on the path to the realization of true unity and equality.

This being one of the deepest concerns in my life, it is with deep happiness that I am able to bear witness to the unfolding fulfillment of the dream of Dr. Martin Luther King manifesting so profoundly in the present time, even as I am remembering the deep impact that the Civil Rights Movement had upon my heart and soul, as I was growing up in the fifties and sixties.

The knowledge that all human beings were created equal, and that equal rights for all were truly worth fighting for was not, however, an understanding that I shared with most of my school mates whose social interests seemed to be more superficial, like dating and going to parties.

I wanted to speak up, without speaking, for what I believed. Every day, I wore a big button on my coat, which said Freedom Now! CORE. This became the name by which most people knew and addressed me. This message is what defined me in the high school, and it is these words that people would call out to me when they saw me. Even if they chanted this as a taunt, it did not bother me, because these words, and all that they represented, expressed what I truly believed in and who I truly was.

It was difficult to find many people of different races and cultures to link arms with in the San Fernando Valley of the late fifties, but the longing for union with Africa and with people of all cultures, countries, and colors was already resonating in my heart. Already my hands and my heart were linked with theirs.

Being somehow deeply aware of this big picture, I could not easily fit in to the somewhat limited life of the student body at Van Nuys High School. Certainly my heart was beating to the beat of a different drummer.

Lennie and Sophie had now moved to Greenwich Village in New York City. That seemed to me to be an appropriate place for me, to continue to expand my horizon. So, when the summer came, I went to live with them. They had an apartment in Washington Square. It was filled as ever with people.

In the absolutely tiny kitchen, where the light would not disturb anyone, I used to read all night long. I remember specifically reading *Portrait of the Artist as a Young Man* by James Joyce, which nourished, inspired, and empowered the artist as a young woman within me. Books such as this were sustenance for the visionary, the thinker, growing up within me, just like the water poured into budding plants which makes them rise up and bloom.

Those were nights of light and days of discovery. I fondly remember roaming through the Village and resonating with like-minded souls. When we are on the path of self-discovery, everyone we meet is a mirror and every word we read is a ray of guidance. That summer in Greenwich Village was full of signs and reflections.

I joined a theatre company in New York called the Fifty-Fourth Street Repertory Company and continued to discover the inner and outer dimensions of self-discovery and the loving art of sharing with others. I wanted to remain there and go to school at one of New York's performing arts high schools, but it was not possible to work out all the details. So, I had to go back and "do more time" (but not too much!) in the San Fernando Valley.

I returned to high school in California, but knew that I could not last there for very long. Not really being able to fit into the "box" of the world, as we knew it then, a culture of pink mini-skirts and American Bandstand, having skipped the sixth grade, I also skipped the twelfth grade. I missed the prom and all related rites of passage, and went to the University of California in Berkeley at the age of sixteen.

2

UC Berkeley—Flying into the Open Sky

Berkeley, California, 1962–69

Onward and upward into the morning, free flash,
O Soul, to the realms of Light.
Move thou in Order, move thou in Harmony,
Freely shalt thou move with the children of light.

Emerald Tablets of Thoth

I was a bird released from its cage, flying into the open sky. Berkeley, in the early sixties, was a marketplace of spiritual teachings, an open-air market where the representatives of all spiritual lines brought their fruit and laid it on the table. I was delighted by this feast, very much energized by the currents of light and knowledge that came flowing into my consciousness.

But not without paying a price, did our generation pass through the door of awakening. I remember vividly standing in the Berkeley Student Union when the news of the assassination of President Kennedy was announced on the loud speaker. This news pierced all our hearts at once. Everyone was paralyzed by its impact. It was a rite of passage that united us all. We lost our innocence and gained knowledge—knowledge of the vulnerability and mortality of all living beings, our President, ourselves.

From that moment on, death was always a part of the picture, as I perceived it—death as the end of a dream, and death as the beginning of the spiritual journey. I saw then how things were inextricably connected, the inevitability of death and the need to gain spiritual knowledge, the need for the liberation that transcends death. The door of the *dharma* was open. I read the autobiography of Carl Jung, the life story of Milarepa, *The Tibetan Book of the Dead*. I will never forget the power and truth of the introductory passage:

> O *procrastinating one who thinks not of the coming of death, devoting oneself to the useless doings of this life, improvident is one in dissipating one's opportunity. Mistaken indeed would one's purpose be now if one returns empty handed. Since dharma is one's need, would one not devote oneself to the dharma even now?*

At this time of the beginning of my awakening, in my sixteenth year and not apparently approaching death, as I was reading the book of my life, I saw that every paragraph was introduced by this phrase. Although young, with my whole life yet to unfold, I grasped with an inner intensity the awareness that life on earth was not permanent. It was but a preparation for an ultimate transformation leading from the impermanent to an eternal life. I wanted to learn and practice that *dharma*, the virtuous way of the higher truth, which would not leave me empty-handed and dissipated at the moment of the coming of death.

Through reading the stories of those who sought the truth, I knew within the depth of my soul the need to find the Master and become a disciple on the Path. But where was the true Master I was searching for, and by what means could I find him? All of the teachers were bringing their fruits and selling them. I tasted them, found some sweetness and nourishment in the teachings, but I knew that none of these teachers were the Master that I needed to find.

I gravitated to the Integral Yoga Institute in San Francisco, which was dedicated to the teachings of Sri Aurobindo. There, I made friends with the director, Dr. Haridas Chaudhuri, and entered the world of the teaching of Sri Aurobindo, a great Indian activist for social justice, teacher, and sage. Reading the writings of Sri Aurobindo about his experiences in prison, where he was interred for a year as a result of civil disobedience, had a stagger-ing effect upon my evolving consciousness.

What impressed me so deeply that I consider it a landmark awakening in my own journey was the description by Sri Aurobindo, of the transformation of his consciousness while he remained in the prison cell. The experience of this teaching was in itself a meeting with the Master. It was not the person that was the guide I was seeking, but the authenticity of his transformative experience, which came through his words, simply ignited my soul and made me yearn yet more deeply for the Teacher and the Path.

As he describes his experience, at first, deprived of freedom, of contact with the books, situations, and people he loved, he underwent the anguish experienced by many prisoners, especially those in solitary confinement. Under these trying conditions, he found it impossible almost to meditate at all. On the contrary, it was necessary for him to experience for himself, the despair and hopelessness of so many people who languish and even go mad under the duress, the inhuman strain of prison life.

This is the catalyst for awakening, as the Buddha also experi-enced it, the deep, empathic comprehension of human suffering. As he continued his journey within the cell, Sri Aurobindo came to understand what he had come there to learn. As his experience in the prison cell continued to unfold, although he was locked in the very same cell where he had suffered so much, he came to the state in which he felt completely embraced by the Divine, and filled with love and wonder, he began to perceive God in every-thing... in the bars of the prison cell, the prison guard, the bird flying outside his window...

This story touched me deeply. In the transformation of one state of mind to the other, I saw the power of the spiritual path, and knew that I must make that journey myself. To further come to the state in which, although apparently imprisoned, one per-ceives God in everything was all the more amazing and marvelous, greatly inspirational to my yearning soul. This was a concept of absolute transformation, which, from the moment I read about it, I have constantly yearned to attain, to embrace all lives as my own, to see God in everything, to perceive the Divine Presence in everything.

This is truly where my heart and soul were at. This was what I was really thinking about, the state of realization that I truly yearned to attain.

But my life was manifesting on other planes at the same time. So, in speaking about this year, my first year at the University in Berkeley, I do not want to convey the sense that everything was so profoundly serious. In fact, life was also delightfully enjoyable. I was free, out of my mother's house, and in my own element. I was going to a university where I did not need to wear shoes to class, studying Theatre, Folklore, Italian, and walking into the mysteries of my unfolding life.

I was walking barefoot along a stone ledge one day, when a man with very long, golden hair and beard and an angelic face began to follow me. He said he would like to play music for me. I went with him to the Pauley Ballroom on the campus. It was empty except for a large grand piano. He improvised galactic music for hours. I lay beneath the piano and then danced across the huge empty ballroom.

Charles and I began to live together in a small cottage on Blake Street and then moved to a house on Parker Street and joined together with artists of all kinds to celebrate the golden age of the sixties in Berkeley. Our life became a continuous series of artistic happenings.

My brother Michael, three and a half years older than I, was an inspired artist in whatever medium he engaged. At this time, his principal art form was creating events, sometimes lasting for as long as twenty-four hours. My brother took the time and care to think about what each person in our circle would most enjoy. He sought to know the inner life of that person and then manifest for him or her, an intricate series of experiences that would reveal to the person most poignantly his or her inner vision. That was truly a beautiful form of art and a deeply caring expression of friendship.

I also have another brother named Steve. He was at the University of Arizona while all this was taking place. I spent time with him, off and on, a little later in life. His love, support and kindness have been continuous throughout my life. His fundamental characteristic of loving kindness has expressed itself, throughout his life, in a love for animals and all creatures.

From the time that I came into this world, I was balanced, by the two aspects that my brothers embodied, both brothers having both qualities. One was a kind of brilliant creativity and the other, compassionate kindness. I have a photograph of myself, as a young girl standing with my brothers on a hillside overlooking a large lake. I am standing with these two aspects of my being, my brothers, surrounding and protecting me, all of us at ease overlooking the lake of existence.

Another very pivotal member of our circle, in sixties' Berkeley was Charles' best friend, a poet named Daniel Moore (who would, upon embracing Islam, become the poet, Abd'al Hayy Moore). It was a spiritual experience even to visit his home. He lived in an apartment in San Francisco's Divisadero district. Daniel was a gifted Blake-like artist as well as an inspired poet. The walls of his apartment were covered with illuminated manuscripts. I felt that these were like the walls of his heart and I was reading his poetry, perceiving his vision from within his heart.

Daniel was the very essence and manifestation of the passionate poetic soul I had known was blazing secretly within me. He was my mystic counterpart whom I recognized and bonded with immediately. The passion was not personal, but collective. We had work to do together, creating a vehicle for the ritual transformation of our extended tribe.

This was Berkeley in the sixties. So many people were searching, but we did not know what we were truly searching for. At the very least, we knew that we wanted to transcend the isolation of the limited nuclear family system that prevailed in America in the fifties and create a truly extended encompassing sense of community, and for the kind of tribe that we were forming, we needed rituals of collective transformation.

So, to channel the energy of so many people who were searching for a meaningful way of joining together not previously found in American culture, not to be found in the gathering of traders on the Stock Market, or at a football game or wrestling match, we created a theatre company called the Floating Lotus Magic Opera Company.

Every weekend, we would perform in an amphitheatre in the hills of Berkeley in John Hinkel Park. We had a large regular audience that came every week for this rite. We began and ended by sitting in a large circle meditating and chanting. In between these two periods of meditation, we would go through the steps and stages of invocation and transformation and then finally serve food to all.

In one play, I had the part of the goddess Kali. In the first half of the play, she unleashes a cyclone of the dark forces that plague the earth. Then, she dies, is placed in a coffin, and is carried on a *bardo* journey around the stage. She is then reborn as the pure regenerated mother earth.

There was a very deep sense in which I had to experience this death and rebirth every week. By compelling confrontation with the force of darkness itself, this period of initiation detached me from identification with the darkness of the Kali Yuga, this age of destruction we are now passing through. Sometimes, in the course of the process, I was unable to move for two or three days in a week, and I would lie still, wait, and pray until the "spirit" rose up again, freed of some more impurities. Then, I would carry on cooking, working with the company, and preparing collectively for the weekend ritual.

Now, as I write about this, forty years later, I have come to see how profound is the darkness of this time of destruction we are living through. As the signs of destruction are manifesting, one after the next, I believe with absolute certainty that we are alive in a time such as this to transmute the darkness into light.

So, it is more important than ever for the earth and all its inhabitants to travel with certitude and focus, under the guidance of a true Master, the guidance of true mastery on the path, which comes from God and leads back to God. We were searching and yearning for this even then in our amazing theater experiences in the Berkeley hills, but it is yet more amazing to consider how we ultimately found it.

Once or twice a week, I taught yoga classes in a very large, light-filled loft that belonged to John Argue, a very fine actor in the Berkeley Theatre Department and a member of our extended theatre family. It was a class for members of the Floating Lotus and for others. Many people came. I had studied with a yogi in San Francisco and was now passing on what I had learned.

At this point in our life and collective journey, we were given the gift of timelessness. We were not bound and constrained by the sense of urgency beating at the door. The class did not seem to take place in a certain defined period, after which we had to get up and go. We entered into the eternity of the breath and allowed it to breathe through us. Our bodies, stretched across the room, were floating in the breath. We would assume one of the yoga postures for a while and then return to the formless peace. As the apparent facilitator of this process, I discovered that I could be a vehicle for peace.

When the theatre company, this assembling of our tribe, began, I was still living with the cosmic pianist named Charles. We had a small house on Parker Street. In the back was a garage that I lined with wood in a rustic style. This became my painting studio. It opened into a very small but very beautiful and magical garden, surrounded by a weathered lattice fence, heavy with fuscia and bouganvilla.

A Lama from Mongolia used to come to our garden regularly to visit. He had many hundreds of disciples in Mongolia. In

Berkeley very few people even knew that he existed. I accepted his appearance in our garden as the most natural thing and was delighted and blessed by his presence.

When he came to the amphitheatre to see our performance, as I was flying across the stage, I looked out into the audience and saw no one but him. His illuminated face filled all of everything and that was all I could see. I believe that it was the purity of his practice, compassion, and intention, which generated the light that made him especially visible to me.

We were also deeply blessed and amazingly graced by practicing meditation in San Francisco in the *zendo* (meditation hall) of the great Zen Master Shunryo Suzuki Roshi. The first time I entered the *zendo*, Japanese televison was filming a documentary. Not really knowing how things were arranged in the *zendo*, I went in and sat down on the men's side. It was a very zen-like way of entering the path of no-mind and no planning.

Suzuki Roshi was, it certainly seemed to us, an awakened person joyously engaged in awakening others. He was shining like the full moon in a dark night sky, illuminating the world with bright wisdom.

Just as a Zen Master would, he spoke words that automatically dispelled the constraints of the ordinary mind. For example, he said,

> "To live in the realm of Buddha nature is to die as a small being, moment after moment. When we lose our balance, we die, but at the same time, we also develop ourselves, we grow. Whatever we see is changing, losing its balance. Then everything looks beautiful is because it is out of balance, but its background is always perfect harmony."
>
> Shunyru Suzuki Roshi
> *Zen Mind, Beginner's Mind*

This perspective, which integrated, into one reality, the state of imbalance and the state of perfect harmony was useful and enlightening at all times and in all situations. Certainly everything that was happening and everything that could happen could easily find its place in the comprehensive understanding that was being transmitted to us by the bright and shining Roshi.

He also taught extensively through the ongoing practice of meditation, called zazen. I remember, in the midst of sitting in a meditation for several days, I was served a meal on a tiny, rectangular ceramic plate. It consisted of one slice of celery, one slice of carrot, one slice of bean curd, and a few other carefully selected items.

In the context of those many hours of sitting, this small break was utterly wonderful, and the meal, I felt, was the most delicious I had ever eaten. Such was the grace of the purity of that spiritual practice, and the subtle teaching about the interaction of imbalance and harmony that was being transmitted. Outside the zendo, I was noticing the teachings at work in life.

Living in the small house on Parker Street with Charles and me was a large golden cat we called Yellowness. Every night, Yellowness knocked over the statue of the Buddha on our shrine and sat in its place. In this too, the living teaching was manifesting.

We also had other mysterious visitors. Once, a German painter named Blalah turned up and moved in. He was very talented and pleasant, but when tear gas filled the streets during the Free Speech Movement demonstrations, something in his past was triggered. I had stretched a large canvas, which I was meditating on in order to bring forth the vision from the whiteness.

While we were out, the traumatized Blalah slashed the canvas with a knife and disappeared, never to be seen again. The slashing of the canvas was more significant than anything I might have painted on it.

We never knew who would turn up. The house was open. At another point, the actor, Roberts Blossom appeared. He seemed to be a very lovely, kind, and luminous being. As an actor, he had appeared in many movies and television programs, such as The Great Gatsby and Northern Exposure, always playing the part of a wizened old man, a seer. Just as he appeared in *those* movies, so did he in ours.

Whatever happened we accepted as the "unfoldment." A clair-voyant and inspired but also schizophrenic woman named Jennifer appeared, moved in, and lived with us for some time. She spoke con-tinuously and transmitted a lot of spiritual teaching from the masters, but she was possessed by different forces at different times, which destabilized our life and household. Then, she too disappeared.

At a certain point, both the house and life there reached their limit for me. I knew that I needed purification, transformation, and elevation. I needed to take the next step. I asked Charles to drive me to Mendocino and leave me in the middle of the wilder-ness, which he did.

I took with me only *The Tibetan Book of the Dead*. I walked deep-er and deeper into the wilderness and became hopelessly lost. Having no idea where I was or how to retrace my steps, I sat down in a grove of trees as the sun was setting. In some sense, having arrived at my destination, I felt that death was overcoming me. It was an over-whelming and frightening experience. Immediately, I became the prey of hordes of insects, each taking huge bites out of me.

I opened *The Tibetan Book of the Dead* and read prayers, which I felt were being said for me and were being said to protect me in the midst of my plight:

> *O you compassionate ones possessing the wisdom of understanding, the love of compassion, the power of acting, and of protecting in incomprehensible measure, one is passing through this world and leaving it behind. No friends does she have, she is without defenders, without protectors and kinsmen.*
>
> *The light of this world has set. She goes from place to place, she enters darkness, she falls down a steep precipice, she enters a jungle of solitude, she is pursued by karmic forces, she goes into a vast silence, she is borne away on the great ocean, she is wafted on the wind of karma, she goes where there is no certainty, she is caught in the great conflict, she is obsessed by the great affecting spirit, she is awed and terrified by the messengers of death. Existing karma has put her into repeated existence and no strength does she have although the time has come to go alone.*

O you compassionate ones, defend her who is defenseless, protect her who is unprotected, be her kinsman, protect her from the suffering in the depression of the bardo, turn her from the storm wind of karma, turn her from the great awe and terror of the Lords of Death, liberate her from the long narrow way of the Bardo.

I read passages such as these. The book I was holding in my hands and reading was no longer a physical object made of paper; it was the vehicle through which knowledge was being transmitted. I began to comprehend the moment of death, the moment of transition from life in this world to the journey that leads beyond this life. I understood very clearly that in that moment of transition, a choice would have to be made between the terrifying manifestations of the illusions of the mind, and the brilliantly clear light of Reality, the state of enlightenment.

The insects consuming me seemed to be manifestations of the dark forces of illusion. I was being instructed not to be afraid of anything, not to be daunted or awed, but instead to stay focused in meditation upon the clear light of Reality, which was my true nature. This experience was a physical and psychological ordeal. But it was truly a glimpse into another dimension of reality, a spiritual opening. I had come to this forest to confront my own mortality, and was brought through this test by an unseen Power, loving and willing me to continue on the journey of my life.

On the next day, when I knew that the experience was complete, I got up and slowly began to walk. Step by step, my feet were guided out of the wilderness onto the path that would lead back to civilization. When eventually I looked in a mirror, my whole face and body were so swollen from bites, I could barely recognize myself. I could see that I had been changed.

No matter what, I knew that my intention to find the spiritual path that leads beyond death had been infused with life. I had to make the journey, wherever it led me, to attain that Goal. Just as I was guided out of the wilderness back to the path leading to the next step in my journey, I knew that I would continue to be guided. But I had to let go of everything that was distracting me from pursuing the real point of my life and journey.

When I finally arrived at our home on Parker Street, I knew I could never live there again. I could not resume my former life, but was impelled to take the next step, deeper into the spiritual journey. I moved out immediately and then into the large wooden hall where Daniel lived, and the Floating Lotus group gathered. We all lived, rehearsed, meditated, and ate together in the beautiful wooden lodge with immense windows overlooking the wonderful gardens and woods of Williams College on the north side of the Berkeley campus.

It was a beautiful place, a grand building surrounded by a beautiful garden, which inspired in us deep nostalgia, as if we had seen it in our dreams. But it did not belong to us. It had been lent to us and was not our real home. One morning when we woke up, the dream was over, and we had to leave.

Next, we moved to a place we referred to as "the land," an abandoned lumber mill where everything had simply stopped functioning. There, we lived a very strange life in semi-habitable dwellings. On the land, we did our prayers, meditations, and performances, as we had done in Berkeley, but our time together was fading out, and each of us was entering into his or her solitary journey.

We had performed many times in Berkeley in a relatively pure atmosphere. Every time, the rite was completed; every time, the regenerated pure earth rose up out of the coffin. Then, one day, we came in from the land and performed in San Francisco at the Family Dog, a famous gathering place for rock music and New Age happenings. Many people in the audience were on hard drugs. We were incapable of processing that. We could not resurrect. The pure earth could not rise up out of the coffin. The Floating Lotus Magic Opera Company dissolved, and each of the core members went into retreat in preparation for the spiritual journey.

I moved into a glass room in my brother's house in Berkeley and went into deep retreat. In search of my true self, I entered into a period of fasting and silence for many months.

The room had two levels. On the lower level, I had a long *puja* table for spiritual offerings, upon which stood the pictures of many teachers and saints. I saw practically no one but them. They were the friends with whom I conversed.

My bed was on a raised platform that was surrounded by glass. The room was like a glass lantern, my soul, in its unfolding process, the light within it. Surrounding the glass room were trees, blowing in the wind, and the light itself constantly moving. I was in a womb, a crucible of light, being guided and prepared for my journey.

In reality, it was my life that was laid upon the altar. I offered it and surrendered in the deep longing to be guided, inspired. I had many dreams and visions. Understandings of the spiritual path and the need to follow it were flooding in. The ancient texts, teachings of all the religions, were alive. I saw them written in light, heard them resonating, and wrote them in my journal:

> *Ageless, subtler far than the mind's inmost subtlety, Universal Sustainer, shining sun-like, self-luminous. I am the Knowledge, the brilliant Lamp dispelling all darkness. I am the End of the path, the Witness, the Lord, the Sustainer. I am the Place of abode, the Beginning, the Friend, and the Refuge. I am the Breaking-apart and the Storehouse of life's dissolution. I lie under what is seen in all creatures, the Seed that is changeless. I am the cosmos revealed and its essence that lies hidden. The man of inner wisdom, I see as My very Self, because he alone loves Me because I am Myself, the last and only Goal, the inner Truth of his devoted heart.*
>
> Bhagavad-Gita

> *God is the Light of the heavens and the earth. His Light is comparable to a niche, wherein is a wick, the wick is in a crystal, the crystal is brilliant like a star. It (the wick) is kindled from a blessed tree, an olive tree, which is neither of the east nor of the west, and whose oil would almost glow forth of itself, though fire toucheth it not, light upon light.*
>
> The Holy Qur'an 24:35

I went into the room in hopes of finding myself, but what I found there was the light of God, the words of God. These were the secrets that I found, as I was being prepared to make the journey which would lead me to the Source of the beautiful words that were resonating through my being.

Another beautiful passage I wrote in my journal, was especially meaningful as it referred to the "book" not written on paper. This "Book of God's Remembrance" was the one I most wanted to read:

> *But not a word is lost, for in the Book of God's Remembrance, a registry is made of every thought and word and deed. Then, when the world is ready to receive, lo! God will send a Messenger to open up the Book and copy from its pages all the messages of purity and love. Then, every man of earth will read the words of Life in the language of his native land and men will see the light. And man will be at one with God.*

The Aquarian Gospel

Such were the words I was reading, contemplating and recording in my journal as a reference to the sea of universal messages that were resonating within my heart and mind, truly inducing a state of awe, wonder, and yearning to make the journey that would lead me to the Source.

I went out very rarely, but periodically the spiritual teacher Ram Dass came to town, and I knew for some reason I had to see him. Each time he spoke, I sat directly in front of him and was amazed to hear that he was reading to these large gatherings many of the exact passages I had been writing in my journal.

It appeared to me that we were getting messages from the same source and that I should make the journey to India to see his guru, Neem Karoli Baba, or Maharaj-ji, who seemed to be sending these messages—of universal love, universal truth—to me as well as to Ram Dass and others.

I shared this feeling with Ram Dass, and he sent me two letters, confirming my instinct that I must go see Maharaj-ji. He wrote:

"Your letter is so full of shakti that it is fairly ablaze in my hands. You certainly need not worry. The seed of the spirit is planted within you and is emerging as fast as you are able to handle the light. Attachment will fall away, burned by the pure light, just as does the skin of the snake.

"There is nothing you can do but be very calm, very patient and persistent in your sadhana. You must even watch your own desire for enlightenment....We are very blessed to have tasted of the sphere within. Each day is a further unfolding. Here we are eternally, Shanti, Ram Dass."

In another letter he wrote:

"I hear in my heart every twist and turn of your journey...our journey. The veil of purification that makes ready the vehicle of ten thousand suns. We are so ancient...almost old enough to be born. When birth is no birth...death is no death...longing and fulfillment are one. Bharat (India) is where we meet... Bharat is the consummation. You write our journey so good... such mellow drama...the love affair with the Ancient One... Dissolving in the Ocean of Love. All the black magicians bow to the pure Spirit...the Devil knows not for whom he works. There is only One. What we seek, we are. When we arrive, we shall be. I love you, Shanti, Ram Dass."

These letters were inscribed as a seal upon the parchment of my unfolding quest. It was clear that India was the consummation of this stage of my journey, and I had no choice but to set out on the journey to that ancient land.

3

Setting Out on the Path

Orient Express and Afghanistan, 1969

*A man is said to be absorbed when the water has absolute control of him
and he has no control of the water. The man absorbed and the swimmer
are both in the water, but the former is carried along and borne by the
water, whereas the swimmer carries his own strength and moves at his
own free will. So every movement made by the man absorbed, and every
act and word that issues from him, all that proceeds from the water, and
not from him: he is present there as the pretext.*

Discourses of Rumi

Having chronicled the dreams, visions, and messages that
made me know that I had to go forth on the spiritual
journey and give myself entirely to it without looking
back, I made a copy of this book of dreams and visions, gave one
to every member of my family and close friend, and then left, as
though I might never return.

From this time when I first set out, I never once followed a
map or really knew where I was going, much less how to get there.
But I discovered that I was perpetually guided and that there were
certain people I had to meet who were in fact waiting for me.

First were the electronic composer Karlheinz Stockhausen and
his companion, a wonderful person and artist in her own right, Mary
Bauermeister. They lived in a house constructed, like his music and
her art, of many floating rooms, many suspended planes and dimensions. It was an appropriate place to begin my journey into worlds
beyond.

I lived in London for a few months and was well into my next journal of paintings and writings of the dreams and visions that were coming in an ever-flowing stream. Mary seemed to understand what was happening. She showed me photographs of her journey to Sri Lanka, a place I was indeed destined to go.

She also created for me two huge accordion-paged journals to be filled with the account of the journey that was to unfold. I left with her my dog-eared copy of the *Discourses of Rumi* and boarded the Orient Express bound east.

I once heard a very useful teaching relating to train travel: When you get on a train with your luggage, put your luggage down. You do not need to carry your luggage once you are on the train, because the train is carrying both you and your luggage to your destination. So, when I got on the Orient Express, I let everything go. I was like a corpse in the hands of the washer. I was being carried. I was traveling in the current, immersed in it, so much that I had no sense of who I was, other than the one that was being carried along on the journey.

Having abandoned the sense of self-direction, being absorbed in that current which was carrying me, I remember little of the externals of that trip except looking out the window and beholding an endless golden canyon filled with turquoise water reflecting the radiant sky. At that moment, the earth, the divine creation itself, opened up for me its splendor and, as the train passed through this fantastic landscape, I beheld the unparalleled artistry of the One Who created it.

At last, the train arrived at its final destination in the east in order to return to the west. That is where I got out. I was in Afghanistan.

I began to travel by bus, but not the modern, streamlined buses we are used to seeing in great numbers in all modern cities. The buses in Afghanistan were, with their plenitude of bells and tassels, hand-painted works of art. Brilliantly colorful and joyous, with no glass in the windows and packed with equally colorful passengers, they were an expression of the culture, the innocent, childlike heart of the people.

I remember an ancient stillness and light pervading the land, which was at that time still untouched and intact. In every city and every village, the people, dressed in beautiful robes, embroidered hats, and turbans, were sitting in circles, communicating, sharing, and drinking coffee or tea. I saw no violence, no festering fires of terrorism, or the bleeding wounds of a country dispossessed or possessed, but a golden haze of stillness and peace. I sensed that the life here was being lived as it had been for centuries. This was holy Afghanistan, where a boy like Jelaluddin Rumi could have been born and begun to grow up.

For me, this was a vision, something revealed to me that I needed to see. I do not know how accurately this vision presented the real state of the land and the people that I saw. I am certain that there were many things taking place there, within that complex culture that I was not aware of. I saw only the dimension of ancient and eternal peace, and I did not want to leave it.

The memory of this holy time and place is poignantly precious to me now, since all things have been changed by the ravages of the times of destruction. The beautiful, golden, gentle, peaceful land of Afghanistan I saw then cannot be found again in this world, but it lives in the hearts of those who were blessed to perceive and internalize the beauty and grace of the Eternal One that was manifested in Afghanistan then.

What was that mystery which I was blessed to behold, to taste and to smell? Longing to return to that place, I have come to realize that it no longer exists. Nothing in this world is permanent, I know so deeply that I had to move on, and could never go back.

When we realize that our true identity is as a seeker, a wayfarer on the path of God, we come to see more and more deeply that it is the *path* to which we are wed, the path to which we always return, and the path never lets us dwell in any oasis too long. However beautiful and enchanting any experience was, along the way, I could never remain there, but simply take the essence of each experience, the teaching, and continue to be carried along.

Now, I was continuing the journey on a bus with bells, beads, and tassels, rattling along as it bounced through the rocky terrain. The bus was wondrous, I discovered, in more than its appearance. I was amazed to see that suddenly, in the middle of the desert, the bus stopped, and all of the passengers got out and laid out their prayer mats in the desert to pray. This occurred on all the buses in Afghanistan at every time of prayer. The call to prayer would come lilting from a minaret somewhere in the desert, and all the people on the bus would get off the bus, lay out their prayer mats in the desert, and pray.

I had never seen anything like this. It was a wonderful, amazing vision, outside of any political context, a vision of peace and piety, of people united in their love for the Creator. Wherever the people were going, whenever they had to get there, the priority and necessity for them was always to stop in the middle of the journey at the designated times, get off the bus and pray. This was the way in which I was introduced to the simple beauty and truth of prayer and of Islam.

This act of bowing down, of stopping in the middle of any journey to praise the Creator, was not something I learned about in a book—it was a reality that my soul witnessed. It was an awakening for the soul, an invitation to pray.

The way that such images are presented today by the media suggests that when you see a group of people gathering together to pray in the Islamic congregational prayer, you should be afraid, for when they rise up from their prayers these people may do something violent which will endanger you. But what I saw in the middle of the desert was the very opposite—absolutely peaceful, natural, and pure. It was for me a revelation of pure existence, in which human beings traveling upon the earth given for them to dwell upon by the Creator bow down upon it in praise of Him, as He has decreed.

What has been decreed, by the Creator, I came to understand, in my discovery of the beauty of Islam, is mercy and kindness and peace, which come through submission and surrender to the Source of all things, the Most Merciful, Most Compassionate. The true believers bow down to praise the greatness and the glory of the One who created everyone, and the root of the word "Islam" is *salam*—peace.

This is what I learned about the nature of true Islam from the people of God I was destined to meet. Those who are in the state of true Islam, do not bow down, beseeching God to destroy others, and then get up from prayer intent to kill. For, just as the Bible says, "Thou shalt not kill," so does the Holy Qur'an say, "If you kill one person, . . . it is as if you killed all of humanity."

This is the truth of submission to the Creator of all, Most Merciful, Most Compassionate, Most Clement, Most Kind. It is a truth, which is hidden in our world, today, behind a terrible veil of war, brutality, injustice, and strife. But what was revealed to me in that moment in the desert of Afghanistan was a vision of peace, not war, a vision and realization, which has constantly guided my journey toward the Source of eternal peace.

Signs are continuously being revealed to us to help us enter the stream of the Divine attributes. For me, that eternal moment, that vision in the desert of Afghanistan was the opening of a doorway of perception that would lead me toward the Source of the stream. The simple, pure message was: "*Stop in the middle of the journey and bow down to the One Who created you and enabled you to make this journey, and then, when you rise up, and continue to travel, know that wherever you think you are going, the real journey is to Him.*"

4

Entrance to India

"The great thing in this world is not so much where we stand as in what direction we are going."

Oliver Wendell Holmes

I found myself in a Pakistani town en route to India. I was in a hotel room with several other people—westerners on their way to the east. They were engaged in various kinds of activities and social games, which I observed as though I were a visitor from another planet.

What I remember is that I received a message there to cease to find provision for myself. I was not to buy any food or look for it, but only to accept what was offered to me. I said nothing, ate nothing, and was simply focused upon the path leading to the goal. I slept only in order to wake up. I slept very little, woke early, and left the hotel.

Immediately, as I began to walk down the road, I came across an extremely elderly man in a horse-drawn cart who said that he was waiting there to take me to my destination. Although he was much older, he had almost the same face as a teacher with whom I had studied tantric art in the Berkeley Hills, Harish Jahori. Seeing my old teacher appear again leading me on the way, I understood the humor, the secret truth, and I surrendered to his guidance, knowing that he was the one designated to take me to the next stage. So, I got into the horse-drawn cart and off we went.

I remember the warmth and sweetness of the day, the fragrance of fires and incense burning, the pervading golden light, the peace, and the pace of the horse gently carrying me towards an unknown destiny. We traveled for some distance. Because it was so much slower than I was used to, and closer to the earth, it is recorded in my memory in an extended timeless dimension to which I long to return. Finally, we arrived at the destination he had in mind, he put me on a bus, gave respects to the light within me, and disappeared.

The bus quickly started filling up with warm, friendly people. They all seemed to recognize and know me and treated me like a long lost member of their family. They were going to a great wedding feast to which they enthusiastically invited me, as though I was an awaited participant.

I imagined, as the bus passed through the lush, rolling terrain, that I was being guided to this wedding feast, where I would certainly find the food that God would provide for me, the food He had told me to wait for, and maybe also find there my husband. I got right into the celebratory atmosphere that filled the bus, not knowing what wondrous events were about to unfold. After a period of camaraderie, the bus stopped, and absolutely everyone but me got out. They all got off the bus without looking back, without saying a word to me.

Then, the bus took off again, at an incredible speed, with just the driver and me. It seemed to me that we were flying through another dimension of existence. The marriage feast was a dream, an illusion that never took place, and this was a dream too, a dream of passage from one plane to another. I was flying across that river of light, deeply alone, but with the bus driver as my ferryman to the opposite shore. The bus seemed to be flying over the ground and moving at the speed of light. This timeless flight ended at the border of India, where he let me out.

I walked over to the border itself and sat down with the guards. There was a full moon in the sky. "*Full moon in the valley of death*," I said to myself. So far, all the stages of my journey had exactly corresponded to the stages in the mystic book *Conference of the Birds* by Farid al-Din Attar. Now I had come to the seventh valley, the valley of death. Dispassionately I observed the signs and knew that in entering the mystic dimension that was India I would have to undergo some kind of death.

As I was sitting with the guards waiting for the border to open, looking up at the full moon, a young man came and sat down next to me and began to speak with me. He was Danish and very friendly and talkative. He indicated that he would like to travel with me, not in an intimate relationship, but as fellow travelers on the path. I knew that my journey was inherently solitary, but accepted his offered friendship as part of the unfolding story.

He said he was going to be staying in the Green Hotel in Amritsar. I certainly knew by then about the mystic aspect of the color green, and I took that as a sign that that was where I was to go next.

We arrived at the Green Hotel in the middle of the night. I looked up and saw the full moon. A small Indian man appeared and fell at my feet and kissed them. He got up and exclaimed, "*Devi, Devi*! How can we serve you?" I sensed that he believed that I was some kind of incarnation of the Divine Mother.

Whatever he may have thought, he certainly was offering me food, the first food offered since I had received the directive to eat only what was offered to me, and I knew that I had to eat that meal. Very ceremoniously, full of devotion, he laid out before me a beautiful meal composed of many dishes. I began to eat.

From the first bite, I knew that this meal was going to kill me in some way. It was a meal that I would never forget. I felt that it was a kind of initiation and I had to finish it. When I look back at this moment, I can think reasonably that it is not wise to eat whatever you may be given in a foreign country. In that moment of the journey, however, it was the initiation I had to go through.

He took us to a room, and as soon as we entered it, it was as though a fiery dragon took hold of my body, and I was entirely overcome by fever, paroxysms, and vomiting. This continued for days, how many exactly I do not know.

After a day or two, the young man excused himself, saying he was not really ready for this kind of spiritual journey and simply wanted to travel around the world and enjoy himself. I was left alone in that room for an unknown period of time.

Thus did I enter India with the *full moon in the valley of death* and passed through the doorway of purification, so that when I emerged from that room and was able even barely to take the next step, it was as one chastened and changed.

I felt like a newborn colt walking on entirely new legs, as I emerged from the hotel into the bright sunlight. Now that I had the strength to proceed even tentatively, the journey must continue.

Since I was in Amritsar, the next stop was the Golden Temple. After seeing nothing but the dark room and the fires of purification for some unknown period of time, I beheld the Golden Temple like a resplendent vision I had seen in my dreams. The temple of gold floating on luminous water was filled continuously with songs of God's praise.

Was this the *Bharat*, Ancient India, about which Ram Dass had written, the place where we would meet? I found my seat in a place overlooking the shining water and breathed in, drank in, the divine music, as I awaited guidance, waited to be found. Incense filled the air, the sweetness of praise.

After some time, a tall, elderly man with a long beard, turban and Indian robes appeared. He was a Sikh elder. He told me that he had been waiting for me all his life and would like to take me to his home nearby, where he had been keeping a bed for me. I went with him to his room and saw the bed, which, he said, had been reserved for me. Then, he offered me food from a large pot covered with a towel. He lifted the towel, and under it was white rice with large black ants crawling in it. I knew that it could not have been *me* for whom he had been waiting all those years. As politely as I could, I refused and said that I could not really stop there but must continue my journey in search of my Master.

5

In Search of Maharaj-Ji

Crisscrossing India and Nepal, 1970

A man sits wakeful through the dark night, resolved to travel towards the day. Though he does not know how he shall travel, yet since he is awaiting the day, he is near to the day. Another man is traveling by caravan, upon a dark night and in a storm of rain. He does not know where he has got, where he is passing or what distance he has covered; but when that day comes, he will see the result of that traveling. Whoso labors for the Glory of God, though he closes both his eyes, his labor is not lost.

Discourses of Rumi

In search of the Master, my feet were next guided to the *kumbha mela,* a gathering of worshippers on the banks of the Ganges. In Indian tradition, the *kumbha melas* are sacred gatherings where gurus and disciples assemble for a time and live with many others on the shores of holy rivers for the exclusive purpose of worshipping God. It was being held this time at the confluence of three holy rivers in Allahabad. So that was where I went next in my search for the guru.

Upon arriving on the banks of the Ganges, I found many gurus. As far as I could see, there were campfires surrounded by gurus and their disciples, many of them naked, covered only in ash, most of them sitting in meditation. Somehow all of this was not surprising or shocking to me. I felt like I had seen it all before. It was buried in my subconscious mind, an ancient vision that was now manifesting before my eyes.

Still, I did not feel that I should walk from campfire to campfire, looking for my guru since, in many of these circles of naked ash-covered men, no one spoke English, nor, I thought, had they ever seen a western woman. The best thing, I felt, would be to leave them undisturbed and simply sit in meditation and allow the guru to find me.

After some time, the chief disciple in charge of Maharaj-ji's activities in Allahabad, having heard that I was sitting there, came to meet me. He had been told that I had come in search of Maharaj-ji. He was a very refined and soft-spoken gentleman named Dada. He took me to his home, which was exceedingly neat and clean. Everything was in perfect order, awaiting the guru's imminent appearance. The people were all patiently waiting, but they had absolutely no idea where he was or when he would turn up.

I stayed with these kind people for several days, but then, since there was no concrete sign that the guru was coming, I felt it would be best to return to the banks of the Ganges, where at least I could meditate with the *saddhu*s, those who had renounced their households and consecrated their lives to God.

Shortly after I had returned to the *kumbha mela* and to the meditation, suddenly my yoga teacher from the Berkeley hills, Harish, appeared. Very happy to see me in India, he invited me to come home with him. He lived on a piece of land owned by a herbal doctor named Vedgiy.

Knowing that nothing is an accident, I accepted his invitation. I had been searching for the campfire where I was supposed to sit, and I found it there. I was given a beautiful adobe-like outdoor house in which to live, pray, paint, and write. Next to the small adobe house was a fire pit, where every night into the night I met with Vedgiy and Harish under the starry Indian sky and discussed many interesting things, such as tantric art and understanding, and Ayurvedic medicine, both subtle, mysterious concepts and very practical teachings which are stored within the treasury of India's ancient wisdom.

For those eternal moments, I was happy on the Indian earth, beside the fire, under the Indian sky. It was peaceful and healing to my body, heart, and soul. I was at home in a way that I had never been in contemporary America. It is in moments like this that we find ourselves truly established in the state of being. There is a cumulative treasure of awareness gleaned from these moments of eternity that we take with us as we travel on. Yet, as contented as I was to be in that abode of peace, after a few days I thought, "I must not forget why I came to India. I must not be distracted by this natural beauty and peace, but must continue to search for the Master."

I had learned that Maharaj-ji had temples in many parts of the country. No one knew at which one he might be at this time, so I would just have to go from one to the next until I found him.

From this point on, I traveled night and day on trains crisscrossing India in search of Maharaj-ji. I did not know that to get a seat on an Indian train you have to get a reservation even for second class. So, for many days, I traveled standing, often near the restroom, which was the only space open even to stand in. It was an ordeal, but I was always inspired by love and faith in the Master, the certain knowledge that I had to find him.

Eventually I came to realize that by stretching out my sleeping bag on a luggage rack, lighting incense, and meditating, I could establish my identity as a *saddhu,* a worshipper, and have my place and general respect. Thus, in the midst of weeks of searching for the guru as he constantly eluded me, I was able to get a little rest on the luggage rack and meditate, undisturbed. For that prolonged period of train travel, this was the only home I had, and although it was challenging, there was also a great sense of beauty and peace.

As I remember it, there was no glass in the windows of the train. The train was just a metal structure, and we were traveling through the rolling plains, across rivers, and by lakes, intimately close to the small boys on the backs of water-buffalo and the monkeys in the palm trees. In every town we passed through, I heard resonating within me the sounds of worship, the names of God that were being invoked there. I was not a limited independent entity but was an interconnected part of everything. I was never treated by anybody I met along the way like a tourist or stranger. Wherever I traveled, I became part of the landscape.

In this way I continued to journey almost invisibly from one holy place to the next, where someone thought Maharaj-ji had been seen. On reaching each destination after days of travel, I found, again and again, that he was not there, nobody knew exactly where he was, but maybe I could try the temple in Vrindiban, or the temple in one hill station or another. So I kept on traveling, following one lead after the next. In each place, when I found that the guru was not there, I sat very still and waited until someone, often a child, would tell me that Maharaj-ji had been seen in one place or another. That was how I knew where to try next.

Such was my quest for the guru. I had no option but to pursue the path, however difficult it might be. I believed in the process, that it was in fact leading somewhere, although there was no external sign of this. As I can clearly see now, so many years later, everything was leading somewhere—leading through countless veils—ultimately to the path that is straight, to the Master, and to the Goal. Along the way, there were many things I needed to see and experience, to understand about the human condition and my own condition as a human being. That was really what the journey was about. It was not leading to the goal I had in mind but to the process of awakening itself.

Then, intriguingly, I received the message to go to Nepal. Harish had told me that I was in some way linked with Bhagavan Das, the American *saddhu* who had introduced Ram Dass to Maharaj-ji. I thought if I could find Bhagavan Das, that could be an important connection that could lead me to the guru. I had heard that he had been seen traveling a lot in Nepal and had been studying with Tibetan Lamas. Not being able to find the guru, no matter where I went in India, I was pulled irresistibly to Nepal at this stage of the quest.

In the high mountain region of Nepal, I felt immediately at home. One of my underlying motives for leaving America was to escape from modernity with all its superficiality and consumerism. Here, in Nepal, I found the antidote to modernity. The beauty of the land and of the beautiful architecture of the ancient buildings and shrines was deeply satisfying to me. Everything seemed hand-made, hand-carved, hand-hewn. There were almost no traces of the modern world to be seen. The mountainous landscape was splendid and the culture full of color.

I wandered around Kathmandu following trails that had been trodden for centuries. I followed one down to a river and sat down to meditate. Sitting on the white stone steps leading to the banks of the river, I looked up and saw all around me huge, ancient, white, and grey stone temples. I wondered about these awesome structures, so old, so mysterious. Under what circumstances had they been built and what was inspiring to the builders as they built them? They were no doubt powerful monuments, but also somehow ominous.

Seated in the midst of these powerful ancient structures, I meditated. When I opened my eyes, I noticed a fire burning with people around it on the other side of the river. Was it another campfire? No. I noticed, as I looked more closely, that a body was stretched out on a bier and was being consumed by the fire. The people surrounding the burning corpse were wailing intensely and inconsolably. I was astounded.

It was an overwhelming sight, but there was nothing to do about it, no one even to speak with about it. It was a tragic scene that deeply troubled my heart. So, I simply surrendered and then, I had to adapt. I chose to see the vision as a metaphor. I gazed upon the body in flames, imagining that it was my lower self, burning in the fires of purification. I sat there for a few days meditating upon this.

Thirty years later, I returned to this very spot, not searching for my Master, but traveling with him. This time, I had come to India, Nepal, and Pakistan with Sheikh Aly and three other disciples on a mission of peace, healing, and liberation. With greater clarity and knowledge, I saw the burning body not as a symbol of my own purification, but in its own actuality. It was the body of a person, being burnt to ash. From teachings received in later years, I had come to understand the inappropriateness of this practice, the anguish it imposes on the deceased. I was grateful to have been led to the purity and simplicity, the sanity and dignity of the Islamic practices of burial.

After a few days in meditation at the burning *ghats* of Pashupatinath, I was inspired to get up and continue to follow the trails of Kathmandu. Next, I arrived at the beautiful Buddhist shrine called Bodhinath.

A distinctive feature of Buddhist shrines is that the base of the shrines is composed of prayer wheels. As the pilgrims make their circumambulation of the shrine, they turn the prayer wheels, thus activating the wheel of the *dharma*, the teaching transmitted by the Buddha. The turning of the prayer wheels is a sign of the turning of hearts in continuous remembrance.

The shrine of Bodhinath is a very large one rising up from the prayer wheel base to a pyramid peak, which is an eye facing in all directions—the All-Seeing Eye. Stretching out from the peak in all directions are lines of colorful prayer flags, blowing in the wind. All around the circumference of the shrine are shops filled with colorful crafts—painted chests, embroidered cloths and pillows, colorful clothing, paintings and prayer beads. In the center of this dance of life, this ever-animated three-dimensional painting, day and night pilgrims are circumambulating the shrine.

I too walked around the shrine, feeling the well-worn path beneath my feet. As I was making this circular pilgrimage, I noticed another practice of the Tibetan Buddhists. For countless miles, I learned, they make their pilgrimage not walking, but in repeated prostrations. I marveled at this and at the fact that the way these people travel, by prostrating, becomes visible in the light shining through their faces and the warmth and compassion emanating from their hearts. After my sobering experiences at the burning *ghats*, I welcomed the shrine at Bodhinath, as a place of light and joy. This transformation of space and time, I thought, is what the liberation of the Buddha brought.

Born into the dark confines of the Hindu caste system, through meditation upon the nature of reality itself, through meditation upon the impermanent nature of illusory existence, and through the compassion for all beings that arose from his enlightened medita-tion, Siddartha Gautama Buddha transcended all the limits of his karmic inheritance and transmitted this path of liberation to others. This atmosphere of liberation, equality, joyfulness, and peace was tangible at the Buddhist shrines to which I now gravitated.

At this point, I had come to understand that the journey I was on was nothing but a reflection of what I was ready to see, what I was ready to comprehend. So it was that I had to see the burning *ghat*, the Nepalese mountainscape, the journey of perpetual pros-tration. All of these appeared before me one by one as a reflection and a teaching.

Circumambulating the Buddhist shrine, the *stupa*, was like going around the world. As far as we may go, we always return to the place we began, the point of our origin. The beginning and end of the circle are merged. This experience of the circle is one that I have returned to throughout my life's journey.

While circumambulating the *stupa*, I was reunited with a girl named Vicki and a sweet and gentle young man named, appropri-ately, Foster Goodwill. I had met Vicki, who eventually became a Buddhist nun, while traveling east on the Orient Express. Foster, who spent a lot of time with me there, read my journal and knew of my love for Rumi. He eventually came across Mary Bauermeister in Findhorn, Scotland and saw, lying on a table in her apartment, my very dog-eared copy of the *Discourses of Rumi*. Seeing the book sit-ting there, he knew immediately that it was the very book I had loved so much and left with Mary when I visited her along the way. How wondrous is the divine plan!

Wondrous too was the simplicity of our life as we lived there in the rooms around the *stupa*. As I remember it, everything was white—the earth and the shrines formed of that earth. Everything was bathed in the bright light of the sun, and we were bathed in the light of meditation and the experience of pure "being." It was a beautiful time and place, especially because our life was so simple and uncomplicated with no other focus than to "sit" as the Buddha sat.

Eventually I met someone who knew of Bhagavan Das, and I was guided to a little house in the mountains, where a friend of his told me that he had left Nepal some time back to go to the west. He then directed me to the Tibetan Lama, Kalu Rinpoche, with whom Bhagavan Das had been studying. He was living in Sonada, a hill station in the Indian Himalayas. At this time, my visa was running out, and I realized that it was time to return to India and continue my quest there.

I arrived at the monastery of Lama Kalu Rinpoche in the Himalayan hill station of Sonada in the afternoon and walked around the hilltop to see what was happening. I found many small boys gathered in an open-air hall. They were Buddhist monks in training. They were turning around on a kind of turnstile, having the greatest time. Every one of them was laughing, every one in bliss. I thought to myself how joyous monastic life could be!

In another one of the vast halls, rows of monks in burgundy and saffron robes were chanting haunting harmonies. It was the reverberation of timeless being, invoking the endless source of compassion and wisdom. It was this chanting by monks who seemed so profoundly harmonized that prepared me to enter into the presence of Lama Kalu Rinpoche.

Eventually I was greeted, by a more official-looking monk who guided me to the Lama. As soon as I entered the small wooden room where he was sitting, I was overwhelmed by his venerable presence. Lama Kalu Rinpoche's face was engraved with the most intricate lines, which revealed the profound journey of his lifetime. He did not speak out loud but whispered. I discovered later that this profoundly gentle, compassionate, and subtle being, who spoke so softly, had established fifty *dharma* centers in his lifetime. He was venerated, by all who met him.

To be in the blessed presence of Lama Kalu Rinpoche was an initiation. One could feel immediately the mystic presence, as well as his profound humility, kindness and compassion. At that first meeting, he formally initiated me and gave me the name Karma Palden Dolma, *Mother of Compassionate Wisdom*. I knew that this was the spirit called by different names—Tara or Dolma, Maryam or Mary—which has always been with me, inspiring my soul in the awakening of enlightened womanhood.

With his blessed hand, he put his seal upon the unfolding process. After that, all speech was in Tibetan. There were a few western people in the room who were fluent in Tibetan. I did not know a single word, but was receiving the powerful transmission of the lama, the transmission of compassion and wisdom.

Eventually I was guided out of the lama's room and into a great hall with many *thankas* on the walls. *Thankas* are complex paintings depicting the cosmology of the worlds as taught in the teachings of Tibetan Buddhism. In the center of the *mandala*, the circular tableau, is either one of the Buddhas or Padma Sambhava, the father of Tibetan Buddhism, seated in meditation. Sometimes the central figure is a female called Tara or Dolma. Surrounding the meditating figure are numerous scenes, the many kinds of demons and also angelic beings one encounters in the spiritual journey.

These intricate paintings symbolize the central place of meditation in the life of every being, male or female. The largest image, which is always in the center, is of the person sitting in meditation, and positioned around that central image are pictures of that person encountering many other beings and situations, positive and negative. The impact of these paintings upon the heart and soul of a spiritual person who sees them is to inspire him or her to meditate and so gain the peace and wisdom to resolve all of the circumstances encountered in life with equanimity and wisdom.

The Buddhist teacher, the late Dilgo Khyentse Rinpoche taught:

> *"Our realization, our view, should be as high and vast as the sky. Once the awakening of pure awareness arises within the vortex of emptiness, conflicting emotions can no longer obscure it, but instead become its ornaments. The unalterable realization of this view, which has no birth, duration or cessation, is accompanied by an enlightened consciousness that observes the movement of thoughts as a serene old man regards children playing. Confused thoughts cannot affect pure awareness any more than a sword can pierce the sky."*

Such is the beautiful state of mind transmitted by the teaching of the Buddha. I saw it manifested symbolically in the *thanka* and experienced it through the venerable presence of the great Lama.

From the transmission of this understanding I received real and lasting guidance. What is transmitted is a liberated state of awareness, which can be accessed at any moment in the journey, no matter what path one is following. I was very grateful to receive this valuable tool.

But I also understood immediately the complexity of the path of Tibetan Buddhism and felt that if I wished to truly study with the Lama, I must enter deep into this study and also learn the Tibetan language as well as the complex system of Tibetan Buddhism. I grasped in an instant that this was not the language I must learn or the path I was to follow. Still, simply to have met such an exalted person as Lama Kalu Rinpoche, to have sat in his rarefied presence and received an initiation from him, invoking within me the *Mother of Compassionate Wisdom*, was a great blessing.

I would have liked to sit forever in that tiny wooden room, filled with fragrance, filled with the blessings of compassion and wisdom, but as always I had to continue the journey. Now I was back in the Himalayas of India. Finally, after months of continuous travel, I returned to the hill station of Nainital, where I had begun my search for Maharaj-ji. Though this was his main center of activity, by this point, I did not know where I was at all. I walked into the mountains and collapsed.

For how long I lay there I do not know, but I was finally woken, by a man smiling broadly and wearing around his neck a sign saying, "I am Happy, Happy! How can I help you?" The sign was actually a wide flat bag in which he kept messages and things to give to people.

He said that he was a disciple of Maharaj-ji and that Maharaj-ji was presently in his ashram in Nainital nearby, waiting for me. He told me that his name was Pakselieri, but everyone called him "Happy! Happy!" He also told me I was very yellow, from hepatitis, it appeared. Collapsed as I was on the hillside, I had not seen myself for a long time, or even begun to imagine in what condition I might be.

Immediately, he made a fire and cooked vegetables, which he fed to me. This was the first meal in India I could actually eat. It was incredibly delicious and wonderfully good for me. After so many miles of travel, this meal signified the beginning of my healing and the celebration of my arrival at last in a place where the guru actually was! After we had eaten and rested in that cool and beautiful Himalayan grove, he told me that he was going to take me to Maharaj-ji, but first he had to take me to the hospital.

At the hospital, I was examined by a doctor. He pointed out that I had a severe case of hepatitis and that I ought to stay in the hospital for a month. I said, "Okay, but can I please see my guru first? I have been traveling for such a long time, and he is waiting for me." The doctor knew Maharaj-ji, Neem Karoli Baba, and said that he was a great saint. He agreed I could go to see him but said I should go back to the hospital after that.

Pakselieri took me to the ashram. When I entered the presence of Maharaj-ji, Ram Dass was there and also a group of western disciples I had known in California. They had all simply got on a plane and flown to India. They then drove directly to this temple in the hill town of Nainital and immediately found the guru. Hearing their description of their trip, I realized immediately that I was on a different kind of journey.

Although apparently a relatively small old man wrapped in a blanket, Maharaj-ji appeared at the same time to be infinite, unlimited, ancient, and formless. He greeted me like a long lost sister or friend that he had been awaiting for a very long time. He embraced me intensely. I was encompassed, enveloped by that blanket of grace. I felt that in reality I was being embraced by the love of God. Through this embrace, all traces of the hepatitis immediately vanished.

He described to me in detail many of the experiences I had just lived through. It appeared he had seen everything, been with me all along. He mentioned, for example, that one of his monks living at a certain temple had thrown me out of the temple, saying I could not stay there.

He scolded that monk and laughingly said he should not have done that, but should have welcomed me with respect. I realized that he had the power to have made everything so much easier for me. He could have guided me to him directly, as the others had come, but the difficulties of the journey were necessary for me and were blessings, deep teachings.

Maharaj-ji assigned to me a large beautiful room overlooking a lake, in the hotel where all the disciples were staying. After sleeping in woodpiles and standing up on trains, I did not know what had happened, in what luxurious dream world I was living. The view of the lake from the large picture window was radiantly lovely, but the dream was short-lived.

The next morning, someone knocked at the door and said that I had to move. I was given a tiny room in the basement, with no windows at all, next to the room where chickens were being slaughtered. Back to the woodpile! There I was interred, abandoned for several days. My visa was about to expire. I needed to see Maharaj-ji to get it renewed, but I was not able to see him at all. Having left everything behind to find him, I was now left in this small room to pray, weep, and be purified, to await *darshan* with the guru, spiritual communion with him.

Finally, after several days of such purification, I was told that he was waiting to see me. He told me that my visa could not be renewed, and I must go back, that I must follow the path of love (*prema*). He told me that my journey was eternally linked with Jesus (Issa). And he said that he the guru and I were one. He told Ram Dass to give me whatever money he had in his wallet, and he blessed my continuing journey.

Maharaj-ji made me feel so much the sense of his oneness with me that I felt I had truly received what I had come for and, after only a few hours in his presence I could now continue truly transformed.

At every stage in the journey with the teacher and the path, I have found that the teacher takes a different form and transmits a different level of teaching or understanding.

From every encounter with the teacher we receive only that teaching we, in the course of our spiritual evolution, are ready to receive. We look into the mirror shining in the heart of the teacher and see our own face in that state in which we are capable of seeing. So, it was oneness—"*Sub eck! Only One!*" as he said it, holding up his forefinger and smiling—that I saw when I looked into the mirror of Maharaj-ji's heart, and, having understood that, I was blessed to continue my journey in search of the Truth that would make me free.

Undaunted, renewed mysteriously in the depth of my being, healed miraculously and instantaneously from severe hepatitis, I returned to the open road. I had left everything, abandoned my life, as I knew it, to search for the guru, had found him finally, after months of arduous travel, had spent almost no time but an eternal moment in his presence, in which I learned that the teacher and I were one.

This knowledge alone was the treasure I had traveled hard to discover. This knowledge, which I felt he was transmitting to my heart and soul, filled my cup in such a way that I could return to the rigors of the solitary journey, full and satisfied, not empty and long-ing, not hopelessly wandering but deeply touched and inspired by knowledge of my connection to the teacher, the spirit of guidance.

Still, I did not know where I was going, but I knew by the guru's words and his penetrating transmission that I was following Jesus and traveling on the path of love. That, along with his pres-ence within me, was a sufficient source of strength, energy, and inspiration to enable me to return to the cold, hard road very much warmed and relieved of fatigue. I was now returning to a still unknown life but with this secret knowledge—oneness with the teacher—glowing within my soul. Now, it was no longer the form of the guru, but the essential truth of the unfolding journey, which was directing my steps.

6

Waiting for the Sheikh

Discovering Islam in the Holy Cities of Tabriz and Mashad, 1970

We will show them Our Signs in the (furthest) regions (of the earth) and in their own souls until it becomes manifest to them that this is the Truth.

The Holy Qur'an 41:53

I had burned all my bridges to go to India in search of the Master, but now I was coming back. This was my first round, my first journey around the globe. By divine decree, the circumambulation of the planet would occur again and again in my life, every time yielding greater compassion for all lives and greater understanding and experience of the Way. This kind of travel, unlike any kind of tourism, vacation, or safari adventure is called traveling *fisabilillah*, "traveling for the sake of God, traveling in the way of God."

I have mentioned that I never followed a map. By this I mean that I did not plan a trip, I did not determine the course of my journey. In this journal, I have tried to recount the events that took place as accurately as I can remember them because each one had some significance that was determined by the Planner of all. Just as I was led to India and to Maharaj-ji, so was I led back. Neither was Maharaj-ji nor India the real goal of my journey, and that is why, having endured so much to get there, it was so easy to leave. I had learned the lessons I could learn at that stage, and now it was necessary to take the next step on the path of God.

We can see the signs of God in ourselves and in the horizons, in everything that occurs in our journey, both within and without. Often I did not know in what town I was or how I had arrived at that place, but what I did know—what I did see—were the signs of my Lord continuously manifesting, and within the signs I came to see more and more clearly that what was shining like the sun through all the clouds, was the Truth, the One Compassionate Source of all.

Everything that happened to me on the journey was a teaching leading me through the veils, my own thought forms, toward the magnet that is the Truth.

Returning from India, I was let off the bus in another dusty town. I noticed people gathering, and, thinking that it was a religious assembly of some sort, I gravitated toward the crowd, only to realize that there was a conflict being fought between the people in the town.

Just as I was drawn into the crowd, some police officers pulled me out, rushed me up a staircase to a hotel serving as a shelter and then quickly locked the door. Once upstairs, I was surrounded, by people, most of whom were weeping. I had a large bag of dried fruit and nuts, which I shared with them, and a zither on my back, which I took off and played, singing *La ilaha ill'Allah*, the meaning of which I did not really know. I simply heard it resonating within me.

The people appeared to be calmed by this strange phenomenon and said they felt an angel had come.

I learned that the conflict in this little town was between Jews and Muslims. It had started when a Jewish man had spoken disparaging remarks about the Prophet Muhammad (saw).

Later that evening, someone gave me a small book about the Prophet (saw) which explained that he had come as the last of all the prophets and messengers (as) sent by God to bring unity amongst all believers, and peace.

I was trying to understand how these two pieces of information could fit together when I fell asleep, and I was still trying to understand the situation the next morning. If the Prophet Muhammad (saw) had come to bring unity and peace amongst the believers, why was this war going on? This question weighed upon me heavily.

I had no idea why, but I had an incomprehensible yearning to go to the Turkish bath. This turned out, not to be a casual stroll through town, but a guided evasion of periodic explosions. I noticed this, but proceeded without fear, feeling with subtle certainty that I was being guided and protected.

Finally I arrived at the baths and went in and bathed. When I came out, I saw a man who was encircled by children he was teaching. He called me over to join them. I do not believe I said anything to him at all. He said to me in excellent English, "What you were thinking is true. The Prophet (saw) did come to bring unity and peace to the believers."

The teacher continued to tell me many other things about the Prophet (saw). I do not remember the exact words that he said, but the way in which he spoke to me, the way in which he knew what I was thinking, and the way in which I was guided to the bath in that area to receive this information made me know that this transmission came from God, Who directed that event. Because the teaching came to me in that way, I believed that what the man said was true.

I went back to the hotel and prepared to leave and carry on my journey. There were two young men from England that I had met in the hotel who were leaving on the same bus as I was. The prospect of actually traveling with others with whom I could speak, after being so long on the road alone, was overwhelming. I felt very much relieved, like someone who has been in the desert for a long time and comes at last to an oasis. I soon discovered, however, that this, too, was a mirage.

After we had traveled a short way and I had just begun to get used to interacting with these fellow travelers, the bus was stopped and some officials got on and asked to see everyone's immunization cards. When they looked at my card, they said I was missing a cholera booster and that I must get right off.

I was taken to a hospital room and placed on a bed, where I wept. I said, *"O God, do You want me never to speak with anyone again? Must I always be alone?"* I knew that the love of God was so great a gift that I would have to give up anything for it, but the limits of my humanity were being tested.

It was not as if I knew those people and had become attached to them personally. It was simply the idea of traveling with anyone, conversing with anyone! That was what I had to give up, not knowing when I might ever have a companion again. So, I sat on the hospital bed and wept.

As I was weeping, I remembered that I was in the town of Tabriz. I was in the town of Shams-i-Tabriz! I thought how much Rumi would have wept for joy to be here. Then, I began to think of Shams and Rumi, to think of their love, and to weep from love. This love lasted long after Rumi's Master, Shams, had disappeared and also long after Rumi himself departed from this world. Until today it is touching and inspiring the hearts of the lovers of God everywhere. As a traveler on the path of love, seeking the Master who would so transform my heart, I felt great comfort and joy when I realized where I was, in the town of Shams-i Tabriz!

> *"O lovers, lovers it is time*
> *to set out from the world.*
> *I hear a drum in my soul's ear*
> *coming from the depths of the stars.*
> *Our camel driver is at work;*
> *the caravan is being readied.*
> *He asks that we forgive him*
> *for the disturbance he has caused us,*
> *He asks why we travelers are asleep.*
> *Everywhere the murmur of departure;*

the stars, like candles
thrust at us from behind blue veils,
and as if to make the invisible plain,
a wondrous people have come forth."

Mevlana Rumi
The Divan of Shams of Tabriz

As I was crying with happiness, contemplating the mystery of my destiny, which had carried me there and that spiritual love which has continued to inspire seekers for so many generations, a hospital attendant came to me, and asked me why I was crying. I spoke of the love of Shams and Rumi. He told me that he was a Sufi and would send me to the Sufis. This was the reason, he said, I had been detained there.

As soon as I had received the booster, the hospital attendant brought an old man to my bed. He said, "This man will take you to the Sufis. Go with him."

So, I got on the bus with the old man, who did not speak English, but who did know where the Sufis were. We traveled some distance and arrived in the holy city of Mashad. We came to the gate of a walled garden and knocked. The door opened and we were very warmly received.

Immediately, a bed was set up for me in the middle of this walled garden. When they learned that I was a vegetarian, they brought a beautiful meal of fruits, nuts, and vegetables. I was introduced to the people of the house, a very large family with many children, all of whom were disciples of a Sufi Sheikh. Everyone was very excited because the Sheikh was expected at any time.

Whoever we were waiting for, it was an extraordinary night for me. I rested on the bed, in a garden under the canopy of the illuminated sky.

This was the second time, after the desert of Afghanistan, that I witnessed *salat*, the ritual of Islamic prayers, being performed. It seemed to me that this large family did not sleep. They alternately played and prayed throughout the night. Everyone in the family seemed to be getting along very well. They laughed and talked, ate and played together all night, except for the two or three periods when they washed and stood together and bowed down together under the light of the starry sky.

It was a very beautiful sight in the moonlit night. The water they washed in was sparkling, like their laughter and their joy. The beauty of their life together, which was clearly divinely inspired, was visible to me on that illuminated night as I lay on the bed in the enclosed garden and watched this family repeatedly line up together to celebrate the praises of their Lord.

It was because Islam was introduced to me in visions like this that I *love* and do not fear it. So, for me, the best word to describe the process of truly accepting Islam is always *"embrace."*

The next day, the family told me I was being moved to another home, that of a wealthy doctor who was also a disciple of the Sheikh. They were deferring to him because they were poor and he was rich, so they felt he could take care of me in a better fashion.

I was very sorry to leave that illuminated courtyard. But, in truth, it is a place where my heart has always remained, and now, I have shared it with you.

When I arrived at the doctor's more opulent home, I found that his family and their friends were also engaged in waiting for the Sheikh. It appeared that nothing else was really going on. Various people came and went. We all sat in a room, we recited various *zikrs* or devotional songs and prayers, occasionally ate, and more than anything else, were actively awaiting the Sheikh. He was expected at any time, but no one knew when, and no one wanted to miss that moment, so everyone had joined together in this prolonged wait.

Frequently, we went to the mosque—a very well known and beautiful one. I do not remember actually going in, but rather standing in a certain place where I became the recipient of the flood of light that came flowing out of the mosque when prayers were over. I enjoyed standing in that place and watching as the venerable, ancient faces emerged radiantly beautiful from the mosque and I felt myself washed over by the light of their being as they emerged from prayers.

As I write about this experience, I do not know what I was witnessing, whether it was a heavenly or earthly congregation— probably both. But it seems to me that it was composed of very luminous eastern men, the heirs of ancient truths which, at that precise moment they were somehow transmitting to a young American woman—me. I know that this experience, of beholding the light in the faces of the worshippers was like the passage through a doorway in my discovery of Islam.

The first pillar of Islam is witnessing or *shahadah*. We bear witness that there is no reality other than the Reality that is God, and we bear witness that Muhammad is the Messenger of God. At that moment, being the recipient of the grace that was streaming out of that mosque, I began to witness these mysteries.

I want to share with the reader, here, how different it is to witness divine mysteries than it is to watch the news. It was only because I was brought into the state of witnessing and experiencing these subtle truths that I came to know about true Islam. That I had been guided to stand on the hillside facing the mosque in the holy city of Mashad as people were pouring out of the mosque after prayers was simply a step in the divine plan to make me see.

To begin with, I saw that the mosque was not at all a frightening, alien building where people were congregating who wanted to hurt me. I could see that it was an extraordinarily beautiful building, marvelously designed and crafted. I wondered who had designed it and what had inspired this beautiful construction.

Even more beautiful were the faces of the people as they emerged from their prayers. I saw the light of God shining through them. So this is the way in which, step by step, I came to see the beauty of Islam and to learn more and more deeply about it in a way that is never shown on the news. However, I still had to truly enter the mosque to find out what mysteries were taking place within it.

We returned from the beautiful mosque to the doctor's house, and there we continued to wait for the Sheikh. After several days of waiting in the living room for the Sheikh, there was consensus among all those gathered that, since the Sheikh did not appear to be coming at exactly that time, I should be sent to a place in the middle of the desert with another old man in hopes that perhaps we might encounter the Sheikh there. Really having no doubt about the process and no fear, trusting in the unfolding of events, I got into a car with that old man I did not know and drove off into the desert.

As soon as he began to drive, the man began to weep. He was in a state of rapture, of overwhelming love for his Sheikh, and for his Lord, as he drove toward an inevitable meeting. He told me how much he wanted me to meet his Sheikh, who he called his *Christ*, and how much he felt I would love him. We drove on and on until we arrived at last at our destination, a teashop with no walls in the middle of the desert. It was full of people. Everyone there was waiting for the Sheikh. So we joined them. We had many cups of tea and sat there for a long time, until finally the old man got up and told me it appeared that the Sheikh was not yet coming here. So we were going to search for him in the place where he lived.

Back into the desert again we went. We followed a course that I would never be able to retrace. At last, somewhere in the middle of the desert, we came upon a large sanctuary enclosed by tile walls. Inside the walls were beautiful mosques surrounded by gardens through which a river flowed. I absolutely could not have believed that such a place existed in the middle of a vast expanse of desert if I had not been taken there.

I was ushered into a room with women. The men were outside in the garden, listening to the Sheikh. When the Sheikh came into the room where I was, all I saw of him was his feet. It seemed that all the women were touching his feet and weeping with joy. Then he was gone. We all went outside and sat on a terrace overlooking the gardens. They wanted to feed me, as all Sufis do, and brought a tray of beautiful foods.

Dusk began to fall in this mystical garden. I was told that the Sheikh would like to see me in his home at three o'clock in the morning and I could spend the evening praying in the mosque. I took a walk through the beautiful grounds that led to the mosque. I looked up into the night sky and saw a perfect crescent moon with a star inside, a symbol of Islam that has many meanings.

Entering one prayer area that was filled with men, I walked through a corridor on the side of the mosque to get to the area where the women were gathered. As I passed through the corridor, I was amazed by the sound resonating through that sacred space, the sound of humanity singing beautiful songs to God.

I arrived in the place where the women were gathered. It appeared that there was a vast illuminated pearl tablet in the center, which was surrounded by women all dressed in black. I was dressed in white. I fell prostrate upon entering; such was the power of God in that space. Eventually someone called my name and I rose up. The rest of the night was filled with remembrance of God and peace and grace until three in the morning, when I was led through the twisting lanes of the small town to the Sheikh's house. It was a very small house and plain, not at all exotic.

I was carrying with me a very big book of paintings I had made of dreams and experiences I had had on the journey. In the center of the book, which was dedicated to images found in all religions and paths, was a painting of a dream of a person of light I thought to be the veiled Prophet. In the dream, angels were ascending and descending, a holy scripture was held in suspended hands, and the *kalimah*, *"La ilaha ill'Allah"* ("There is no deity but God") was transmitted.

The Sheikh knew about this page in the book and was very interested in it. He wanted to see it. He asked me many questions about my journey. I told him that my heart remained in India with Neem Karoli Baba, Maharaji-ji, and the teaching of oneness he transmitted.

He said to me that as far as I might travel all around the world again and again, I would not escape the *kalimah*, but would come back to it. Though I was not ready to accept Islam there and then, I never forgot his words and came to realize more and more throughout my journey how true they were.

He told me that when I was ready, he would always be ready to receive me and to teach me the Sufi path but would want to teach me first, for forty days, about Islam. I would remember that offer many times in the future, but I had no idea either who he was or where this had all taken place.

7

Saved by Grace

Iran, Turkey, and Bulgaria, 1971

"Fear ends where faith begins."

Georgio Dano

I had learned all that I could at that moment and had to move on. I had caught a glimpse of the beauty of Islam, but it was not yet time for me to fully embrace it. As Maharaj-ji had indicated, I had to find Jesus first. I was being carried along. Where exactly I was going or what lessons I must learn I did not know.

I took trains and buses until I reached Tehran, but by then the money, which had been given to me from Maharaj-ji out of Ram Dass' wallet had almost run out. So, I went to a trucking company to see if I could find a trustworthy truck driver with whom to travel to Turkey. I knew of no other way to get back.

After some hours had passed, someone from the trucking company told me that they had finally found someone that they felt I could trust. They introduced me to a truck driver, a young man who told me that we would be traveling with his sister and her baby, that we would eat dinner and stay overnight in a hotel and then leave all together early in the morning. I accepted this proposed plan as that which was being provided.

A room was given to me, and dinner was served. I did not catch even a glimpse of the sister or her baby and wondered where they might be. As we were finishing the meal, I noticed that the trucker seemed to be looking at me in an inappropriate way. Throughout my journey, I had been absolutely celibate. My unrelenting certainty of my position was a great protection in this situation.

I looked at that man with such a glare that he instantly became terrified, got up, and ran out of the room, and I never saw him again. I have wished, in the years that followed, to master that gaze and address it to Satan, the dark seducer, in all the forms he has assumed, so that he would run out of the room as fast as that trucker did.

The next morning I went back to the trucking agency to try again, since that appeared to be my only option. We waited for a while for a reliable candidate. I studied the truckers who came in until I saw one who seemed clear and responsible. We talked about Islam. He said that he was a faithful Muslim, a believer, and he looked like it to me.

So, invoking the protection of God, the Merciful, the Compassionate, I climbed into the cab with him, and we set out. Long stretches in the desert and plains were punctuated by stops for refueling. We seemed to be riding parallel with another truck, which we encountered at every truck stop. Riding in that truck was a French hitchhiker. He and I spoke quite a lot and were looking out for each other in this potentially dangerous situation.

Dangerous it was when the trucks stopped at a café in the desert in the middle of the night. The energy was such that I felt I should bring my zither into the café and sing to God. This was an absolutely sincere call on my part, but also a reminder to these men that they were Muslim and should act like it. I was sitting next to the hitchhiker from France.

We noticed that strange things were happening in the café. The driver of the truck I was riding in was standing against the back wall of the café and was approached by another man with money in his hand. They were furtively glancing at me. My driver seemed to refuse several times. Then, he seemed about to accept the money.

Very slowly and steadily, the Frenchman and I got up and walked out of the café. He led me to where my things were. I picked them up, as though I was clearly going somewhere, but truly we were in the middle of nowhere. A group of men came out of the café and approached us.

Suddenly, a Volkswagen van appeared out of nowhere. It was filled with a group of Europeans with whom the Frenchman had traveled in the past. He waved them down, and they stopped. He beseeched them not to take him, but to take me, explaining quickly what seemed to be happening. They agreed.

I jumped into the van, pulling my things with me. They shut the door, and we zoomed off into the desert with a throng of men running after us. I managed to get all of my belongings into the van except a carved metal staff I was carrying which I had been told was to ward off evil. That was all that they could get from me. The van sped off into the night, crossed the border, and dropped me off in Bulgaria.

I certainly could not recommend this mode of travel to anyone. I would not encourage anyone—and certainly no young woman— to test fate like this. It was, however, important for me to live through it. I still remember vividly the feelings I experienced on that night and the way in which the Hand of God whisked me away from certain doom.

With so many clear signs, which have manifested directly in front of me, I do wonder why I continue, from time to time, to worry and fear, instead of being a constant witness to the Mercy, the Compassion, the living Presence, the Omnipresent Power of the One Who perfectly protects those who truly love Him, those who journey for His sake:

> *"The Lord is my light and my salvation; whom shall I fear?*
> *The Lord is the strength of my life; of whom shall I be afraid?"*

> Psalm 27:1

8

Who Am I?
In the City Flowing with Light

Amsterdam, 1971

Observe the wonders as they occur around you.
Don't claim them. Feel the artistry moving through,
and be silent.

Mevlana Jelaluddin Rumi
The Essential Rumi

G rateful to be alive, and unscathed by this test, I traveled from Bulgaria back to Cologne, Germany, from where I had originally set forth on the Orient Express. Arriving in the region of Cologne, I called Karlheinz and Mary with whom I had stayed en route, but they did not answer their phone. So, the only place I was able to stay that night was on a steep hill. I had to fit my body between rocks into a position that resembled a cross and sleep in a semi-vertical position. Faced with this particular circumstance, I found that this, too, was possible. From nights like this, I learned, for the rest of my life, to appreciate having a bed to sleep in.

The next morning, I crossed the border from Germany to Holland. Even the sky in Germany seemed dark and foreboding, while the sky directly on the other side of the border was sunny and bright. I thought about how many Jews and other refugees had begun to taste the sweetness of refuge and release from their immense ordeal when they arrived in this benign land.

I, too, after the duress and fatigue of a long journey with no resting place, returned to Amsterdam with great happiness and found a place flowing with light and goodwill, such that simply setting foot on the land was healing. I went back to the home of a Dutch dancer with whom I had stayed en route.

It was very beautiful there in their quaint farmhouse on the emerald bank of the canal. The painter had a lot of friends who visited, all of whom spoke Dutch, which I did not speak at all. After several evenings of listening to conversations in which I could neither receive, nor give anything, I saw there was no reason for me to stay there and so I packed my bags and got on a tram one morning, having no idea at all where I was going.

I stayed on the tram until the end of the line and then got off. As I was getting off the train, I heard someone calling my name. It was a young man I had known in Berkeley.

He said he was waiting for me to get off before greeting me. There was someone he was sure I should meet. I was pretty sure of this too, since I was waiting for a sign and had no other idea what I was supposed to do.

Jeffrey took me to the apartment of a Dutch painter named Albert Jan, who, Jeffrey said, was a Sufi. When we entered the room, the painter, who had been sitting on the edge of a large bed, leapt up and ran over to embrace me. He greeted me like someone whom he had known forever and had missed for a long time.

He was very tall, very vulnerable and open, like a very large child. He spoke to me as if he had been in isolation for a long time and had finally found someone to talk to. He spoke mostly about Sufism and his experiences in Jerusalem, but also about his experiences with the teachings of the great Indian Master, Sri Ramana Maharshi. Most of what he said was closely related to my journey and to what would happen to me in the future. I did not know this at the time, having no idea what the future would bring.

Now, in looking back at the map of my life's journey, I see where I was destined to go and receive the teachings waiting for me there. Those were the places of power that I had to visit, and all of this had been decreed. The Dutch painter who loved Sufism was simply one of the many kind beings I was destined to meet, through whom, stage by stage, I became aware of the way I was to follow.

He became for me an agent of the divine mercy. He told me that he had created a prayer room in the attic, where he did not have much time to go, and he would be very happy and honored if I stayed there and prayed there as long as I liked. That was a clear sign of where I was supposed to stay next, so I accepted with deep gratitude.

After so many miles of being on the road, often sleeping on the road itself, in woodpiles, and on the luggage racks of trains, what an experience it was to be in a room in which I could begin to contemplate what had unfolded in the months of continuous travel. Only in not having any place at all and no one to speak with throughout the journey, did I begin to sense the profound inherent blessing in everything.

During this part of my life, in which I did no business, had no idea of my identity or where I was going, and pursued no goal but the search for truth, I experienced a fundamental state of existence in which I had nothing and was utterly dependent upon the grace and guidance of God.

In later years, I built many things, a business, a family, houses, communities… but I never forget, in the core of my being, the experience I had during those years of travel, the experience of being invisible, indigent, and dependent for everything upon the grace of God. I had nothing to hold onto. It was not a vacation after which I would return to a "known" life. The life I knew I had abandoned. I had no plans at all. Every new step of the journey was revealed by the grace of God.

I believe that it was because of the purity, the poverty, and absolute dependence of my state, the fact that "I" determined nothing, I knew nothing about where I was going, that I was very clearly guided, and as much guidance as has been given to me in later years, by the grace of God, the core experience of being, as it is described in Sufism, "a corpse in the hand of the washer" was revealed during this time and in this way.

Many of the teachings I learned later from the teachers whom I was blessed to meet and study with were first transmitted during this essential journey when I was guided by nothing but the grace and love of God.

Now, as I walked down the streets and along the canals of Amsterdam, the light of guidance was taking the form of the face of the illuminated sage, Sri Ramana Maharshi, and the guidance that he was transmitting took the profoundly simple form of a question, "*Who am I?*" This question, and the self-inquiry that is generated by it, was posed to us by the great sage, but truly arises from the depth of the mystery of our being. It is one of those phrases like "*Seek, and the truth shall make you free*" that is always relevant and must always be applied to the endless process of self-discovery and the search for truth.

While asking myself this question repeatedly, I found that all of the roles I had played in my life were not really who I was. So, the question remained, perpetually probing, evoking the mystery of existence, itself.

> *What is the means for constantly holding on to the thought "Who am I?"*
>
> *When other thoughts arise, one should not pursue them, but should inquire: "To whom do they arise?" It does not matter how many thoughts arise. As each thought arises, one should inquire with diligence, "To whom has this thought arisen?" The answer that would emerge would be "To me." Thereupon if one inquires "Who am I?" the mind will go back to its source; and the thought that arose will become quiescent. With repeated practice in this manner, the mind will develop the skill to stay in its source.*
>
> Sri Ramana Maharshi

Engaged in this process of self-enquiry, seeking the source of my thoughts and the knowledge of who was thinking them, I almost glided down the streets of Amsterdam, not really focusing on the outer sights but on the inner mirror of the face of the luminous sage, dwelling as I was, in the process of self-inquiry he had proposed.

Although this advice was given to me, by someone I had never met, it was invaluable to me. Not defined within the context of any specific religion, as I saw it, it was a powerful psychological and spiritual tool, one that helps the seeker to dispel the illusion of egotism, himself or herself.

It was a gift I was given along with the gift of refuge in the home of the Dutch painter. Yet, even as we become aware that our thoughts and perceptions are unreal in relation to the eternal reality of God, still the thoughts and perceptions are there, like words on the page we are reading.

From the time that we begin to be aware that there is a transcendent Reality, and that is the reality of the true Self, which is in contrast to the illusory world of the ego, from this point on, we may begin to perceive the counterpoint, the inner light of truth, the eternal light of the inner sage, in contrast to the darkness of the sorrows accumulating in the illusory world.

I discovered after some time, that while I was enjoying the sweetness of inner reflection in the home of the Dutch painter, within the home there were some deep problems. My gracious host, even while extending such kindness to me, was struggling with the dissolution of his marriage, which was causing confusion, pain, and conflict in his family and home. I tried to see if there was any way I could help, but found there was none, other than to pray for the peace of all.

Feeling that I must continue on the journey, not knowing where to go next, I had one of a series of quest dreams that I had throughout the journey. In each of the dreams, I began in a house with many rooms, often filled with light and warmth and a lot of people congregating, sometimes around a fireside, and I was told by a voice that I had to leave all this, leave the world as I knew it, and make the journey alone.

The next part of the dream was a long, solitary trip, often through a desert or on a narrow mountain path. This solitary journey would lead to the next station of spiritual understanding or experience I was to reach. In the "quest" dream that I had in Amsterdam, I was in the very apartment where I was living with the family of the painter. They were struggling with the same problems I had sensed in waking life.

Again, I felt helpless to improve their situation. I was told by the voice to leave the world and return to my solitary journey, and I began to walk through the night. I walked and walked and came at last to a beautiful forest of large, bluish and grey-green fir trees against a luminous, pre-dawn, blue-grey sky. The voice said, "Here is He for whom you seek." I woke up from the dream but did not remember it until several days later when I arrived in the forest.

The next day, I heard the voices of monks singing a very beautiful eastern liturgy on a tape playing in an adjoining room. I was moved by this and inquired where the tape came from. Learning that it had been recorded in a certain monastery in Chevetogne, Belgium, I immediately went upstairs and painted a scroll on parchment paper to send to the place where this tape had been produced. I framed the letter with paintings of the Himalayas and a seeker traveling through them. I said that I was a traveler searching for truth. I had heard the sound of the monks singing and felt magnetically drawn by it, that the journey was leading my soul to the monastery.

I sent this little scroll to the monastery in Belgium, and within a few days I received a response. One of the monks, Father Theodor, who was the doorkeeper of the monastery, told me that in a few days they would be celebrating the festival of the baptism of Christ and I was warmly invited to attend. The monastery was a famous gathering place of Christians of many denominations. It was so ecumenical that even a formless wanderer, a seeker of truth, a Jewish girl returning from the Himalayas was definitely welcome, invited without hesitation.

As soon as I received the invitation, I accepted it and set out to locate the place from which that beautiful sound had emanated. I took a train from Amsterdam to Brussels, a bus to Namours and another bus to Ciney, where Chevetogne was located, arriving late at night in the middle of a snowstorm. I got off the bus and could see nothing but snow, thick snow on the ground, snow flying in the sky.

It was, as St. John of the Cross tells us, *"On a dark night, kindled in love, with yearnings, O happy chance! In the happy night, in secret, when none saw me, nor I beheld aught, without light or guide, save that which burned in my heart."* In the darkness I could see nothing, nor could I be seen, but I was not afraid, because the light of faith and yearning was burning in my heart. Then, gradually, very faintly in the distance, I perceived a tiny light. Since that was the only sign I had, I followed it, up a hill, through the storm, to a small house.

There I found an old woman who indicated the direction in which I should find the house where the sisters lived, where I was to stay. It was quite a trek through the blizzard.

Finally arriving at the door, I was very warmly and sweetly welcomed by a nun, Sister Raphaelle, who was wearing a blue denim habit that matched her large blue eyes. I knew I had already seen her before, but in what world or dimension of consciousness, I do not know.

She took me on a tour of the small house. It was equally familiar. Everything, it seemed, was hand-hewn and aglow with light. The interior of the house was made of golden wood. It was illuminated, by candles dipped by the nuns and decorated by icons painted by the nuns. I would be fed bread baked by the nuns and vegetables grown by them.

I was taken to a room where I was to stay that was very comfortable and aglow with the same light and warmth, not a cold and austere cell that we imagine to be essential to monastic life. After a few hours' sleep, I was woken and sent out on a path again alone, this time the one leading to the churches where liturgies were being sung. It was about four in the morning. There were two large, domed buildings, one where the Eastern rite was being performed and one where the Western rite was being performed. I was attracted to the Eastern rite in the Byzantine Chapel.

As I entered the vast, glowing church from the dark path, I was inundated with light. I had attended many churches in my child-hood searching for a light I intuitively felt was somewhere in the church, but finding darkness. Now, here it was, a church filled with light! There were candles burning everywhere and beautiful vision-ary icons on every surface of the arched cathedral, but the truly luminous dimension of the experience was shining within me.

I realized immediately upon entering that resplendent church that the "man of light" I had seen so long within me was, it seemed, directly connected with Jesus (as). This is obvious to everyone who knows it, but until that moment, I had not grasped it. So, that moment—the entrance into that place of light to which I had been invited to celebrate the baptism of Christ—was for me an immer-sion in an ocean of light and understanding. This moment was reve-latory for me in the sense that it was the first moment in my life when the inner light of my being was clearly aligned with the pro-phetic manifestation.

When the liturgy was completed and I left the church, a cool and radiant dawn lit up the forest through which I walked from the Byzantine monastery to the warm, glowing house of the Sisters of Bethlehem, where I was staying. I realized in the early morning light that this was the forest I had seen in my dream in which I heard the voice saying, *"Here is He for whom you seek."*

9

Life in the Monasteries

Chevetogne, Belgium, and the French Alps, 1972

Lay not up for yourselves treasures upon earth, where moth and dust doth corrupt, and where thieves break through and steal. But lay up for yourselves treasures in heaven, where neither moth nor dust doth corrupt, and where thieves do not break through and steal. For where your treasure is, there will your heart be also.

Matthew 6:19–21

"I have held many things in my hands, and I have lost them all; but whatever I have placed in God's hands, that I still possess."

Martin Luther

Every morning before dawn, I would walk through the forest that I had seen in my dream. At one end of the winding path was the house where the five sisters lived, and I with them, and on the other side of the forest were two large churches, one where the Western rites were being observed and one where the Eastern rites were being observed, several times a day.

The church where the Eastern, or Byzantine, rites were being practiced was a huge, domed cathedral, the inside of which was covered with paintings of the saints and mysteries. In my generally altered state, I saw everything happening three-dimensionally in trans-historic time. That image which most attracted my heart and soul was the rendering of Jesus, ascended with arms outstretched, as though in flight.

I was strongly drawn to the Byzantine church and attended all the services held there. In the vast cool cathedral, full of mysteries, surrounding the central area where the priests performed their duties, there was a semi-circle of ornately carved wooden niches made of rich, dark wood.

These were the niches where the faithful were invited to stand and observe the liturgy. Other than the three monks, I was often the only person present to respond to the divine invitation, and I felt perfectly at home, blessed and protected in that niche to which I returned day after day, many times a day.

Father Theodor looked like Saint Nicholas in a Russian Orthodox robe and was always giving gifts of kindness and love. It was he who had received my letter and welcomed me to come immediately. I am still struck to this day by the quality of unconditional openness with which he received me. He was the manifestation of non-judgmental, universal acceptance. In addition to these meetings in the church, I met with him for one or two hours every day to discuss dreams, understandings, and experiences which were arising within me in this holy place, all of which he seemed to welcome with interest.

I also met every day with Father Gabriel, who was another of the monks at the services. He was a towering figure with long red hair and beard and green light-filled eyes. In his long black robes and tall hat, with such grace, dignity, and mysticism, he was truly a man of my dreams. He was a deeply internal person radiating mystic presence. I sensed that he was directly linked with the Angel Gabriel, as with Jesus and Mary.

So, this is where Maharaj-ji was sending me, to this beautiful wellspring of Christian mystical life!

In later years, I was traveling through Europe and sought out Father Gabriel. I was told that he had entered into a state of permanent contemplation, never to be seen again by a human being. I felt very much blessed that I was one of the human beings that had seen him before he disappeared from view.

Every day, I traveled back and forth between the fathers, the sisters, and the liturgies in the Eastern Church. Then, one day, I began hearing that a very special woman was coming to the monastery. She was the Mother Superior in charge of the sisters who were taking care of the house where I had been given refuge. She had given birth to a large order of sisters called the Sisters of Bethlehem.

I had already noted the special quality of the women I was living with. They seemed very happy, very open, fulfilled, grounded, creative, and at peace, not rigid or repressed, as stereotypes of nuns would suggest. Now, they were all awaiting the coming of Sister Marie, their spiritual guide.

Since the monastery in Chevetogne was a well-known centre of ecumenical assembly, there were always many people visiting. I looked at all of the women as they appeared, walking across the emerald grounds, wondering which one was the much-awaited Sister Marie. I saw various women with impressive-looking formal habits, but each time I thought, "No, that could not be Sister Marie!"

In the house of the sisters, which was called Bethlehem, the tables were laid in a circle for meals. We ate in silence, but beautiful music was played. I felt that the Holy Spirit was singing. One night, as the meal was unfolding, I noticed a striking woman. She was very tall with many deep lines engraved upon her face. She was dressed in the light blue denim habit of the order. Her habit, like her face, was well worn.

More striking than her appearance was the way she was standing over her food in prayer. It was a strange thing to behold the interiority of another person's prayer. I was powerfully drawn to her as she stood for a long time in silence before sitting to eat. She was emanating a sense of deep worship, meaningful service, and submission to God. I felt that she was the foundation of this community upon which it was resting, not the "Mother Superior." She did not have the dress, the demeanor, or the attitude of a Mother Superior, but the demeanor of a servant of God. In her humility, there was immense strength. I wondered who she was.

I finished my meal. As I was taking my plate to be washed, I felt a strong hand on my shoulder, and I was impelled into a small room. The door was closed. It was she who had led me there and sat down facing me, her face about two inches from mine. She said, "Jesus wants us to set the whole world on fire with the love of God! Mary is the Master of love! And the Father is searching for lovers! What does God, who is the Plenitude of everything, search for—only those who truly love and worship Him."

She then told me the story of her life and mission. In her youth, she was living in a convent, when many blessings descended upon her. She was filled with the love of God and deeply inspired. One day, she looked out of the window of her room in the convent and saw a barber on the street below. She wondered how she, enclosed in the convent, could be the recipient of so much grace, while the man below in the street had no access to this grace. This perception catalyzed her mission.

She left the convent and went into the world. In various locations, she gathered people and asked them if they would give a year of their lives for the love of God. In each place, with the community that she had formed, composed of people consecrated to the church and also lay people, men, women, and children living and working together, she built a center. In this way, she built centers all around France and Belgium, all of which she called *Bethlehem*.

These communities of people, dedicated to working together for the sake of God, had become a great success. I saw how beautifully the experiment was working in Chevetogne, but the price she had paid for bringing forth these communities was that, in constantly traveling from place to place and working constantly with people everywhere, she had to some extent sacrificed the depth of her contemplative life.

When she saw me, she told me, she remembered the life of her soul. She told me that Jesus and Mary spoke to her about me. She was guided to give me refuge and also the spiritual freedom, as she said, to serve God and God alone. As she had been instructed, she must extend to me refuge and protection in all of her communities, but unlike the other members of her communities, she wanted me to focus not on daily chores and interactions but solely on the path of contemplation, to learn to listen to and obey the voice of the Divine.

She took me with her to her community in the French Alps in a village called Les Voirons. The community gathered in the monastery was composed, like her other communities, of a great assortment of people. I was simply another one of the multicolored threads in the beautiful tapestry she was weaving.

Every day, we gathered in a circle to pray for everyone. Each person was invited to specify any individual or group of people to add to our collective prayer. Sister Marie was very touched by the fact that I was of Jewish origin, and every day at prayer time, she made reference to this fact and, inspired by my presence and the fact that God had sent me to join their circle, she prayed for all the children of Israel.

That she prayed for me in this context and for all the children of Israel (*Bani 'Israil*) is significant in the context of this story, and it reminds me that I, as a journeyer through deserts in search of Divine Guidance, must not forget the original journey of my ancestors through the desert in response to the Divine Command.

All the revelations that came later completed the revelations that came earlier. And this ongoing divine reality, remembrance of the people, throughout the ages, who have traveled on the journey guided by God, is what Sister Marie was honoring when she brought the children of Israel into the circle of prayer.

Now, the feast of Easter was approaching. A Bishop was coming to celebrate the feast in this monastery high in the Alps. Sister Marie felt that I should be baptized, by the Bishop on Easter Sunday. She said that she would be my godmother and I her spiritual child, although this was very unorthodox, since in general she would take this responsibility only for the sisters within her order.

Another unconventional aspect of this baptism was that I had received no catechism at all. Until today, I have learned almost nothing about the structure and the rules or dogma of the Church; I have been taught, only by the light, and the spirit of Christ.

But since she was functioning in the realm of truth, the realm of light and inspiration, Sister Marie was not concerned that I had not memorized the rules. Simply, the Bishop was coming, Easter was approaching, and my baptism, she said, had to occur at that time. She asked me what name I felt I should be baptized with. I said, "Miriam Arunati." "Arunati," a word I had learned in India, means, "full of grace."

Sister Marie, and all those brought up by her, transmitted a very powerful sense of the reality of Jesus (as) and his mother, who for them were not idealized greeting card figures but absolutely revolutionary beings, courageous and fearless servants of the Truth.

This was a very liberating and galvanizing approach. Jesus (as) was not as the world portrayed him. As dedicated and sincere disciples of the spirit of Christ and his teaching, the Sisters of Bethlehem conveyed to me how serious and great a spiritual Master he was and how profound a taskmaster, which I understood and experienced more and more deeply as I read the words he spoke to his disciples.

What I began to understand, from the transmission of these followers of Christ, in contrast to what I had seen in Christian churches in my childhood, is the difference between Jesus (as) the man with his pure teachings and the vast complex of Christianity, which evolved after he left this world.

Just as the Prophet Abraham (as) and the Prophet Muhammad (saw) were the greatest threats to those in the "idol business" in their times, Jesus (as), who threw the money lenders out of the temple and was the greatest threat to the worldly authorities in power because of his absolute purity and submission only to God, had strangely become the symbol behind which, for so many centuries, those worldly powers have rallied.

To a magnitude that defies comprehension, he who was free of egotism and idolatry had become an idol worshipped by multitudes. This is the great paradox apparent in every religion, and the reason why the sincere seeker must go beyond all worldly appearances into the essence and the living truth, which all the representatives sent by God have brought.

I loved the Sisters of Bethlehem because they took my hand and walked with me into the garden of the heart where Jesus (as) taught. They helped me to receive and experience fully the teaching that he brought.

On Easter Sunday, Sister Marie asked me to bathe as the disciples of Jesus (as) had bathed. I have thought about that request for the rest of my life. How did the disciples of Christ bathe? In retrospect, I see that this community, the Sisters of Bethlehem, was living very much as the disciples of Christ lived, in the reality of his presence and his teaching. That was why I had been guided directly to them, to receive and imbibe this living tradition.

That night, we went out into the snow-covered Alps. There, a huge bonfire had been built. It was like a pillar of flame, reaching into the night sky. I was baptized in the snow, and then Sister Marie lit a very long, white candle, igniting it in the bonfire, which represented the light of Christ, and she gave the candle to me.

Having received the flaming torch and been baptized in the snow of Mount Blanc, the White Mountain, I went into retreat for forty days. Sister Marie was guided not to allow me to become distracted by housework and social contact; the overpowering priority at this stage of my journey, she made me know, was to dedicate my life to the service of the Divine.

I lit the huge candle everyday to remind me of the eternal light shining within me and within everything. Just as the light of the candle that had been placed in my hand was ignited by and drawn from the huge bonfire, so was the light of each soul ignited by and drawn from the infinite plenitude of the Light of God.

In the depth of that solitude, with nothing but the majestic white mountains to see, no one to speak with, nothing to do but to pray, I read the words of the Bible inwardly and experienced within my soul the story of the life of Jesus as deeply as I could, dwelling upon his experiences in the wilderness and facing my own tests and temptations in the wilderness of my inner being.

When the period of forty days of solitude was complete, Sister Marie sent me into the Alps every day with Sister Claire. Sister Claire had huge, shining, brown eyes and a brilliant, yet very gentle spirit. She was a maker of beautiful puppets and puppet shows, an artist and a poet. She was supposed to teach me catechism on our daily journeys into the Alps. In reality, all that we spoke about was Jesus (as) and Mevlana Rumi (ra). She shared with me the spirit of Christ, and I shared with her the stories and teachings of Rumi (ra) I had read.

Every day, we sat amongst those great white peaks and celebrated the presence of the men of God who in spirit sat with us. I never once contemplated the "Trinity" or Jesus (as) as the "Son of God" or Jesus (as) "suffering for my sins on a cross." All that we thought and talked about were the ever living, eternally inspiring and life-giving spiritual teachings of Jesus (as) and Rumi (ra), which, as we discovered, were interlinked. Such was my catechism.

Otherwise, under the direction of Sister Marie and her inspiration that I must focus principally upon the contemplation of God and the inner work, rather than focusing upon housework and other more worldly activities, I spent most of my time in the monastery in a kind of retreat and then created a room for retreat in the monastery, which I heard later, was regularly used in the future by the sisters for individual periods of contemplation.

Sister Marie wanted me to stay forever with her and the Sisters of Bethlehem. I did not want to leave them, but one day I looked out into the courtyard of the monastery and saw a man, a woman, and a child walking together. It was beautiful and compelling, and it was a message for me. I knew that I had to leave the monastery and continue my journey. My journey had more dimensions, which had to be fulfilled.

I sent this news to Lennie and Sophie, who immediately sent me a plane ticket. It was one of the very few times in my life I have ever traveled first class. There was only one other person in the cabin, and he was sitting next to me. He was a very refined, educated, and devout person. He had a lovely face and manner.

We were served platters; it seemed a feast, of the most delicious fruits and vegetables. Throughout our journey through the heavens, celestial music came pouring through our earphones, a Magnificat to Mary and other divine music. I felt that even these details of the journey home, were orchestrated by the Divine.

10

Short Stay in America,
Culture Shock,
Longing to Return to Sanctified Land

California and Taos, New Mexico, 1973

"Never look down to test the ground before taking your next step; only he who keeps his eye fixed on the far horizon will find the right road."

Dag Hammarskjold

I returned to the America, from which I had fled. Re-entry, with its culture shock, was softened by Sophie. When I had been living in the monastery in Chevetogne, Lennie and Sophie had come to visit. Lennie had insisted that he be in the church for all the liturgies, starting at four o'clock in the morning. Although he thought of himself as something of an agnostic, his soul was insisting that he not miss one time of prayer.

Sophie too had seemed to enjoy going into the church. After all, she was an artist and the church was full of art. She was also amazed at the delicious food prepared by the Sisters of Bethlehem.

When I returned to America, it was through the gracious portal of the house of Lennie and Sophie that I entered. They were now living on a beautiful, wooded property near the ocean in Pacific Palisades. Adjoining the main house was a small glass house surrounded by trees. There, by hanging up the icons she had purchased at the monastery, Sophie created a small chapel in which I could live.

Whenever anybody, even people coming to work on the house, would come over, she brought them to this little chapel to meet me and played a tape of the monks singing at the monastery. Such was the nature of her acceptance, creative thinking, and religious tolerance.

Later, when I had embraced Islam, and I came home with Ahamad Kabeer, an *imam*, it was with equally great ease that, having invited Muslims from the neighborhood to join, he was able to perform the *jummah* prayers (congregational prayers held every Friday) in the living room of Lennie and Sophie. That was just the kind of thing that you could imagine happening in the living room of Lennie and Sophie. I mention this in response to the often-asked question: How did my Jewish family respond to my embrace first of Christianity and then of Islam?

It was all like a river naturally following its course into the sea. It was as though my course was predestined. All that was to happen to me was already present within me from the time of my childhood, the time of my birth. Nothing at all that unfolded in my journey was surprising, shocking, or unsettling to my family because the sense of the unconventional, extraordinary things that were to take place in my life were present within me from the beginning.

It was very peaceful in the little glass chapel surrounded by towering eucalyptus trees, but I had to get on with my life and journey, whatever that entailed. I went back to Berkeley and moved into the house of my brother Michael, where I had lived before I left. This time, the glass lantern room, like all the other rooms in the house, was occupied, and there was only a small space available in the basement.

So, I moved into one side of the dark basement. It was like living in a hole in the ground and also like being in a womb. I was gestating, processing all that had been revealed to me on my quest. Because the inner work was so strong and deep, I did not go out much. But one night, I was invited to a *zikr*, a circle of remembrance of God, and in the spirit of divine celebration I went.

The Sheikh, who was visiting Berkeley, spoke first, introducing the *zikr* in a broad and tolerant way. He said that the most important thing was to remember God, to love God, and to keep God in your heart. That certainly resonated with me, and I went into my heart, and felt the wellspring of love for God, which was opening up within me. As the *zikr*, or chanting, was unfolding, I thought of all the beautiful things He had revealed to me and given to me on my journey, and I was deeply moved with gratitude.

I have no idea how I was manifesting externally because I was immersed in the inner world, surrendering to the love of God as the Sheikh had instructed. Suddenly, I was shocked out of that state of contemplation by one of the male disciples, whose hand was on my knee. He touched me so as to let me know that I must stop doing what I was doing. I think I must have been swaying. Shocked into alertness, I looked at the Sheikh, who was staring at me with disdain. Instantly, I realized that this was not the way in which he wanted me to remember and love God.

After the sitting *zikr*, we stood up and formed circles, one for the men, one for the women, and we began a standing *zikr*. This was a practice of saying the names of God in Arabic while moving. The movements were, for me, very fast, strong, and intense. I could not keep up with them at all. I had a scarf on my head, but could not really keep it on correctly with all of the movement.

Once again, there was a hand, this time on my shoulder, telling me to stop, and again the Sheikh was looking at me with marked disapproval. I was asked to leave the circle and sit down. Truly, being unable to keep up with the movement and longing for the stillness of meditation, I was greatly relieved to sit down and meditate.

When the *zikr* was over and we were leaving, I thanked the Sheikh, and apologized for any way in which I might have offended him or disturbed the practice. I knew that he was not happy with me, but what could I do? I went home to my dark hole, very much affected by this meeting. I had been so deeply internal and alone in my worship and love of God. This step into the more formal world of the remembrance of God was absolutely shocking. I was almost paralyzed by the intensity of the encounter with the Sheikh.

The next morning, still very much affected, I was strangely inspired to go to a small store in Berkeley called *Tail of the Yak* where artifacts from around the world, but mostly from Tibet, were sold. I had a Tibetan cape on layaway there, which I thought I should pick up. I walked slowly to that store, with every step praying with my Russian Orthodox black cloth prayer beads the prayer of the heart, I arrived at the store and went into the back room to inquire about the cape on layaway.

There, in that backroom, was the Sheikh I had met the previous night and several of his disciples. What a wonder! I apologized again for anything I had done that might have offended anyone.

He seemed to be waiting there for me. He seemed to have called me there so he could tell me more strongly what he thought. When I said that I was sorry, he said, "You should be sorry! If you continue in the way you are going, they will have to tie you up in a straitjacket and wheel you away!" After that shocking statement, he spoke to me about Islam and the necessity of embracing Islam, indicating that I should learn about this from him.

Whatever else he said, I do not remember. I was completely stunned, assaulted. I was barely able to get home, and once I did get back to the dark basement, unable to move at all for several days. It was the association of the behavior and the advice of the Sheikh with his proposal that I must embrace Islam, which disturbed me most deeply, causing me to stop functioning almost entirely.

This was severely troubling because part of what he said was true, and it *was* necessary for me to embrace Islam. This knowledge was deeply planted and hidden within me. But I could not enter the holy door of Islam at the hands of this Sheikh. Although his approach was helpful to others, including some of my dearest friends, it was not the way for me. This dichotomy literally paralyzed me psychologically. I could not move. The people who were living in the house with me were very concerned. Nobody could do anything to shake me out of that state.

Finally, after several days, a few friends came down into that dark basement and literally picked me up in their arms. They said, "We are taking you to Mount Shasta to see a psychic named Pearl." We drove to the mountain, and when I walked into Pearl's room, she exclaimed, "O India! O Israel! The orthodoxy will never understand what you have to do! To be one with God is to be in the majority!"

The meeting with Pearl was the remedy. Through her nondogmatic openness and subtle reflection, I was able to find my center again, to reclaim my heart with its love of God intact, wild and wooly but sincere. Not every teacher and every teaching approach is good for all students. Each of us has to follow our own true path. In reality, I did continue to go the way I was going, sincerely searching for the way of God, and the deep inclination of the heart led me with certainty, in the time and the way decreed, to the path of Islam, and not to a mental ward, as the Sheikh had warned.

After being in Berkeley a short while, I reconnected with Ram Dass and his community again. We had weekly *kirtan*s, singing and chanting the names of God, and did a lot of meditation. With Ram Dass and a teacher of Vipassana meditation, we held a meditation retreat in the Santa Cruz Mountains. We also formed a band, *Amazing Grace*, and made an album. One song I remember from the album, written, I believe by Parmahamsa Yogananda, went:

> *"Who is in my temple?*
> *All the doors do open themselves.*
> *All the lights do light themselves.*
> *Darkness, like a dark bird, flies away, oh flies away!"*

The formless dimension of the meditation was very helpful to me. I entered into the practice of Vipassana meditation for sixteen hours a day, several days in a row. The practice is one of sweeping through the body with a current of awareness and dispelling all congestion, density, illusion, or disease with the consciousness that all is impermanent.

For me, this was an immensely effective practice. All of the confusion and pain, wherever it was lodged in the body, heart, or mind, seemed to be dispelled by the current of consciousness that was passing through my body. For this practice, and its powerful cleansing and transformative effect, I was very grateful.

Otherwise, I found life in America difficult because of the lack of clarity, the lack of morality, the absence of guidelines that were being followed.

Eventually, many of the group went to Boulder where Trungpa Rinpoche, a lama from Tibet who was quite westernized, was teaching his students. I had read his book *Cutting Through Spiritual Materialism* and found that it was brilliantly written, but I was baffled by the apparent effect of the teaching on the behavior of the disciples. This was an approach, which taught, as I understood it, that the disciple could do whatever he liked, as long as he did it with "wisdom." Almost anything could be done, it seemed, as long as one was using "wisdom" and cutting through spiritual materialism while doing it.

Having been back in America only a short time and somewhat re-integrated into the "spiritual scene," as I observed the way teachings were often being transmitted, I was shocked by how loose and how lawless the spiritual communities seemed to be. I had become sensitized to and transformed by a completely different way of existing.

Although it was not yet revealed in its completeness, the path was now beneath my feet. In my heart and in my body, I knew that rules, discipline, and spiritual guidance were fundamental and absolutely necessary for real spiritual development.

I was profoundly homesick for the purity of existence I had experienced in the monasteries and throughout my journey. After only a short time in America, I wanted to leave again, to escape the cultural pollution and corruption that was rampant, even in the spiritual movements, and continue on the journey of my soul towards God. I had heard about initiatic orders in South America and was thinking about going there, when I took a side trip from Boulder, Colorado, to the Lama Foundation in the mountains above Taos, New Mexico.

There, I discovered my next step. The Lama Foundation, in the San Cristobal Mountain range, is built on elevated, blessed land, which stands like a high island surrounded by an ocean of space. The endless view, the space one breathes and beholds, is majestic and mystical. One gets the sense, as the Native Americans did, that one is standing on sacred ground.

I had passed through and lived for a while at the Lama Foundation some time before. Cooking in the round, hewn wood and adobe Lama kitchen with its windows overlooking infinity was for me an initiation into cooking and service. With the hundreds of *chapattis* that we cooked there, it was the birthplace of my love of serving food and, after the house of Lennie and Sophie, it was a real training ground in the beauty and sweetness, as well as the challenges, of communal living.

Now, as I was returning to Lama for a brief visit, I wanted to express my gratitude for the blessings I had received there, those blessings, which were actually seeds of awareness growing within me. I visited the beautiful buildings of Lama, which were mostly domes built of wood and adobe and filled with light.

They were created to exist in harmony with the nature that surrounded them, so that the light within flowed without obstruction into the luminous space surrounding each building and extending into the boundless vista. Walking through the buildings of the Lama Foundation was for me a lesson in sacred architecture and in the Tao, or effortless being, the natural state.

I walked over to the Lama garden. There, in the midst of the flourishing garden of organic green vegetables, was the Green Man himself, Nooruddeen Durkee. It was he, whose name means "the light of the way, the light of religion," who had put up most of the buildings with his wife Asha, and who had envisioned and facilitated the construction of each of the illuminated spaces I had just passed through. Nooruddeen, an impressive figure with long red hair and beard and green eyes, was standing in the greenness of the garden, wearing a green and white sarong and a red shirt.

I was carrying in my arms a huge tome, the journal I had made of my journey.

Nooruddeen told me that he was preparing to go very soon with a small group of people to Jerusalem to write the fourth book in a series he had produced, working with a small group of people from around the world whom he called *"Companions of the Palm."* He was waiting now for whomever God would send to work on this project and at the same time preparing to go.

Arriving with my stone-covered journal in my arms, it appeared that I was one of the people he was waiting for, one of the members of the team. Since I was longing for the purity I had experienced in the monasteries, it seemed that a journey to Jerusalem would be the perfect next step.

We spent the next week together in a state of transcendent communication. This encounter was an oasis, in the midst of the vast desert of my solitude. On the second floor of a small, domed building, filled with plants and sunlight, we met and shared much, so many dimensions, in one eternal week. I found in him a man of vision and action and light.

It was the light of God that I saw in him, that was guiding me to the Mount of Olives, where Jesus (as) had prayed, and to the grandfather who lived near the tomb of Abraham (as), and to the embrace of Islam. When the eternal week in the light-filled dome was over, it was time to return to the road.

Nooruddeen and another brother who was going to work on the book, Abd'al Ahad, and I traveled by car across country. From New York, I flew with Abd'al Ahad to Venice and from there we crossed an ocean of shining water to arrive in Haifa. We then found our way to Jerusalem and to the blessed Mount of Olives, on which we were to live for a sacred time.

11

Embracing Islam in El Khalil, The Place of Abraham (as), Friend of God

Jerusalem and Hebron, 1974

And a voice came out of the throne, saying, praise our God, all His servants, and ye that fear Him, both small and great. And I heard as it were the voice of a great multitude, and as the voice of many waters and as the voice of mighty thunders, saying, "Alleluiah: For the Lord God Omnipotent reigneth."

Book of Revelation 19:5–6

The day I arrived in Jerusalem, it so happened that my beloved Sister Marie arrived too. She had come to visit her mentor, an illuminated priest who was to give a seminar in a monastery on the Mount of Olives. The subject he had chosen was the Book of Revelation. So that was where I spent my first week in the Holy Land, and it was truly a holy land that I was transported to by the priest as he made the Book of Revelation real for us, as it was for him.

I remember the subtle intensity of light in the room, the feeling of spiritual energy coming through him and filling the room as he read passages from the Book of Revelation. The priest never looked at us. He was facing another direction. I sensed that he was turned away from this earth and toward the Celestial Jerusalem. I was amazed at the rays of light I saw descending upon him.

In the normal world, if one was to give a seminar every day for a week and never looked at his audience, he would lose his listeners, but this priest enthralled us with what was enthralling him. I went with him to the world of revelation and saw, to some degree, what he saw. As he described the images in the Book of Revelation and explained what they signified to him, exploring the meanings that they could have for a follower of Christ, I felt the Divine Presence manifesting through these images, creating a city of celestial peace.

That is how I entered Jerusalem, not as a militarized secular city which has endured centuries of conflict and strife, culminating in the present tragic conditions, but as a place of light in a plane of light, a place sacred to people of all religions, Jerusalem, the Holy, that we the believers have yet to make real on earth.

When the seminar was over, I joined Nooruddeen and the others he had gathered together to work on the book on Jerusalem. We all lived in a large airy house on the Mount of Olives. I stayed in half of a long room, which I shared with Shahida, who would later become Noura Issa and also the wife of Nooruddeen. We had nothing in that room but light and space. With barely a suit-case full of possessions, the basic necessities, and no possessiveness, I very much enjoyed sharing that space and light with her. It was a sign of the way in which our souls were linked.

As we assembled on the roof of the house on the Mount of Olives and were bathed in soft golden light at sunset, and as we walked upon the golden earth where the prophets (as) had walked, I felt that I had returned home. Although I had been born as a Jew, it was not to a specifically Jewish homeland that I had returned, but to a place of sanctity, holy for me, and others.

Our life and research went on. The book was to be called *Jerusalem: A Garden in the Flames,* and, very much aware of the flames encircling the city, we were searching for the eternal garden, which lay hidden in the heart of the city and its people. This being our intention, we were guided to the lovers of God in all the faiths.

We spoke to many people, recording interviews with Rabbis, Priests, Sheikhs, and simply the believing people of all the faiths. We were searching for and finding the common threads and fundamental truths. Many of the people, both Palestinians and Israelis, expressed that they had lived in peace with people of the other faith until outside forces, such as the British, had come in to foment conflict.

One day, wrapped in a large blue shawl that completely enveloped me, I was sitting outside Damascus Gate, waiting for Sister Marie. I was very much immersed in the inner space but little by little felt something drawing me out. When I opened my eyes, I saw a man with intense green eyes gazing at me, a very slight young man but with a fervent spirit. His eyes were riveted to me. He said, "Are you Mary from California?" I said, "Yes." He said, "My grandfather is waiting for you. When you are ready, I will take you to meet him."

The young man's name was Hassan Al-Sharif. He came home with me that day, and we spent the rest of the day in our home on the Mount of Olives. We talked and talked and talked. I do not remember what we said, but I felt the beautiful, gentle, holy presence of his grandfather in some way entering my heart.

I was also deeply impressed by something Hassan did. When he heard the call to prayer, he took everything out of his pockets and took his watch off, before he did ablutions and prayed. It was a teaching about preparation for prayer and prayer itself that I have never forgotten.

Probably a week later, when we were ready, I set out with Hassan, Nooruddeen, and Abd'al Latif to go to the place where his grandfather was waiting for us. We traveled in an old rickety bus from Jerusalem to Hebron, known as El-Khalil in Arabic. It is the holy city where Prophet Abraham (as) and several members of his family are buried.

The land between El Quds (Jerusalem, the Holy) and El Khalil (short for *Khalilullah*—friend of God, the title of Prophet Abraham (as)) is very beautiful, fertile land, sculpted into many-layered terraces. I strongly felt the presence of our father Abraham (as) during the journey, that he had not only walked on this land, but had also cultivated it and planted seeds in it that were still bearing fruit. If only his descendants could find this fruit and eat it together!

Something about the land was extremely familiar and healing. I felt again that I had been returned home. I was caressed by the care that had been shown to this earth and was greatly refreshed. But the peace that came to us as we traveled through this sacred land was disturbed when we arrived in El Khalil. In the bus station, many people were passing through and milling around, and one could instantly sense the tension and the strain of the inhabitants of this holy city.

We went into the mosque, which is also a synagogue, the so-called "tomb," more accurately called *mazhar*, or place of the presence of Abraham (as) and several of his relatives. It was a place of pilgrimage for Judaism and Christianity as well as Islam, and was full of pilgrims of all three faiths.

Upon entering that place of power, I fell prostrate, not because I had heard I should do it, but because it was the natural, inevitable thing to do. I arose eventually to find that I was surrounded, by worshippers on all sides—angelic and human worshippers, it seemed—of different faiths and understandings, but all descendants and heirs of one father, worshipping together in one sanctified space.

Blessed it was, and deeply meaningful, that I should enter Islam on the earth where Prophet Abraham, *Khalilullah*, Friend of God, (as) had lived and was buried. He was the exemplar, the leader for all the peoples, and one whose descendants, God said, would be like the stars.

Feeling his presence so strongly here in *El-Khalil*, I wondered why all of us, the descendants of this great man, are not shining with the light of certain faith that illuminated his way and following the beautifully clear example he set for all humanity in his understanding of and surrender to the One God. I prayed that I might become a daughter worthy to follow in the footsteps of such an exalted father.

After bringing us to meet our one father, Hassan took us on a journey through the ancient narrow winding lanes, through many arches, doorways, and gateways to the *zawiyyah* (gathering place), where the grandfather was awaiting us. The grandfather, Sidi Sheikh Abdul Muttalib (ra) was one hundred and thirty-five years old, Hassan told us, and was the caretaker of another *mazhar*, the tomb of the Sufi saint Ash-Shibli.

We entered at the level of the road and went far down into an amazing complex until we reached the *zawiyyah* below. Everywhere, there were beautiful plants, flowers, and squash, incredibly healthy vines, and creepers growing up and down the walls. Later, I saw the grandfather, although he was blind, lovingly tending them one by one. I came to realize that I too was one of the plants, which he would nurture and bring to life with the loving tenderness of his divinely inspired touch.

There were two sides to the *zawiyyah,* one was a cave-like room where the grandfather, the Sheikh, lived with his wife, and the other was a larger room where he gathered every day with his disciples. We found the Sheikh with some disciples in the larger room performing *zikr,* invoking the divine qualities. The Sheikh was ancient, venerable, and pure. He was wearing a white and green turban and an ancient long black cloak. In place of a shawl, he was wearing a towel.

I was utterly happy to be in his presence, feeling that I was reunited at last with my true father and friend. His being emanated not a trace of egotism, but only great sweetness, kindness, and grace.

The disciples were sitting in a semi-circle and welcomed us to join them as soon as we entered. We sat down with them and joined the circle. The fact that I was a female and that we were apparent strangers from another part of the world did not seem strange or awkward at all; our presence seemed to enhance what the Sheikh was doing, and we were integrated into their circle in the most natural and harmonious way, as though they had been waiting for us to complete it.

Sheikh Abdul Muttalib (ra) and his disciples were invoking the name of God, *Ya Latif, the Most Subtle, the Kind*. The *zikr* went on and on, so gently and so deeply, with many subtle shifts and permutations. It was the most beautiful invocation. I have wished for the rest of my life that I had a recording of it, so I could listen to it again and understand why it moved me so very much to hear them and join with them. But it is recorded in my heart in accordance with the secret of that name, *the Most Subtle*.

It was a moment of initiation into that beautiful Name of God, and the reflection of that Name in his actions, words, and resonance was the Sheikh, Sidi Sheikh Abdul Muttalib (ra), whom God had brought us here to meet.

After the *zikr*, the Sheikh welcomed us very graciously and introduced us to the way of his *tariqat* (spiritual path). When our meeting was completed, we gave *salaam*s and started to leave. Nooruddeen and Abd'al Latif were out of the *zawiyyah* and I was at the doorway when one of the elder disciples stopped me and told me that the Sheikh wanted me to move in. I accepted this invitation without hesitation.

I went back to the Mount of Olives, got some things, and returned that day. I began living with grandfather and his wife in the cave. She sat on the floor in a corner and cooked the food over a small flame. He frequently placed the food in my mouth. Many blessings, which have come to me later in my life may be traceable back to the *barakah*, the blessing, of receiving and eating what grandfather put in my mouth.

The grandfather gave me his bed to sleep in. I later realized that he did not sleep, but sat up the whole night, throughout which he blew on my head and prayed. I had a dream. I was living in a high mountain kingdom where there was a war going on between two tribes. I was making a spiritual retreat for forty days, alone in a cave, praying for reconciliation and peace.

One day, a man came to the cave and brought a rose. The next day, he came again and brought another rose. This continued for days until the cave was full of roses. Then the man who had been bringing the roses told me that he was a messenger of the king. The king was asking for my hand in marriage. To fulfill the marriage, I would have to jump off a cliff. This offering or sacrifice, this *leap of faith*, would bring about peace in the high mountain kingdom where the two tribes had been warring for a very long time.

I told the dream to the grandfather. He said that the King was the Prophet Muhammad (saw) and that to fulfill the marriage, I must make *salat*, the ritual Islamic prayer. This, he said, was the leap of faith indicated in my dream.

Having been immersed in a "contemplative state," which I thought was continuous, I was not eager to get involved with the "exercise" of *salat*, so I had managed not to hear the command to make *salat* from anyone who had told me about it in the past.

But for grandfather to tell me to do it was as close to a divine transmission as could come in human form, I felt. The sweetness, kindness, and subtlety with which this blessed man invited me to surrender to the will of God engendered in me the deepest sense of happiness and peace I had ever experienced in my life. There was no doubt about accepting this invitation and no struggle at all. I felt I would join again with my ancient family and we would all worship together the One God, Most Merciful, who created us out of His Mercy.

If I had to jump off a cliff, it was into the unknown, but I felt in this secret holy enclave, to which I had been guided by the "*hand*" of God, that the unknown realm into which I was now entering was the realm of God's infinite Grace. I had no choice and no desire but to surrender and enter.

And so it was in this small, ancient, and exalted congregation that I, a Jewish girl born in Hollywood, began to make *salat*. At each time of prayer, a small, lace curtain was hung in the tiny cave, separating the male side of the line from the female side. Standing close to the middle, I was at least fifty years if not a hundred years younger than everyone else in the congregation.

Although so small, it was a wonderful congregation composed of exalted beings. How could I fathom the mercy and loving kindness of the Guide who led me to discover the sweetness of prayer in such an assembly, full of blessing, hidden from the eyes of the world?

Now all of them have left this earth, leaving me alone the sole witness of what took place there. I know that everything I experienced in that cave, the purity of true Islam, the sweetness, kindness, harmony, and peace, all were manifestations of the mercy of the One Who created us all and Who sent all the prophets (as) bearing His message, to make me know that true Islam—Islam revealed by God to the people of God—is peace and light.

Every chapter of the Qur'an, except one, begins, "In the Name of God, the Merciful, the Compassionate." What a great irony it is that the word "Islam" has become inexorably linked in the media world with words such as "terrorism" and "fanaticism."

This media stereotype is certainly fueled and sustained by people who, in the name of Islam, do things, which are condemned and forbidden in the Qur'an, antithetical to the way and religion of the Creator, Most Merciful. For example, the act of committing suicide in Islam is forbidden, as is the killing of women and children in war. In the clearly defined rules of war, fighting is only permitted in defense against attack, and even trees along the way must be protected.

In the present world in which people are committing, in the name of Islam, things that are absolutely forbidden in Islam, and the media is amplifying and promulgating this falsehood, we are conditioned by the forces of darkness and ignorance, which want to keep us from the truth, to associate Islam with things that are totally forbidden in Islam.

But the lovers of truth, the seekers of truth, will find it, and the truth will set them free. It was unquestionably the magnetism of the truth—the magnet that is truth—that led me to grandfather, my first Sheikh, Sidi Sheikh Abdul Muttalib, may God sanctify his secret. No map, no guidebook could have led me to him, only the Divine Guide.

For, although I had encountered Islam several times earlier in my journey, it was only in the presence of such a being that Islam was revealed to me with such sweetness, beauty, and integrity that I had no choice but to embrace it.

In embracing the message brought by the Prophet Muhammad (saw) there in the place of Prophet Abraham (as) I embraced all of the messages brought by all of the messengers (as) sent by the One Creator of all. In embracing the tree and cherishing its fruits, I also found my ancient Jewish roots planted here in the Holy Land.

All of these understandings were transmitted to me, by the grandfather. He did not make me know or accept this through the force of his personality or the eloquence of his words. Few words passed between us. Yet, he gave me so much.

I had dreamt of the ancient ones blowing upon me, blessing me, guiding, and inspiring me. Undoubtedly, that dream led me to him at whose hands I was to embrace Islam, and because that was the door through which I entered, I always have the most joyous, peaceful, and pure associations with the path I was guided to embrace. There was not a trace of compulsion, not a trace of politics, pressure or oppression. There was only sweetness, kindness, light and grace, manifesting in the form of a human being fully dedicated to the service of his Lord.

Because I was guided by the One Most Merciful to embrace His path at the hands of such a person, in such a beautiful way, this is the way in which I hope I can share it with others, as light upon light, love within love, truth within the heart, which loves the truth.

12

Praying in the Dome of the Rock

Jerusalem, 1974

Glory to God who did take His servant for a journey by night from the sacred mosque to the farthest mosque whose precincts we did bless, in order that we might show him some of our signs: for He is the One who heareth and seeth all things.

The Holy Qur'an 17:1

J erusalem is a city of many gates, many passageways, and many mysteries hidden in unexpected places and accessed by unexpected means. There is a garden hidden in the city, but one must pass through flames—centuries of conflict—to enter.

Having received from grandfather, Sidi Sheikh Abd'ul Muttalib (ra) the beautiful gift of Islam and the practice of the *salat*, one day, when I had been making *salat* for only a few months, I was guided to go to the Dome of the Rock and pray. It was not at a given time of prayer, but I knew that I had to do it then.

So, I strode through a gateway leading to Temple Mount, without hesitation and without seeing the guards standing at the gate. They came running after me and with their bodies blocked my way. "You cannot come in here!" they insisted forcefully. "Only Muslims can enter." "I am a Muslim," I said. "I must go to the mosque to pray." They insisted that I prove this by reciting the fundamental verses of the Qur'an, which I did, not for their sake, but for the sake of God who had asked me to pray. Still they did not want to let me enter.

I knew that I had to go in. I was being drawn, by an irresistible force. They could not stop me from doing what I was going to do, nor could I stop them from doing what they were doing. Finally the guards said, "We are taking you to the police." They took me to the police office on Temple Mount.

When we entered the building, a man, who turned out to be the Chief of Police, saw me with them and said, "That is Maryam, you must take her to the mosque to pray. She has to pray." I had never met this man and had no idea how he knew that or why he said it. But, *Alhamdulillah*, I was then escorted by the guards to the door of the mosque. So I entered that amazing place, as I had known I must that day.

There is no adequate way to describe the rock around which the mosque is built. It is the place on earth from which the Prophet Muhammad (saw) rose on the night of his ascension. It is referred to in the Qur'an as the *"Farthest Mosque."* Upon entering, I beheld an extraordinary place. The rock from which the Holy Prophet ascended is immense, luminous, and appears to be in flight. It does not look like any other piece of earth I have ever seen. I saw it only that one time, and the memory of it is practically blinding. It is awe-inspiring.

I realized then why I had to go there. Once you enter it, you do not leave; you have been there forever, and there you remain. It was a place I felt linked to, a place I truly belonged. On the day that I walked into the mosque, it appeared almost no one was there, and I walked straight to the *qibla*, where the *imam* leads the prayers, and prayed there. While I was praying in that holy spot as the Creator had willed, my soul was inspired to beseech the Lord to entrust to me a child that would serve him. Many years later, after I had passed through six miscarriages, my son Issa was born.

Whether he is such a child who will serve his Lord, only God knows and will reveal. I continue to pray every day that my original supplication may be fulfilled, and in the midst of all the trials of bringing up a son as a single mother in a world full of strife and corruption, I perceive subtle signs, such as the deep love and understanding of Islam, the love for God and compassion for the creation developing in him, which indicate that my supplication is being granted. The earnest seeker and lover of God that he has grown up to be is indeed the sacred legacy and harvest of my life and journey. It is the fulfillment of the intention that rose up from my soul as I was blessed to pray in the holy mosque from which the Messenger of God ascended. In every matter, it is only the will of God that is done.

Whatever may be the ultimate result of the prayer and supplication I made that day, there is a dimension of my soul that remains awestruck by the power, the majesty, and sanctity of that space and the opportunity I was given to enter it and find my place there.

I am also amazed, having witnessed and experienced that divine wonder that exists in the heart of the Holy City, when I notice that this sacred dimension is never mentioned on the news about the city. It seems to be almost entirely overlooked by, or hidden from the view of, the inhabitants of the city and the world. It is the resplendent secret of the garden hidden behind the flames, which are presently consuming Jerusalem, Darussalam, *"the place of peace."*

May the celestial Jerusalem, upon which such a name has been bestowed, become the place of peace for those who follow the Prophet (saw) on the path of ascension; and as the inhabitants in the celestial Jerusalem unite in the realization of divine peace, may the rain of *rahmat*, the rain of God's grace, descend upon the earthly Jerusalem and extinguish the flames which engulf it.

While living on the Mount of Olives, we frequently ran into another Sheikh, Sidi Sheikh Muhammad al-Jemal. We met him one day riding on the bus that goes down the mountain. From that point on, he came almost every night to our house to share teachings with us. These were Sufi teachings, which very much interested us all.

The time came for Nooruddeen, Shahida (Noura Issa) and the others in the group to return to their homes in America and Europe. By this time Grandfather, Sidi Sheikh Abdul Muttalib (ra) had transmitted Islam to me, but very little verbal communication was possible between us.

So, at this point I moved into the *zawiyyah* of Sidi Sheikh Muhammad to receive more of these teachings. Sheikh Muhammad was able to speak enough English and I was able to understand enough Arabic for there to be ongoing communication between us. Sidi Sheikh Muhammad often gave the Friday sermon in Al Aqsa Mosque, and he spoke frequently about many interesting subjects. Because these subjects intrigued me, I felt impelled to remain in his *zawiyyah* for a time to learn more about Islam and *tasawwuf*, the Sufi path.

The *zawiyyah* was a very large, empty basement on the lower level of the house of the Sheikh. The door opened onto the desert, and the desert wind would come in. Because there was almost no furniture, all sounds resonated beautifully in that cool open space.

It was a very good place in which to recite *surah*s and do *zikr*. It was here that I began to enter into the resonance of the Qur'an and the prayer.

One beautiful gift the Sheikh gave me was the blessing of my first *khalwah* (guided spiritual retreat). He put me in a room with a beautiful set of five hundred prayer beads, and instructed me to visualize the word of God in Arabic written in light and not to sleep through the night. That was for me a beautiful night journey, the first of many I would be blessed to make.

For the most part, I lived alone in the *zawiyyah*, though from time to time, someone would come to stay for a while and then leave. Often, the sweet children of the Sheikh would come to visit. The real quality of my experience at this time, however, was in the solitude and in the sense that I had been here centuries before and my soul had returned home.

On certain days in the week, I took the bus down the Mount of Olives to Jerusalem where I taught English in a school called *Dar'ul Awlad*, the Place of the Children. The children were orphans of Arab origin from the streets of Jerusalem.

Given their situation, they were wonderfully bright, open, and untroubled. It was a blessing and a delight to get to know them and share with them. It was also always a joy and a spiritual education to explore the narrow, winding lanes of the Old City after school and discover what treasures lay within the shops and within the hearts of the people. In this way, I continued the work on the project, interviewing the people of the city and continuing to discover the garden within the flames.

On certain days I went to the Temple Mount to pray. One day I was walking there and I ran into an old friend named Aaron who was studying to be a Rabbi. He wanted me to meet the Rabbi with whom he was studying. I met with the Rabbi. He wanted to know why I, a Jewish girl, was studying with a Sheikh. I told him that the Sheikhs were transmitting to me deep mystical teachings about prayer and life, things that I very deeply yearned to know and to put into practice.

I asked him if he could teach me what the Ba'al Shem Tov, a very illuminated Rabbi, taught his disciples. He told me that he could certainly not teach me. He arranged for me to meet with a Rebbitzen, a female Rabbi. It did not appear that she knew anything at all about the spiritual knowledge I was yearning to learn.

This, then was the answer to the Rabbi's question. I was studying with the Sufi Masters because they had the knowledge of the journey to God and were very willing to share it.

On the other days of the week, I walked along the ancient mountain paths to Bethany, where Lazarus was brought back from the dead. There I had a job working with handicapped children. It was not in the Holy Sepulcher or in the designated tourist sites where I felt the presence of Jesus (as) most deeply but on these walks on the mountain paths between the Mount of Olives and Bethany. I had the strong sense that he had walked along the same paths and he was walking with me.

"How had he lived here?" I asked myself, as I walked along those ancient paths. "By what means, by what power, did he give life to the dead? How does a human being, living and walking upon this earth, become the instrument of the One and only Being Who can give life to the dead? Then, how can I and each of us become an instrument for that life-giving Power?"

Such were the questions inspired in my soul by that journey back and forth between Bethany, where I learned about the healing power of love, and the Mount of Olives, where I learned to pray. I had received a great candle lit from a bonfire on one mountain, there for the purpose of understanding who Jesus (as) truly was and what message he truly brought to this earth. Now, I was walking on another mountain where the presence of the prophetic manifestation was even stronger.

I felt, as I walked, his humanity, his love for the poor, and his willingness to go everywhere to find them and do everything to feed them and heal them. I did not envision him hanging on a cross or dying for our sins, but truly and eternally living that we may follow his example and live eternally in the presence of God. He, who was the pure servant of the Eternal One, did not die, I felt, so that our sins may be forgiven; he overcame all the temptations of Satan, thereby conquering sin and evil, and he taught all of his disciples, all of us, that in following him we must do this too.

Jesus (as), "*son of man*," as he humbly called himself, went ahead, along with all those sent by God as our prophets (as) and guides. We must walk on the same path behind them and be judged for what we do, not for what they did. For, as the Holy Qur'an tells us, on the Day of Judgment, we will each see every atom's weight of good that we did and every atom's weight of evil. The scales of our judgment are balanced by our own deeds.

Walking on the path behind Jesus (as) was, as I was experiencing it, powerful, dynamic and profound. As I walked in those hills where I felt, certainly, somehow, I had walked before, always I saw signs that the teachings were alive.

One day, I met a family along the way, a very large and poor family, but full of faith and light. One of the many children in this family was from birth unable to move or talk, and in a completely altered state, that is, totally different than the state in which we expect a human being to be. This child, unable to speak or move, was emanating great light and love.

All the activities of the family seemed to center around him. Far from feeling that this was a tragic circumstance, the whole family seemed lit up by love. They told me that the child had been sent to them, by God and he was like Christ to them. He was their inspiration, the center of their focus, and the means by which the whole family was blessed. I could see that all the affairs of the family were being conducted in an atmosphere of divine peace and submission, and the child, without speaking, was the guide.

In situations like this that I encountered in my journey through the Holy Land, I came to understand and to see that the light of Christ, and the life-giving power of God, whom he served, manifest on many different levels and in many different ways.

What made the Holy Land holy? I asked for inner understanding. Not only Jesus (as), but so many of the messengers (as) of God were sent to this land. I asked myself why, as I walked upon the narrow pathways, along the red-gold cliffs, which were then as they had been when the prophets (as) walked there. What about the words they said, the words they were commanded to speak? How were those words to be fulfilled? How had the prophets (as) been received, as they came one by one, bearing the divine treasure to humankind?

As I walked through the olive trees in the Garden of Gethsemane, where Jesus (as) had walked and taught his disciples, where he had stayed awake while others slept, and as I looked down from the wall on the Mount of Olives over the extraordinary view of the city of Jerusalem with the Dome of the Rock in its center, I contemplated the terrible, bloody history the city had endured, and the wondrous divine mysteries contained at the same time within its walls.

Gazing upon the panorama of the walled city with its stone gates and ancient dwellings, I pondered how many references had been made to it in scripture and how many messengers (as) had been sent here carrying both good news and a warning, directly from the Source.

Yet, time after time, age after age, they were persecuted, rejected, and denied. The prophets (as) looked down upon the city, upon the condition of humankind, and wept in lamentation. They knew where things were leading, the repercussions of the choice made by the majority of the people to whom the message was addressed.

All human beings are inhabitants in the city of God. Why have we persecuted and denied the messengers (as) who came to us with the honorable task of bringing to us the living Word of God? Why have we not honored the One Who sent them and heeded their advice?

The grievous condition of the world today, I thought then, with the divided city of Jerusalem at its epicenter, is the inevitable outcome of the rejection of the messengers (as) of truth, and the Truth, *al-Haqq*, who sent them. Nevertheless, the Scriptures tell us that the situation is not irreversible. The redemption is also foretold by the One whose promise is eternally true.

In the center of the city is the mosque wherein lies the rock from which the Holy Prophet (saw) ascended. If only we listen to our Creator Most Merciful and do what He is telling us to do, we can rise up through the flames and be united with His peace that transcends all wars.

I, a daughter of Zion, from the tribe of *Bani Isra'il*, to whom the greatest number of prophets (as) had been sent, had come to the Holy Land to perceive these things. In the cave of the grandfather, the tomb of the Sufi Master, I had a dream.

I dreamt there was a war in a high mountain kingdom and I entered a cave to pray for peace. One day after the next, a man came to this cave and sent in a flower, a rose from the King. When the cave was full of roses, a proposal was presented. The King was asking me to marry him. For the marriage to be completed, I would have to plunge off a cliff—sacrifice myself—so that there would be peace in the kingdom.

The kingdom was Jerusalem, the kingdom of the heart, the city of God. The warring people in the high mountain kingdom were the Jews, Christians, and Muslims, all children of one great father, the Prophet Abraham (as). "Why must this war go on between the children of this great man, who served and worshipped nothing but the One God, Most Merciful?" I asked myself. "How can I make an offering of my life so that it may become an instrument of peace, an instrument of the reconciliation of the children of Abraham (as)?"

The grandfather, Sidi Sheikh Abdul Muttalib (as) told me in the softest and strongest possible way that what God wanted me to do, was to bow down. The Sheikh's communication to me was strong because as softly as he spoke, there was no way I could refuse the message he transmitted to me.

In bowing down in submission to the one and only Lord of all, the Jew within me, follower of Moses (as), the Christian, follower of Jesus (as), and the Muslim, follower of Muhammad (saw), were all perfectly reconciled. There was no conflict at all, only one Message, one Truth.

Many years later, what I sensed then about the messengers (as) and the One Truth was explained with beautiful clarity. The prophetic Message, that Truth brought to humankind by all of the prophets (as) is like a glass. At first, the glass was empty. Then, Prophet Adam (as) put water in it. After that, every prophet continued to fill that glass with the water of the teaching he was charged by God to bring. When the Prophet Muhammad (saw) came and put the Revelation of the Qur'an into the glass, the glass became full and no more could be added to the water in the glass.

What is most important to realize is that all the teachings brought by all the true messengers (as) of God are now merged in the water in the glass and cannot be removed or separated in any way from each other. The unity of all the divine messages and the absolute necessity to bow down and pray in accordance with the commandments of the One Lord of all were amongst the great gifts bestowed upon me on my journey to the Holy Land.

Now that the knowledge had been implanted, I knew that I must return to America. I had maintained contact with Nooruddeen and Shahida. They were building the Intensive Studies Center at the Lama Foundation and working on the Jerusalem book there. After all, I had come to Jerusalem to work on this project, and it was time to go back, reunite with the circle, and move the work along.

As I was heading back to America, on a long ride across Europe, the train stopped in Bulgaria, where it was delayed for several hours, and there I began to experience the impact of what I had received in the Holy Land. The time for prayer arrived. I did not begin to think about where I was. Simply, knowing that the train was not going to move, I went onto the side of the train tracks, laid out my prayer mat and prayed. When my prayer was over, and I gave salaams to the right and the left, people came running from both sides, weeping, to embrace me. We were, after all, in a Communist country, where praying was illegal. Regardless of what religion these people were, they were overjoyed and profoundly moved to see someone praying.

13

Building the Adobe Mosque

Lama Foundation, Taos, New Mexico, 1975

What shall we say the kingdom of God is like, or what parable shall we use to describe it? It is like a mustard seed, which is the smallest seed you plant in the ground. Yet when planted, it grows and becomes the largest of all garden plants, with such big branches, that the birds of the air can perch in its shade.

Gospel of Mark 4:30–32

I returned to Lama with a bundle of Bedouin clothes and a bag full of transcriptions and tapes. There, I continued transcribing the tapes as I had been doing in Jerusalem. This was work I had to do, but it was also my therapy. It was a way I could continue to hear the voices of Jerusalem, continue to feel, blowing upon my face, the softness of the desert air. My soul was still there, walking on the path to Bethany.

At the same time, slowly, my body was habituating itself to the earth of New Mexico. Earth it was that I found in my hands many hours a day, as it was in the earth that we needed to plant the sacred seed. On my return to Lama, I discovered major building going on. The *Companions of the Palm*, having transmigrated back to Lama, were now building, out of adobe, the Intensive Studies Center.

The I.S.C. to be distinguished from the Basic Studies Center of the Lama Foundation, was a five-minute walk away from the large dome and many small houses. It would be a semi-circle of rooms built of adobe surrounding a central gathering space. The center was to be for intensive spiritual work, and all of these rooms were in the process of being built when I arrived.

Sculptor that I was, with the love of clay forever in my hands, I threw myself into the "mudding" to such a degree that I became known as the "holy mudder." Nooruddeen was a focused taskmaster. We worked many hours a day, "no ifs, ands, or buts." It was very helpful training for which I am indebted to him. Having tendencies to space out and dwell on other planes, I learned from him how to live on earth and to work with it.

I was assigned to cell number five in the semicircle and given the task of adobe-ing that room, as well as others. The other rooms were heated by wood-burning stoves. There was no electricity at Lama. So, when it became cold, especially in the very cold, snowy winters, we greatly appreciated and needed our fires.

With the help of Henry Gomez, the son of the great Native American elder Grandpa Joe Gomez, I built a traditional southwestern rounded fireplace, and then spent a great many nights sitting beside it, often in his company. I appreciated very much the purity of sitting with him and the subtle way that the Native American tradition he had inherited was transmitted just by sitting in his presence in silence and looking at the fire.

Having sculpted it as I wished, caressed the curves, and brought the sculpture forth, I was happy to live in my adobe room. Lying in my bed and gazing at the fire under the skylight, through which I could see the star-filled sky, I felt a kind of ancient peace. There were also, I confess, many nights in which I felt lonely, filled with longing. The room I had sculpted was the kind of romantic space, so simple, unadorned, and of the earth itself that I would have loved to share it with "my beloved." But where on earth was he?

Such was the test of solitude, a desert I traversed for years upon years. Although it was difficult to cross alone, the desert was not arid and barren but filled with gems and treasures, the treasures of awakening to the knowledge of being, the jewels of gratitude for exactly what God, in His mercy, had given me to live through on the journey leading to Him. For, once our life becomes consecrated to Him, if He wills for us extended solitude, the treasures of His love can be found within that, and if He wills for us marriage, the treasures of His love can be found within that. Everything unfolds in precise accordance with His merciful decree.

Although I passed, in my adobe cave, some lonely nights, it must be remembered that we were living in cells for the purpose of intensive study. It was not a romantic vacation. We were in a school, to learn how to focus, how to become disciplined, how to work. I see now that the real goal of our study was to come to know, to understand, and experience the great, multi-faceted treasure that we had found in the Holy Land and brought back with us—the way of Islam, which, as we came to understand it, was the completion of the way of life and worship transmitted by all the prophets and messengers (as) throughout time.

Surrounded by the individual cells, the central area of the Intensive Studies Center was the place where we all gathered. It was constructed of wood and adobe, like all the buildings at Lama. On one side of the building was the kitchen and table where we ate, and on the other side was the place where we prayed.

So, as God willed it, Nooruddeen, Noura, and I, who had memorized the *Surat'ul-Fatihah* at the same time, while walking on the Mount of Olives, now grew in our love and understanding of Islam in this humble, rustic, hand-built mosque. Thus does the light of true Islam, the way of God transmitted by all His prophets (as), spread, from the Source of knowledge to open spaces, open hearts, in which the seeds of knowledge, can, by God's will, germinate and bear fruit.

True Islam, that peace which comes with submission and surrender to the will of God, being the natural state (*al-fitrah*), it was very appropriate for it to grow within us in the midst of nature. I sensed within our tiny congregation and with our very initial efforts, the purity of the first mosque built by the Prophet Muhammad (saw) in Medina. It was the purity of the love of the truth of God, the beauty of the revelation, as it was being born within us.

It was like that in those days and nights at the Intensive Studies Center, fires burning in the middle of the brilliant cold winter, the men in their row, and the women in their row, pressed together, shoulder to shoulder, on the large *kilim* prayer rug upon which we all prayed, with the love of the community, the love of the Way that was dawning within us, an even a greater source of warmth.

I remember this time with great fondness and nostalgia because the Islam we were discovering was independent of any political or worldly context. There was no cultural or political overlay. We had been searching for the Way, the path of truth, for union with the Divine. Our Creator had answered our yearnings and supplications by revealing to us the Way that all the prophets (as) had followed, each in his own time, in accordance with that time. How does the light of truth travel, but as God wills, from open heart to open heart? As Sheikh Bawa Muhaiyaddeen (ra), whom I was soon to meet, would later explain,

> *"Faith alone can capture another heart. Faith alone can rule the world. The qualities of God that exist within the heart of one with determined faith must reach out, enter the heart of another, and give him comfort and peace. It is seeing God's compassion, His equality, His tranquility, His integrity, His honesty, and the manner in which He embraces and protects all lives with equal justice, which can bring a person to the state of harmony and compel him to bow in unity. It is these qualities that can conquer people and nations. They begin by capturing the hearts of a few, then they reach out to all those in the village, then the city, and eventually these qualities reach out to the entire population of the country."*

That faith had been transmitted to our hearts in the Holy Land. We were traveling in the current of the divine transmission. As it had been decreed for us to receive the seed of Islam in Jerusalem, so it was decreed that we continue the journey, guided to different places of training in which the seed was to be cultivated. Nooruddeen and Noura were guided to Mecca, where they were to live for several years. As for me, in order to fertilize and cultivate the soil in the garden of the heart, thus enabling the pure seed of faith to grow, I was guided to Sheikh Muhammad Rahim Bawa Muhaiyaddeen (ra), in whose company I was blessed to live for several years, until he passed from the world in 1986.

14

Meeting the Ancient Sage

Philadelphia, 1979–1986

"Open your heart! You have to open your heart, discard the dunya, this world, and remove all the veils of the world. Keep God and His kingdom within yourself, keep God's justice within you. You must know today the judgment that God will pass on you tomorrow. Know your faults and try to correct them. Before He raises you on Judgment Day, before He passes judgment on you, judge yourself while you are here."

Sheikh Bawa Muhaiyaddeen
The Tree That Fell to the West

During the week or so I had spent at Lama before going to Jerusalem, an enigmatic, impassioned, determined person turned up on Lama Mountain. He was a man with a mission. His name was Ahamad Muhaiyaddeen, and he was inspired with great fervor to speak to me about his teacher, Bawa Muhaiyaddeen. Before he left, he gave me a book by his Sheikh.

The title alone intrigued me very much, and I carried the book with me from that moment on, along with the knowledge that such a person, an ancient sage, was living in Philadelphia and teaching people there. I carried it with me, feeling that it was something of value, but did not actually read it. I simply knew within my heart that there was a Sufi Master living in Philadelphia and that one day I would meet him.

In 1979, the Jerusalem book had evolved to such a degree that we thought it could be submitted to a publisher. Since Nooruddeen and Noura had left the project and gone to live in Mecca, I had continued to work on it with a small group of people in Santa Fe, and now I was going to take the fruits of our labor of love to the East Coast to begin looking for a publisher.

From a Sufi teacher named Reshad Field with whom I had spent a little time in New Mexico I received some names of people of the path that it would be good to see on the East Coast. One of them was Abdul Azziz Sayyid, a professor at the American University in Washington, D.C. I called his office and went to see him as soon as I arrived in Washington.

There was a couple sitting in his office at the same time as I was, named Walter and Vicky, who lived in Philadelphia. Walter was a Sufi student of Professor Sayyid. I mentioned that I had heard about a Sufi Master living in Philadelphia and would like to meet him. I hoped to interview him for the book on Jerusalem before going to the publishers. They kindly invited me to stay with them while I was in Philadelphia. So, that was clearly my next move. Walter, it turned out, was the connection between Bawa and Professor Sayyid. Bawa (ra), at this time, was writing letters to President Jimmy Carter. Walter would pick up the letters and deliver them to Professor Sayyid, who would pass them to the President.

We went to Philadelphia, and Walter took me to the Fellowship. While I was sitting in the meeting room downstairs in the Fellowship house, waiting to meet Bawa (ra) in his room upstairs, many Fellowship members greeted me. I mentioned that I was working on a book on Jerusalem and would like to interview Bawa. Because of this, I was treated temporarily like a "media person," someone who is coming specifically to interview Bawa (ra).

Then I was led up to Bawa's (ra) room. He was seated on his bed. He was a very ancient man but with a very young, beautiful, eternal face. Though he was physically very small and very humble, his presence was great with the light of purity and wisdom. Bawa was speaking in the Tamil language and his words were being translated into English, yet his words affected me directly and intensely.

He did not treat me like a media person at all. That mask was quickly discarded. He addressed other aspects of my identity—*who* I thought I was, what I thought I was doing with my life and journey. Very quickly he penetrated many veils and left me nowhere to stand comfortably. Thus did he reveal to me, behind the romantic veil, which was stripped away, the deep, hard, fundamental work of which the real spiritual path consisted.

Bawa (ra) looked not at me but through me with the laser beam of divine wisdom. He was not politely engaging various aspects of who I thought I was, but powerfully penetrating veils, discarding whatever could be discarded, and showing the way to the goal: *"La ilaha ill'Allah."* The *zikr*, *"La ilaha ill'Allah,"* was the powerful medicine and tool of transformation. The way that we become liberated from all our illusions and all the negative qualities we have been often unconsciously sustaining within ourselves is by contemplating with the breath that only God truly exists.

The Sheikh spoke for a long time and said many things about my life and journey. One sentence that I remember is, "You have read many books, but you cannot cook a paper squash." This statement led me to wonder what real squash he was referring to.

I was overwhelmed by the intensity of this encounter. It was certainly not that he spoke loudly or forcefully, but his words were annihilating to at least some of the false identities I had been attached to. For the next several days, I could barely speak or move. It was like the tip of the sword of *al-Haqq*, the Truth, was pressed into my heart and I was paralyzed, awaiting the Grace of God to resurrect me in the next dimension or phase of my journey. There being no reality but the Reality which is God, my existence and the continuation of my journey were totally contingent upon God.

I was wearing a long maroon skirt and shawl at that first meeting. I was so much stopped in my tracks by the reality of meeting with the Sheikh and the profound challenge that was being posed that I was unable to do the simplest things such as change my clothes. So I wore those same clothes day after day. I was staying at

Walter and Vicky's. He would drop me at the Fellowship, and I would remain there for the day, simply waiting for the words of the wise man that would guide me to the next step.

On about the third day, in the middle of a discourse, Bawa (ra) said, "You are like a person who has worn the same clothes for three days." I was shocked into awakening by the words. He was not looking directly at me, but suddenly I realized my condition, felt certain that he was speaking about me, and became greatly embarrassed.

Then he said something so extremely helpful I have never forgotten it, but I have understood its application to so many situations in my life and in the lives of others: "You need to put these clothes in the washing machine and wash them." From this teaching, I understood that I myself was not dirty. Only my clothes were dirty. All I had to do was to remove them and wash them. It was like that also with the veils, which were covering over my soul. They too could be removed. The soul was pure.

I came to see many times later in life how often I, and others, become attached to guilt, regret, unworthiness, and other garments and veils, which are covering up the purity of the soul, as though they are inseparably attached to us, and therefore, if they are bad, so inevitably are we.

But what Bawa (ra) revealed to me at that moment, which I sometimes remember and sometimes unfortunately forget, is that all of these "clothes" can be taken off and cleaned. Only the soul is eternal, the essence of reality, and that cannot be "taken off." As soon as I understood this, I was able to let go of my attachment to who I thought I was and begin to tune into the transmission that was coming through Bawa (ra).

Within the first few weeks of meeting Bawa (ra), I had three profound dreams. The first was the dream of the Emerald Child. In this dream I found myself surrounded by children at a fair in the yard of the Fellowship. They led me to a big field full of flowers. In the middle of the field was a large bed with a baby sitting on it. The baby was sitting in an erect posture. His skin was translucent and he was composed of emerald light. All of the organs and inner workings of his body were visible, light within light.

They were saying about the baby that he had no parents. It was clear that he was a most unusual, beautiful child. From the distance, he saw me and bowed to me and I to him. When I approached him, he was somehow drawn to my heart, came into my arms, and then entered my body and disappeared into my heart.

The next day, when I gave the Sheikh salaams, I remembered the dream and felt the presence of the emerald child within me. I told him about it. Bawa Muhaiyadeen (ra) said,

> *"Whoever can raise that child with love is the one who must raise him. All the other children you saw are children who have parents, but that child that you saw, from that time until today, is an orphan. For the person that can bring up that child, hell and the difficulties of life will be very, very far. To be able to rear that orphan child, you need to show lots and lots of love. You must take care of him like your own life. If you nurture him like that, that child will grow. Otherwise, he will leave and go to play with the other children.*
>
> *The other children that you saw playing in the yard are children, no doubt, but this orphan child, this wonderful child, is the gift of God. Whoever rears this child in this world, in the world of souls, and in the kingdom of God, will have happiness. They will see the victory of their lives and hell will be very, very far away. God's grace, God's light, and God's blessings will be with them. If you can bring up this child properly, if you can keep it where it has to be kept, and then rear it, that will be very, very good."*

My second dream was the dream of the mosque of Mankumban. In the dream I entered into a building, a holy space that was vast and empty, filled with awe and wonder. There was great silence, but also an intense battle was going on invisibly. All the molecules in the air were charged.

The power was so great, it took a great effort to walk from one side to the other. You had to be deeply immersed in the state of remembrance to gain the strength to make the journey. I entered the sanctified space and made *salat*. Some people came to me and asked if I would teach them how to make *salat*. I said, "The *waqt* (time) is over; we will meet at the next *waqt*." Then, I began to walk through the mosque. It was a very hard journey just to get across the room.

Along the way, I passed by some people who were speaking about *zikr*. Although a few people were there, there was a great sense of emptiness in the mosque and also fullness in regard to the unseen realms. I came to a stairway and began to ascend. It required great energy to take each step. When I approached the top, I saw a very tall, very beautiful woman, veiled in light, standing and making *salat* at the top of the stairs. She was a powerful presence, completely cloaked in a very majestic way.

Bawa Muhaiyaddeen (ra) explained to me,

> *"This is a real secret, a real mystery. That is Maryam (Mother of Jesus)."*

I had sensed that the majestic, luminous woman I saw praying at the top of the stairs was her, and Bawa confirmed this mystical awareness. He then went on to speak about his deep relationship with her and the building of God's House, the mosque he built by the ocean in Jaffna with the help of many of his disciples from America.

This mosque is, as I had seen in my dream, a place of great power, mysticism, and light. I was very blessed to have visited it in my dreams, and later to go there and pray in that radiant space in waking life. It was as Bawa continued to describe it, in response to the dream I had just shared with him:

> *"Within that mosque there are so many spiritual beings who are protecting it. All the prophets and awliya (friends) of God are there. The person you saw praying and another person are always there praying in that mosque. Although it is a small mosque, it contains many, many secrets. In two and a half months we completed the work that should have taken two and a half years. That lady you saw praying— that is Maryam. It is the eleventh place for the Qutb (the pole) to rest.*
>
> *"You visited that place. So therefore, there is some connection for you also there. It is because of that connection that you have come*

here. You have had that search and you have had that connection
and that is why God has brought you here."

My third dream was the dream of the man of light in the mirror.
In this one, I was in Jerusalem in the tunnel, which goes beneath the
Temple Mount. There is a stream which flows there called Silhuane.
The Prophet Jesus (as), it is said, healed people there. In the dream,
there were people sitting in wheel chairs who needed to be healed.

It appeared that the spirit of Issa (as) stood up (within me)
and began to move quickly and powerfully down the tunnel alongside the stream. A white shawl dropped into my hand. I put it on
my head and looked into a mirror that suddenly appeared. I saw
the face of Christ looking back, his beautiful, glowing eyes shining
through. His face appeared in place of mine and I looked deeply
into his gaze.

Some of the people of Jerusalem, in biblical dress, walked by. I
looked away from the mirror, so they wouldn't see, feeling it might
be too much for them to bear. They left and I looked back into the
mirror. After some time, the man of light continued to move down
the tunnel. He returned to the healing spring. Two men were
attempting to urinate into it. He said, "This is the pure spring. You
should never do anything like that here." I woke up at four in the
morning, with body, heart, and soul shaking.

Bawa Muhaiyaddeen (ra) commented,

> *"Very, very good. The mirror. There is no other mirror. God alone is*
> *the mirror. Only His 'eyes' are the real eyes. We have to have faith*
> *in Him. The water is His rahmat, His benevolence. That benevo-*
> *lence is the light of the Qutb, which is divine luminous wisdom.*
> *That is the water, which is called the rahmat of God. It is by drink-*
> *ing that pure water, the water of pure rahmat that you can make*
> *yourself pure, and through that you can establish the firm iman of*
> *certitude. It is only that water that can quench the thirst.*
>
> *"That mirror is the mirror of God, which has no form. What we*
> *see in that mirror is He. If we look in the mirror here, all we see is*
> *our own figure, and all that we see in that mirror is like urinating*
> *in the purity. Only the rahmat of God can heal. All that we do,*

saying we are doing it, is impurity. What we do is that we urinate into the purity. We bring the differences of 'I' and 'you,' 'my religion' and 'your religion' and put these things into the places of purity. No one is worthy of worship other than God Most High.

"We must go and die in God. That is what you saw. Everything else—I and you—all differences are removed. When one goes and falls into it, that is the purity. You must become that light. That is what you saw. All other things are things that make the purity impure, the differences of 'I' and 'you.'

"Jerusalem, from the time it came into being until today, has been a battlefield. All the prophets came to clear this place, which is the central spot, but still it is the battlefield where the prophets were killed and people were made to suffer. All this happened in Jerusalem. It is the battlefield, and from then until today, it has been flowing with blood. 'Yeru salam' in Tamil means 'fire-water.' Whoever wants to grab that place, as his own, will get burned. They were all destroyed.

"In truth, that place belongs only to God. Peace and equality are there. In Jerusalem, you can (also) find earth, fire, water, and ether. The people you saw urinating into the spring are the ones who wish to grab Jerusalem as their own. But you can also find there, the arsh'ul muminun, the throne of the believers, the throne of God.

"So, let us clear the Jerusalem that is within us, the place of purity, paradise, heaven. Let us organize this house within us. If we can organize this house within us, that will be good. The other Jerusalem is just burning water."

Bawa's first name for me was *"Jerusalem Poullai,"* or "Child of Jerusalem." He said that I had spent seven years (much more than I had actually spent in physical time) in Jerusalem, and it was a very profound experience for me. He too was engaged in speaking about Jerusalem a great deal, which I was aware of from the time I arrived, but when I asked him about the book we had planned to publish, he said clearly not to publish it.

Imagine, he explained, that we were to take out a full-page ad in a newspaper in which we put passages of the book. We say that we want peace in Jerusalem. We put quotations from the Scriptures and from people of different religions, advocating peace. We put our telephone number at the bottom of the page.

Then imagine if people called and asked for advice about *how* to make peace in Jerusalem. We would not be able to tell them how to do it. He then said that instead of publishing the book, I should build Jerusalem, the place of peace, in my heart. He told me further that if I could build the holy city within myself, honey would develop there, and then, many bees would come to get that honey.

I understood. I knew that I could not bring peace to the outer Jerusalem but must first bring peace to the inner Jerusalem as he had indicated. I knew that I had no choice, but to surrender to this guidance and, God willing, learn from him as much as I could about building the inner place of peace.

After working for many years on the Jerusalem book, I knew I had to simply let it go and then focus upon what the Sheikh was showing me about the world within: how to get all the money-lenders out of the place of prayer, the place of peace, and how to look into the mirror of God and be healed by the water of His benevolence, rather than urinating into that pure spring.

I knew that I had no choice but to do the inner work that was being demanded and that there could be no real success without real purification. As the Qur'an tells us, *"He will be successful who purifies it (the self)"* (The Holy Qur'an 91:10).

But I had not come here prepared to move in, only—I thought—to get an interview with the sage. In fact, as the media person that I temporarily appeared to be, I had not had the opportunity to ask him even one of the questions I had prepared!

Not knowing that I would have real spiritual work to do in Philadelphia, I had left all of my somewhat humble belongings and a certain amount of unfinished business in New Mexico. I needed to go back and put things in order before I could really settle into the work that had to be done here. So I went back for a brief visit, hoping to resolve what remained unresolved, and found in New Mexico that whatever I hoped to find there, I would have to go through dense snow to get it.

I started in Santa Fe, intending to share with the small circle with whom I had been working on the book the depth and significance of what Bawa (ra) had transmitted, both about the book and about the path itself. I had written a little to them about the unfolding events and hoped now to share fully what had happened and to bring my relationship with the project to a kind of closure and peace.

But the door was totally closed. It seemed that they were very attached to the project and to my involvement in it, and did not want to hear at all what Bawa (ra) had said. I was prevented from even entering the house. It made me sad, but I knew that there was no way that I could reject the guidance that had been directly transmitted and attempt to finish the book in hopes of pleasing them. My test, which had begun by meeting with Bawa (ra), was continuing to unfold.

Next, I had to go from Santa Fe to the Lama Foundation high in the mountains above Taos in the freezing New Mexico winter. I was able to get a ride part way up the mountain and then climb up through thick snow the rest of the way. I went directly to the Intensive Studies Center and, after being warmly welcomed by some very dear old friends, took refuge in one of the cells. Somehow I had to regroup, re-establish my inner balance, find the center. I had to ask again, "Who am I? I am not this, nor this, nor this."

For example, I was attached to a style of living and a concept of myself within that style of living. I would never have wished to leave the mountains of New Mexico to go live in a city like Philadelphia. But how could I deny the truth that was beckoning me to move forward, and choose instead to hide in the mountains or in the "book," as if these things had any inherent reality, any verification by the Divine? Now I saw that I could not define myself as a person who had traveled around the world seeking God and was writing a book about Jerusalem in the mountains of New Mexico. It was a false identity.

All the things I had identified with had been real for me and spiritually valid only until I had entered into the presence of the man of wisdom who was now directing me towards another goal, another dimension of the spiritual path. As always, it was time to let go and move on, but I needed to come back to the mountain in order to let it go.

There, by the fireside, in the middle of the dense snow, I made one final retreat. I made peace with the mountain, made peace with the past, left behind what could be left behind and took with me a small bag of external possessions, and many more internal possessions, which were still coming along with me into the life to come. Then, I made the journey back from the mountain of earth to the mountain of spiritual transformation, which Bawa (ra) referred to as Mount Sinai, the mountain, which every spiritual seeker must ascend.

Now, I began to settle into the life of the community, but it was not an easy, natural fit. Appearing in the meeting room in Bedouin clothes, which were still covered with the dust of Jerusalem and New Mexico, I felt like someone from another generation, someone who had been sleeping in a cave for hundreds of years and then woke up one day and walked into the modern world. Even the currency I carried in my pocket was money from a different world.

Although I did not quite fit in to the life of the Fellowship, there was a reason that I had to be there. I had to hear the words that came flowing through the mouth of the sage.

Bawa Muhaiyaddeen (ra), although he was very, very old, and often very ill, at this time in his life, spoke abundantly, morning, noon, and night. He was "unlettered," so the knowledge he transmitted he had not acquired through reading. It was knowledge transmitted to and through the Sheikh in his profound experience on the path of God.

At various times of the day and night the word would spread throughout the house and community that Bawa (ra) was speaking. Immediately the disciples came running from wherever they might be and assembled around his bed. The words flooded through him like a current. No one listening to the discourse could remember everything that he said. Of the rain of words, which fell upon us each caught what he or she could catch and understood only what he or she could understand at the time.

Within the flood of the teachings that came pouring through, there were also some that appeared contradictory to others. This ultimately caused some of the disciples to understand the teaching in a very different way than others.

Dusty traveler that I was, having wandered so long in the desert, I stood, with arms outstretched in the rain. Listening as one in love with the light and beauty of Islam, I was amazed to hear the inner explanations of so many of the dimensions of Islam. Day and night the Sheikh was speaking about the profound and wondrous mysteries and truths of Allah and His Messenger (saw) and the light of the Revelation sent by the Creator through His Messenger (saw).

And yet, it was time to pray, and no one was making *salat*. I turned to God. What should I do? The message was unequivocal—"This is My House. So you must pray!"

I put down my prayer mat in the Fellowship meeting room and prayed at every time of prayer. I was not aware of it then, but have heard since, that many people, seeing this sight for the first time, were stunned. They thought that I was a fanatic or simply completely crazy to think that I could do such a thing in the Fellowship meeting room. But for me it was the simplest action, the fulfillment of my covenant with my Lord. It had nothing to do with anyone else, and so I was unaware until many years later of the response of those people.

Now, as I am writing this, many years after the Sheikh left this world, a beautiful mosque exists, which was built on his order and explicit direction, a place where many people gather daily to pray, confirming the message I received—"This is My House. So you must pray!" But at that time it seemed it was a message that I alone had received.

During my first month at the Fellowship, when all sense of self-importance was being clearly annihilated, and I was permitted only to clean the bathroom if I was lucky enough to have any duty to perform, I saw people walking around with large manila envelopes, which contained discourses that they were working on.

When I saw those envelopes, I realized how much I yearned for the chance to work on a book again. Then I found out that I could volunteer to type discourses. Every time I typed something, it happened to be one of the earliest discourses Bawa (ra) had spoken to me, always annihilating my sense of self-importance. That was a very necessary phase.

Then, suddenly, about a month and a half after I had arrived at the Fellowship, the Sheikh called me into his room. He said that since I knew some Arabic, he would like me to edit a book that he had dictated in the sixties. I had heard from many of the people of the Fellowship that it was a great work.

The Sheikh told me further that he would soon be going to Sri Lanka and he would like me to go too and work on the book with him there. As he placed this book in my hand, entrusting it to me, he said, "Every word has seventy thousand meanings. If you change any one of them, the *blood* will be on your hands." How staggering and impossible a task he had given me! I came to understand the seriousness of this statement more and more as time went on.

The transcript I was working on often consisted in many parts of solid text with no paragraphs. A whole page could be one sentence, with concepts building upon concepts, made into a sentence only by a small phrase at the bottom of the page. What did these words mean?

I began to read and read. I entered into the text and attempted to decipher it. It was not at all like other books. It could not be grasped with the intellect. It was like an ocean, and one had to dive completely in. It created its own universe, and you had to be within it in order to comprehend its spiritual logic.

In accordance with the Sheikh's instruction, I immersed myself in this ocean and began to think with a "new" mind. I continued to swim in it, discovering the pearls within it as God permitted me to, and doing the best I could to edit it, which really meant that I was being *edited by it*, for the next twelve years.

With this mysterious book in my arms and a foam bed rolled up on my back, I arrived in the airport in Philadelphia and set off with a small group of people to join the Sheikh in Sri Lanka. Ready for whatever was to unfold, I was so happy to be back on the road again and going to work with the Sheikh!

15

The Resonance of Allah, The Deepening Experience of Prayer

Colombo, Sri Lanka and Philadelphia, 1980-1982

"My children, if the truth contained in the resplendent explanations that come from God's grace could be made clear and printed in books, and if you wanted to understand it, you would need the wisdom of the resplendent Qutb which is God's grace. My brethren who have been born with me, it is with that wisdom that you should delve into those books in order to learn and understand what is contained within them."

Sheikh Bawa Muhaiyaddeen

Arriving in Sri Lanka, I was picked up at the airport by the translator with whom I would be working on the book. The first thing he said was, "Bawa has been waiting for you so we can get started on the work." What a wonder, I felt, that such a person would be waiting for *me*! Now, this work was going to take place in Sri Lanka, a small island beneath the lower tip of India. In the past, this island had been called Serendip, and Bawa named the community he had formed here Serendip Sufi Study Circle.

The little island of Sri Lanka is, like every part of the holy creation of God, blessed with unique mysteries and miracles. One of these undoubted wonders is the majestic mountain called *Adam's Peak*. It is venerated, by Christians and Muslims, who believe that this is the place where Prophet Adam (as) first laid his foot on the earth, as well as by Buddhists, who believe that the footprint of the Buddha is imbedded on the mountain peak. The mountain is a place of pilgrimage, the small island, a place of peace and refuge for many, as I found that it was for me, as soon as I set foot upon the blessed land.

We left the airport and began to drive through a relatively undeveloped expanse of light-filled jungles. I sensed the presence of the ocean, although I could not see it. The air was warm, soft, and welcoming. Once again, I felt that my consciousness was being rearranged. I was so happy to have arrived and, as we drove along, I tuned into the land, the light, and the energy of Sri Lanka, and the joy of arriving at the next stage of my journey, joy, which arises from working closely with the Sheikh.

One of the miracles of traveling across the earth in the way of God is that one becomes a witness to the miraculous artistry of the Creator as it manifests in His creation in wondrous diversity. It is amazing to behold His vision that manifests before us: that He willed there to be jungles, deserts, mountains, oceans, all kinds of climate, all the kinds of animals, all the colors and kinds of flowers, and all the colors and shapes of human beings which arose in the context of all of the different climates He created in which human beings were to live.

We learn as we travel that we do not belong only to the small piece of earth where we were born. For that piece of the earth is connected to the piece next to it, and that piece to the one next to it. As you see more and more of the pieces, you experience more and more profoundly that the earth is one. It is round, not flat, and when you come to the edge of the country you call your own, you do not fall off. All national frontiers and borders are artificial, not inherent.

Every life we encounter as we travel through the lands is a mirror in which we see our own life reflected. This is a truth that I learned when I was a very small child and my father sang,

> *"Close your eyes and point your finger.*
> *On the map, just let it linger.*
> *Anywhere you point your finger to,*
> *There's someone with the same type blood*
> *As you."*

I took my father's advice literally, and journeyed to so many different points on the map, everywhere finding only human beings like myself with blood flowing in their veins just like me! No matter what the color of their skin, what their language, nationality, or culture, I see all the living beings I am blessed to meet as I travel, as my brothers and sisters, members of my own family, all children of Adam (as), the *family of man*.

For our Creator has not revealed to us any divisions that should be acknowledged between the children of Adam (as), except the difference between those who believe and those who do not believe. He has told us that He made the creations diverse intentionally, and no creation is superior to another except for those who have the greatest *taqwa* (consciousness of Him).

Therefore, when arriving in a place I have never been before, I do not consider it as a foreign land but as the next dimension of His creation that the Creator is unveiling to me.

And now, it was the island of Sri Lanka, to which I had been invited by Bawa Muhaiyaddeen (ra), which was the next dimension for my soul to discover. As Allah says in the Holy Qur'an, *"Every moment, We manifest a new creation"* (The Holy Qur'an 55:29). Whenever you arrive in a new place in this state of mind, you too are *new*. You are ready for the next dimension of your own unfolding, ready to see what you can see and to learn what you can learn. This is especially true when you are working with the Sheikh.

I felt the soft tropical jungle air wafting through the car window, sweet air filled with peace and blessings, as we drove through the gentle lands en route to Colombo, and the house of Dr. Ajwad and Amin Macan-Markar, where Bawa was staying with the disciples.

As I was working on this chapter many years later at the end of 2004, we had just witnessed the beautiful island of Sri Lanka, and its people, covered by a devastating tidal wave. We were all stunned by what took place. Much of humanity was profoundly moved and united, if temporarily, in a common concern. People at last began to unite in charity and prayer, inspired by compassion for those members of our human family who on that day were taken back to their Lord and those who remained on earth, the survivors after the flood.

We have learned from all the Scriptures and the great teachers that natural disasters such as these earthquakes and floods are a warning and a call for humanity to return to the Way of Truth. Have we not learned from the story of Noah (as) to listen to the message and follow the directions of our Lord before the deluge covers the earth, before death, in whatever way is destined, overtakes us? How can we truly respond to the immense magnitude of the events, which are shaking the earth, challenging in so many places and ways our hopes that life on this earth has any kind of lasting stability or permanence?

I know that the earth that God showed me in Sri Lanka will never exist in the same way again. Nor will the beautiful lands and cultures of Afghanistan or Kashmir or Tibet ever exist again as they did before each was tried, invaded or possessed and inevitably changed.

We are witnessing the transformation of our world before our eyes and before the eyes of our heart and the eyes of our soul. As the signs continue to unfold, we see that the whole earth is in radical transition, and the only place whose beauty, safety, and peace are our certain refuge, not subject to devastation and destruction, is the land of God, the Divine Presence, and that is where our real journey must lead.

We need to receive the guidance of the prophets (as) and the saints, the guidance of God, in order to learn how truly to prepare, how to die before death, how to cut our attachment to the destructible, perishable, illusory aspects of our being, before destruction and death strike us. I knew that it was for the development of this training, and not for a holiday in an earthly paradise, that I had come to the island of Sri Lanka.

We arrived at night. Bawa (ra) was sitting on his bed awaiting us. I felt as if I was meeting him for the first time and also that I had known him forever. Bawa often addressed his disciples, "Jeweled lights of my eyes, you who were born with me ...."

In Philadelphia there had always been so many people and so much of the institution present that I was only able to see Bawa (ra) from time to time, and there was a certain formality about our meetings. But in Sri Lanka at this time there were only a handful of Americans, and I had come here to work directly with the Sheikh at his request.

So, from the very moment I arrived in his room, there was a kind of intensity, a sense that the corn kernels, which had been sitting in heated oil, were about to pop.

The next morning, I was sitting on the floor in Bawa's room, when the call to prayer for *fajr*, the early morning prayer, echoed from the nearby minarets. At the Fellowship in Philadelphia, when I prayed, I was downstairs in the meeting room, while Bawa was upstairs in his room. At that time, I was not in a relationship with him in which I could ask him if I should pray. I had to have the courage to make that decision apparently "on my own."

Now, in Sri Lanka, I was sitting in his room, in his presence, looking at him, while listening to the call to prayer. I believe I said nothing out loud, but asked him internally what I should do. He said to me, "Yes, of course, you should pray. Amina Hannum will show you the direction to turn, and others will follow you."

I was guided in the right direction, did my prayers outside Bawa's room on the second floor of the house, and, as he said, people started gathering behind me. Through the love of Islam and dedication to its practice that the Creator had instilled in me, I was thus used as an instrument to activate this practice in the community of Sheikh Bawa Muhaiyaddeen (ra). That was an honor and blessing. But for me, truly, it was simply the most natural thing to do—perform the prayer when it was time to pray! Of course, as a woman, I could not be the *imam* of the ritual prayer. I was simply performing the prayer and then joined by others; an *imam* was needed.

In addition to Amina Hannum, who was an elderly woman and the wife of one of Bawa's (ra) translators, I had noticed someone else praying in the corner of the living room. He was one of the disciples of Bawa (ra) and had been with him for a long time. He seemed to be close to Bawa (ra) and was always sitting at his feet, making talismans for people at the Sheikh's request and doing other kinds of prayers and blessings as Bawa (ra) directed him. He generally wore a white sarong and a white shirt. He seemed unusually untouched by worldly influences. His name was Seyed Ahamad Kabeer, and he was often called Ahamad Kabeer or just Kabeer.

After some weeks, I mentioned to Bawa (ra) that I had noticed Ahamad Kabeer praying. Could he not take over the duty of *imam*? Bawa (ra) called Ahamad Kabeer in and asked him to do this. He resisted at first, but finally surrendered and became the *imam* of our tiny bourgeoning congregation.

At a certain point, both Ahamad Kabeer and I went to India, he to visit his family, and I, along with some other disciples, to renew my visa. After we left, Bawa (ra) scolded the men and implored them to learn how to lead the prayers. Several of the brothers then learned, and when we came back, everything was put into balance in the correct configuration, and thus the mysteries of the prayer continued to unfold.

Bawa (ra) asked me to teach classes about the prayer. Many more people from America had come, and Bawa (ra) wanted the knowledge to be shared.

This was a challenge, because in order to share the information it was necessary to face and hopefully help to transform the resistance that many people had been developing all their lives against their conception of Islam and its practices.

For the first seven years of his mission in America, Sheikh Bawa Muhaiyaddeen (ra) transmitted the very essence of the remembrance of God through the *kalimah*: *La ilaha ill'Allah*. From the time he came to America in 1972, he had been transmitting to his disciples the awareness of perpetual prayer, exhorting them to focus on the *zikr* with the breath, so that they might abide in the state of remembrance, prostration, and submission with every breath. He was teaching the disciples to breathe out all falsehood and illusion on the out-breath and breathe in the light and grace of God.

There were several years in the mission of the Holy Prophet (saw) also before the actions of the *salat* were revealed and taught. Following the prophetic model, Bawa (ra) now introduced the *salat*, the formal Islamic prayer, to his disciples. He also began to transmit and explain the significance of the other obligatory duties (*furud*) and other dimensions of Islam. Those years in Sri Lanka, the last years of Bawa's (ra) life, were filled with the transmission and explanation of the inner and outer meanings of the way of Islam.

Our days and nights were filled with prayer and instruction. We usually had three two- to three-hour sessions of *zikr* a day, the last one from eleven at night to two in the morning. Then, we would awaken a few hours later for *awwal-fajr* and *fajr* (dawn) prayers and get ready for the next day of prayer and teaching about prayer. We were truly engaged in a course of intensive studies with the Sheikh, the goal of which was to make every dimension of prayer as vitally alive as possible.

There were many of Bawa's (ra) "children" who were surprised by this course of events, by the way in which Bawa (ra) was now teaching, specifically in regards to the integration of the practices of Islam. They did not understand that what he had been teaching from the beginning was the essence of the path of pure Islam.

He spoke about this in the context of the evolution of the human being (*insan*), explaining that all religions existed at different levels within the body of the human being, and Islam, or the Criterion (*furqan*), was at the level of the head, the crown.

When Bawa (ra) returned to America in 1982, this teaching about prayer and the practices of Islam led directly to the building of a mosque behind the Fellowship house in Philadelphia, a mosque of light whose building he overlooked and supervised down to the last detail.

Bawa (ra) taught extensively on so many different levels, no one could grasp or summarize the depth and extent of his teaching. Some of the things he said seemed contradictory to others. As a result, there is significant diversity amongst those who followed him. What I am reporting is based upon exactly what *I* saw and experienced. Coming to the Sheikh as a devoted Muslim, my experience and practice of Islam was deepened and strengthened by the teachings I received through him.

Others among his disciples did not seem to hear what I heard. Not all of Bawa's (ra) disciples embraced Islam. He spoke to each in accordance with the level and capacity of that person's faith, understanding, and wisdom. While people of all religions, and even, no religion, were drawn to him, to the light of wisdom that was manifesting through him, he did not build a temple, a synagogue, or a church. By the decree of God, he left as one of his great legacies a mosque, which is truly an inheritance of light.

When I met Bawa (ra) in 1979, I wondered why I had not been guided to meet him when he first came to Philadelphia in 1972. But, as time went on and I contemplated the configuration of my life and path, I saw that Allah had willed for me to embrace Islam and become imbued with its fragrance before meeting Bawa Muhaiyaddeen (ra). The pillars were already established within the mosque within my heart that were clarified by the explanations he gave, explanations which did not come from him, but from the Divine. It was because the light of Islam was already shining within me, that I was able to greatly appreciate and utilize the teachings, which flowed through him day and night.

Through the *kalimah,* he transmitted the wisdom which, filtering and filtering, led us to the Source of purity. And every aspect of the obligations (*furud*) of the practice of Islam was explained in the context of the fundamental role of the *Kalimah* to absolutely transform the consciousness of the sincere worshipper.

Thus did the holy seeds of Islam, which had been planted, by the grace of God, within the garden within me, continue to be nurtured by the blessed "hand" of the Master of all the worlds, as He intended and decreed.

I worked continuously throughout this time in Sri Lanka and altogether for a period of twelve years on Bawa's (ra) book, *The Resonance of Allah*, which was the esoteric explanation of many dimensions of prayer, the true state of the human being, and the soul's journey to God. In this deep treatise, words regularly understood in Islam in a simple, direct way, such as *shariat* and *iman*, were presented as multi-dimensional mystical realities, containing meanings within meanings.

Doors of understanding and experience were opened for me by being in close proximity with the Sheikh day and night and committed to fulfilling the work he had asked me to do. I was able to ask many questions about the book, and so I received a lot of knowledge and understanding directly.

This dialogue with the Sheikh did not only continue throughout the day; very often I continued to ask him questions and receive explanations while I slept. People told me that I would often sit bolt upright on my sleeping bag, and say, "*Alhamdulillah!*" and have a lively, lengthy discussion with the Sheikh in my sleep. This was a sign of the depth of the engagement of my psyche or soul in the dialogue with the Sheikh on the project.

I once had a dream that I discovered all the chapters of the book separated and out of order, on yellowed pages, tied up in packages in a dark dusty attic. I was deeply troubled to see this great book in such disarray. Then a powerful, clear voice spoke to me and said, "Do not worry. This book has already been encoded in your DNA."

Bawa (ra) told me on more than one occasion that the reward for the selfless effort I had put into this work would be given in the hereafter, not in this world. I have come to realize again and again that no valuable gift is given to a seeker on the way of God that is not also a test and purification.

Having received the blessing of working so intensively on this project with the Sheikh, while he was alive, I had to give it up completely after he left this world. After Bawa (ra) passed, there was a complete restructuring of the project in which I, and others who had been working on it for many years, were replaced by other people.

After the book was published, a film was also produced about the process of accomplishing it. My involvement was never acknowledged in any way. This was a blessing for me. I came to understand more and more clearly what Bawa (ra) had been telling me. Whatever had taken place in the process of my working on this project, whatever part of my service to this work was pure and good, the reward was not to be found in this world but solely in the world to come.

As for what will be revealed in the world to come, the account is with God. In the light of the day when *"every atom's weight of good will be seen"* and *"every atom's weight of evil,"* we pray only that we can learn, through all these challenges and tests that we meet along the way, to serve the Creator more purely with worship and service that He will accept.

When we realize that the reason God created us is solely so that we may worship and serve Him, we must cut away all thoughts and intentions that have been grafted onto the original intention and thus dispel within our consciousness the illusion that we are here to get our reward in this world. This is what I came to understand and experience from what Bawa (ra) told me and from all that I went through attempting to fulfill the assignment he had given me.

Another situation arose during the time spent with Bawa (ra) in Sri Lanka that, like everything else on the path to God, was a lesson and a test. From the beginning, through the prayer, Ahamad Kabeer and I were connected. What touched me about Kabeer, was his piety, his simplicity, and his devotion to the Sheikh. This was the wealth and knowledge that he had, nothing else.

He once showed me a trunk in which he had all his treasures. He had saved every small gift, down to the tissues, given to him by the disciples of Bawa (ra) visiting Sri Lanka. I was touched by his unspoiled attitude. During this period of his life, at Bawa's (ra) request, he had stopped doing any work in the world so he could focus entirely on his service to the Sheikh. He was thus at the mercy of God, the Sheikh, and the disciples for every material thing he received, and he seemed very grateful for the smallest gift.

What really brought Kabeer and me together was the prayer. Having started to do the *salat* upstairs outside Bawa's (ra) room, where I had been originally guided to pray, we had now moved to the large living room downstairs because more people were tending to come. Sometimes there were several people in the congregation, and sometimes just he and I and one or two others. Our connection was thus established in the congregational prayer and in communication about prayer.

Relationships which are meaningful, in the way of God, are those that bear fruit, and that fruit, when eaten, brings people closer to God. Thus, our joining in the prayer was useful in the way of God, as He had decreed, since more and more people came to pray together, following that example.

There was another fruit also destined for us to bear. This was revealed, like so many of the unfolding mysteries of my life's journey, in a mysterious way. On the trip to India, where we went to renew our visas, I had the pleasure of meeting Kabeer's holy mother. Her name was Maimuna Umma, but we called her Babicha (grandmother) in Tamil. She was one of the ancient ones that I have been so blessed to meet on my life's journey. I felt the sanctity, holiness, in her soft-skinned hands like in the hands of the other ancient ones I was graced to meet. You feel that this ancient hand has touched no impurity, and you are so blessed that it is now caressing you. As soon as she met me, she took hold of me, held me, and prayed over me for a long time.

Though nothing had come to pass that would indicate marriage between Kabeer and me, I seemed to sense that she was praying for our offspring. Kabeer had never been inclined to marriage at all. This was the one and only chance that she might see his progeny. I felt the intensity of her embrace and knew that there was a blessing in it. It was not for nothing that she lived her entire life in a state of prayer and purity. What she intended would come to pass, but not right away.

The meeting with Kabeer's mother was deep. The intensity of her desire made me realize that I also was in some way inclined to that union, and especially to the fruit that it would produce.

When our visas were ready, we returned to Sri Lanka. Bawa (ra) knew about the subtlety of what had taken place in my meeting with the mother of Kabeer. He called me into his room and spoke to me for more than an hour explaining why, specifically and in depth, I should *not* think about marrying Kabeer. It was a searing discourse, which nearly made my hair stand on end.

As he spoke about so many details I could not possibly know, I realized again that the Sheikh knew what I knew not. Once again, I had no choice but to follow his direction. And then, entering more deeply into the teaching, I asked myself: *What is he really saying to me? And how can I be truly obedient with my heart and soul and understanding to what he is teaching me?*

To begin with, I needed to control the mind, desire, and imagination. This was the real inner work, the most fundamental and necessary level of submission to the Divine Will, but also the most difficult to achieve. Who I am to marry, when, and how—all of this is in God's "hand." The destiny is already written. Why should I attempt to project any fantasy I may have onto existence? It is much better to let the story unfold by itself.

Bawa (ra) then showed me that I did not know really who Kabeer was. I saw how much we project our mind and desire onto others and do not know who they really are. Such is the power of our mind and desire to make us see what they want us to see, but the Sheikh wants us to see something else, and to see in a different way.

It was a very intense communication with the Sheikh, as he exposed to me these forces within myself, and the tendency I had to project them onto others, especially in the context of looking for a partner. Once again, he placed me in a state of shock.

Bawa (ra) often spoke about the state of metal, which needs to be transformed by the blacksmith. As long as it is in the heat of the fire, it is malleable and can be reshaped, but once it is out of the fire, it becomes fixed and cannot be molded. On that day, he kept me in the heat of the fire for a long time, and when I came out, I wanted nothing but to let go of any idea I may have had and surrender deeply to the Divine Decree.

For the following year that I was in Sri Lanka, as carefully as I could, I followed the advice Bawa (ra) gave me that day. I regarded Kabeer respectfully at a distance and spoke to him as infrequently as possible.

Approximately a year later, however, two weeks before Bawa (ra) left Sri Lanka, I walked into his room wearing green. He said to me, "Green Maryam, are you dressed for your wedding?" He then told me to prepare for the marriage to Kabeer, which would take place in about twenty-four hours.

I had barely looked at or spoken to Kabeer for the past year in obedience to the Sheikh's instruction. Once he had cut the attachment in me, I was able to look at the situation much more objectively. Kabeer barely spoke English and had no training to work in America, nor would it be easy for him to integrate with the culture and life there. I felt the weight of all the responsibility as a burden lying upon me. I sat in front of Bawa's (ra) bed, stricken by this awareness, hoping for some kind of clarification or reprieve. The fantasy had long before been dispelled. Now I was facing reality.

Nevertheless, there did not seem to be anything to discuss. Bawa (ra) told me to get ready, and that was all. I believe that this was so—he did not ask me what I thought or felt about the idea—because it was a thing ordained. Kabeer had to come to America, and Issa had to be born.

On that day, when I realized that I had twenty-four hours before the destiny would be fulfilled, Lennie and Sophie called and said that they were in China and would like to come visit in Sri Lanka in a few days.

Our wedding was the last one ever performed by Bawa (ra) in Sri Lanka. The house was packed with people, people sleeping everywhere, even on all the steps of the staircase, since everyone knew that the Sheikh was leaving soon. In reality, he would never return.

When Bawa (ra) performed the wedding ceremony, the room was filled with *imams*. Bawa's (ra) discourse was grave. He said that all the weight, all the burden, all the responsibility would rest upon me. He said that everything rests on the earth, and so the earth must not shake, or everything will fall. He told me not to expect anything in the marriage from Kabeer, but to take responsibility for everything myself.

When I saw how our life unfolded in later years, I understood the truth in his words. As heavy as it sounded, that was how it was. But, as I have learned again, again, and again, in all the circumstances of my life, *surely* with difficulty comes ease. The very fact that I had to bear so much responsibility made me learn how to take care of many things, and I became independent as a result of this marriage, able to take care of almost everything by myself. That was part of the blessing of what I had to learn at this stage in my life. So, the only word I can say about it is *Alhamdulillah*—all praise be to God for all the lessons we learn and all the challenges we meet!

The next day, my parents arrived, as well as the Ambassador to Sri Lanka from Pakistan and his wife, friends of Bawa's (ra) close disciple, Fuard Utteman. Fuard, my parents, the Ambassador and his wife, and Kabeer and I went off into the tea country in the hills of Sri Lanka to celebrate our honeymoon. Bawa (ra) specified that this trip could not last longer than two and a half days.

Once we were out on the road and traveling up into the mountains, true to form, my father started to sing. Several times, he sang the call to prayer. I do not know where he learned it, but he was definitely inspired to sing it on that trip. Then he sang his old favorites, such as,

> "*If we could consider each other*
> *A neighbor a friend or a brother,*

It could be a wonderful, wonderful world,
It could be a wonderful world,

Oh yes, it could be a wonderful world!
If there were no poor,
And the rich were content,
If strangers were welcome
Wherever they went,
If each of us knew what
True brotherhood meant,
It could be a wonderful world,
O yes, it could be a wonderful world!"

The wedding was done, the honeymoon was a group adventure in the hill country of Sri Lanka, and what was really being celebrated was the wonderful world that could exist if true brotherhood reigned.

When we returned to Bawa (ra), he asked Kabeer what had happened on the trip. Kabeer said, "My father-in-law sang many songs," and he attempted, with some help, to sing a song that Lennie had sung. Bawa (ra) laughed and laughed and said that was very good. Soon after, he went back to America, and Ahamad Kabeer and I followed about a month later.

We arrived in the middle of winter. When he saw that all the trees had no leaves, Kabeer, who had always lived in a tropical climate where the trees do not lose their leaves, was shocked. He thought that a great fire must have devastated the land, and, out of respect and sympathy for us, he did not want to say anything about this disaster. He only told me about his initial perception much later.

We arrived in Philadelphia and before too long rented a room in a house down the block from the Fellowship. All the work, the focus on prayer, the building of the mosque in the heart, which had been galvanized in Sri Lanka, continued to develop in Philadelphia. Kabeer and I were actively engaged with the work. He was leading prayers and doing blessings; I was teaching classes of all kinds— prayer, Arabic, and so on. All of the activity, of course, was centered around the Sheikh.

Day and night, Bawa (ra) would give discourses revealing the light within true prayer, Islam, and the Qur'an. For example, he said:

> *"Brothers and sisters in Islam,*
> *No matter what changes occur throughout the ages, the Qur'an is one thing that never changes.*
> *It is immutable.*
> *It offers an explanation appropriate for every period of time and for every level of understanding.*
> *All the meanings it contains could not be written down even if all the oceans of the world were made into ink and all the trees were made into pens.*
> *To comprehend the Qur'an,*
> *First we must establish our absolute faith, certitude, and determination; then we must acquire wisdom; and finally we must delve deep inside and study it from within.*
> *If we look into the depths of the Qur'an, we will find the complete never-ending wealth and grace of Almighty God. We will find the light of Allah, the resplendence of Allah.*
> *We will not find racial or religious prejudices, battles, or fighting of any kind. We will find only the benevolence of all the universes....*
> *The Qur'an is a treasure, which continually speaks to our faith.*
> *Its verses were sent to Muhammad one by one, according to the needs of the people, the difficulties they were undergoing, and the questions they asked.*
> *These verses and chapters were sent to bring clarity to man, from the time he appears as a fetus, as the mim, to the moment he reaches the shore of the hereafter.*
> *They cleanse man stage by stage.*
> *Whatever state he is in at one time of prayer, the Qur'an explains the state he should achieve by the next prayer time. In this way, the Qur'an lifts man up, causing his wisdom, his beauty, and his divine knowledge to grow little by little.*
> *The Prophet said, 'Even though I depart from the world, I leave you the Qur'an. That is your evidence. Please keep it close to you.'*
> *The Qur'an will be a teacher and a learned one to the innermost heart. That is why its verses were sent to humankind. Step by step the Qur'an elevates man; chapter-by-chapter, it cuts away all the things within him that need to be discarded."*

The words coming through the Sheikh day and night upon his return from Sri Lanka galvanized the community step by step into the building of the mosque, both within and without. Bawa (ra), who was not strong enough to go downstairs, was informed of every step of the building process through videos. The labor was done almost entirely by members of the Fellowship.

It must be acknowledged that both before and while the mosque was being built there was a lot of resistance to it in certain members of the community. Bawa (ra) had been teaching for so long the necessity to transcend religious differences, saying, "That which separates us from our fellow man is that which separates us from God." He taught that all the religions represented stages of the development of the human being and that all these levels of development were united in the true human being. He also taught that the true place of worship is not an outer building but the innermost heart.

But along with the repository of inner teachings, he also left, as part of his eternal legacy, the mosque and an abundance of teachings about the mosque, about true prayer and the Qur'an, such as the text I have quoted above.

For me, there was never any choice but to go deeper and deeper into the state of prayer and submission. All the Sheikhs, all the teachings I have encountered have guided me unfailingly in this direction. This is what our Creator, Most Merciful, created us to do, and explains in His words when He says, *"And I did not create the jinn and humans except to worship Me"* (The Holy Qur'an 51:56).

So that is , I believe why Sheikh Bawa Muhaiyaddeen (ra) left a mosque as a legacy: to enable those who came after him to understand and experience the meaning of this beautiful *ayat*, as well as all the verses of the Holy Qur'an.

The mosque was completed and opened in a ceremony, just before Ramadhan in 1984. Sheikh Bawa Muhaiyaddeen (ra) left this world, at a very old age, in December 1986. I have not heard of anyone who could say that he or she knew exactly how old he was. The extent of his life, and the mysteries it contained were known only by Allah.

At the moment that he passed, for a fraction of a second, there was an intense cry uttered by a few, but it was immediately overpowered by powerful *zikr* that filled the house and, I sensed, the universe. What I felt was not sadness that he had left, but blessing that he had come. A few days earlier, while sitting at the doorway of his room, I had felt his spirit speaking blissfully within me, "Do not be concerned; I am simply taking off the shirt."

On the night of his passing, I sat at the head of Bawa's (ra) bed and played Qur'an tapes, throughout the night. There was a beautiful, gentle, peaceful smile on his face and light and peace emanating from his form and filling the room. People came circling around the bed throughout the night, including many children. I saw no fear or distress in the people coming through that night. There was a transcendent sense of peace covering over everything.

Bawa (ra) left many beautiful gifts as his legacy, many teachings yet to be received and realized. What he did not leave, apparently, was a *successor*, someone who had received the full transmission and was complete, liberated, and authorized to totally transform the lives of others.

Most of the disciples feel that the spiritual presence of Bawa (ra) and his teachings, the thousands of hours of video taped discourses, his beautiful *mazhar* (shrine) in the countryside, as well as the unity of the community blessed by his spiritual presence, are the living transmission of the Sheikh.

For me, as much as I respected and loved the Sheikh, I knew for certain that my journey was not complete and I needed further training and transformation, more experience in the journey through the stages of the Way, in order to attain complete realization and liberation.

I cannot evaluate the state of any of the followers of the Sheikh or estimate the level that each has reached. Assessing my own state and knowing that I was certainly not completely realized, I felt that

I had to journey with a living teacher until I was annihilated and completely merged with the Truth.

My life's story, the journey through ten thousand veils, was not finished. In this endless tale, there were more chapters to come.

In the time that followed his peaceful passing, I missed the Sheikh very much. From his bed he had generated so much of the energy, the transformative life force we experienced, and, after he left this world, it was not the same.

This was especially apparent in my marriage with Kabeer. Truly, we had both been much more deeply related to the Sheikh than to each other. It was he whom we loved and who inspired us always. That power and that passion were not present in our relationship without him. After Bawa (ra) left, I became aware of a stagnancy and a kind of void which could never be filled in my relationship with Kabeer.

This does not mean that I do not respect him for the work that he does with the purity of his heart for God, the Sheikh, and the community. But the marriage simply was not vitally alive and spiritually nourishing for me. It was not half of my religion as it should have been. From the time of Bawa's (ra) passing, little by little, I became more and more profoundly aware of this.

But, there was one important thing we had to do together. It was one of two things that Bawa (ra) frequently asked me about. These were two "in-jokes" or spiritual secrets that we shared, and they were part of the personal legacy he left to me. First, very often he asked me, "How are you?" Whenever he asked me this question, immediately I felt that I was in the divine presence, that God was gazing upon me and asking me this question. Every time this happened, I was overwhelmed by love and awe and gratitude, and said, "*Alhamdulillah*, Bawa! I am very well!"

The Sheikh never asked me the question when I was depressed, disturbed, or too far away from contemplation of the Divine to know that God was gazing upon me. He would completely ignore me when I was in any kind of negative state. He was targeting the state of divine joy, the plenitude of contentment. Then he would often say about me that whenever he asked me how I was, I always said, "*Alhamdulillah*! (All Praise be to God!")") In this way, he trained me to know that this is what I must always say, that this was the state in which he wanted me always to abide. And I extend this invitation, with all my love, to you.

Another thing that Bawa (ra) said to me almost every time he saw me was, "Maryam, where is Issa?" He asked me this so many times, all I could do is smile, and say, "You know, Bawa." Then, one day, he asked me if I had any questions. I said, "Yes, Bawa, where is Issa?" He said, "Issa is the light of the soul."

He gave a very beautiful, exalted discourse about the light of Issa, *ruh'Allah*, the soul of God. So, this was one of the dimensions that he was referring to when he asked me the question. But he was also referring to Issa, my son, who was to be born. He said some very deep things about him and then kept asking me where he was. I really did not know. I felt him very much too, but I could not seem to bring him in.

Bawa (ra) had given us instructions about how to conceive a child consciously in the state of prayer. We were following them scrupulously, targeting the correct times, and then following the protocol, but Issa was existing comfortably in the world of souls and not ready to come in. I miscarried six times. In all of the miscarriages, I did not feel that a child had come and left. No, the same child was there, but he was not ready to come. I had to go through the doorway six times, so that my intention could be purified and faith strengthened. But after the sixth time, I did wonder!

Bawa (ra) had asked about Issa so many times, but by the time that he left this world, still Issa had not come. Where, O God, was Issa? On the day of Bawa's (ra) burial, I laid my head on the rocks covering his grave and placed the matter of Issa entirely and absolutely in the "hand" of God. I had tried as much as I could, but I could not bring him in.

That was on December 8, 1986. Very soon after, I became pregnant for the seventh time and the due date for the baby was December 8, 1987. Issa was born, however, one week later on December 15, 1987.

His personality and energy were very noticeable, even when he was in the womb. This was especially so during the twelve days in which we celebrated the *mawlid* (birth) of the Prophet Muhammad (saw) and during the month of Ramadan. It was as though he was doing flips and somersaults for joy, or maybe, he was praying.

Since the journey in the way of God was such an important and valuable part of my life, I could not but share it with my child. He began to travel with me when he was eight months old and we went to New Mexico. Many short and long trips followed. In general, he was a very happy traveler.

When he was four and a half, Issa, Kabeer and I went to the south of India, so he could get to know his father's family, and to the north of India to visit my friends in Kashmir from whom I had been importing tapestries. Issa fell into the arms of everyone and merged easily with his cousins, uncles, aunts, and beloved grandmother, Babicha (whose prayers had now been answered) in Madras, as well as with our beloved friends in Kashmir. That was the first of many international journeys that he, son of a much traveling mother, would make.

16

The Vale of Kashmir,
Crown Jewel of the World
—Imprisoned but Free

Srinagar, Kashmir, 1992

Did ye think that ye would enter Heaven without Allah testing those of you who fought hard (in His Cause) and remained steadfast?

The Holy Qur'an 3:142

"Soaring mountains, limpid lakes and gardens enhance its aesthetic appeal. This is the place, which boasted of a wealth of flora and fauna, beauty and serenity and attracted great saints and rishis. Today, alas, it is desperately struggling for survival and peace."

Partha Bannerjee

The journey of descent into the Vale of Kashmir is breathtaking. As we flew down, the pilot was inspired, flying like a cosmic dancer up and down and around the magnificent, amazing sculptures of snow. This could only bring forth, in the beholder, awe and contemplation of the inspiration of the Sculptor, Himself. There are rare moments in our life when we are permitted and blessed to see such things—all awesome signs of the grandeur of the Creator and that which He has created, which is simply the manifested sign of the greatness of the One who made it. As we descended further between the snowy peaks and entered the valley, we passed through layer upon layer of emerald light.

The spectral beauty of the land, with its intensity of color and light, was awe-inspiring.

I have descended by plane into many lands, but none more radiantly beautiful. In addition to the elemental beauty of this magical valley, the spiritual energy was intense. Upon landing in this realm, I felt as if the top of my head flew off and was replaced by highly charged, luminous air. From the moment of arriving in this energized sphere, my heart was seized by a kind of nostalgia. I do not know in what way, but in some way, I was connected with this place.

The land and the people were extremely familiar. They recognized me instantly, as I did them, and so deep was the attraction between us that, during most of my stays in Kashmir, I remained consciously inside the house because I felt if I went out even into the marketplace, the love and longing inspired by being in the midst of these people would be more than my heart could bear.

The political situation of this remote yet strategic valley is, itself, heartbreaking. In stark contrast to the great natural beauty of the landscape and the luminous intelligence and warmth of the people is the darkness of the force of occupation that oppresses this land. It reminds us that although we can see an image of it, paradise has not yet been attained on this earth.

The Kashmiris, who were given the right to self-determination by the United Nations in 1948, until now have not been able to exercise that right. On the contrary, these noble and gifted people have been severely oppressed, and, in a sense, held hostage in their own land. While Kashmir is a tourism-based economy, much of the time tourists cannot get into the country, and a major source of its income has thus been cut off.

The people have endured so many ordeals, there is no way that we, who are not living through this with them, can truly fathom their trial and their suffering. This must not be forgotten, even while we appreciate the beauty of the land, the people, and the unique artistry of Kashmir.

On our second trip to Kashmir, we were vividly aware of this. We sat in an airport in London, waiting to take off to fly there.

Although we were told that a strict curfew was being imposed and no one could get in, we continued to wait, like someone who knows that the sun is hidden behind the clouds on a very cloudy day and that it will inevitably shine again. Only a short while before our plane was scheduled to take off was the curfew lifted, and we were able to fly under that black cloud cover of oppression and to land in our beloved imperiled paradise.

We were met at the airport by two large families, our original suppliers, and those with whom we were currently dealing in tapestries, all of whom we loved very much. They were now very politely vying with each other for the blessing of hosting us, and no doubt for our business also. We went home with our present suppliers, an elegant, princely man, kind and lovely, named aptly Jelaluddin As-Sufi and his beautiful wife, Shahnaz, who became my dear friend, as well as her brother, Yousuf Shah, with whom I would continue to do business for many years in the future.

Traveling the relatively short distance between the airport and their home was an experience fraught with danger. One could feel a confrontation, something oppressive, taking place nearby, and it turned out that some violence had occurred five minutes from their house that night. Our hosts knew the parties involved and were very saddened and concerned by the news. They knew also that the people injured could, at any time, be themselves.

I looked at these beautiful people, drank in the sight of them, and appreciated their presence deeply. I understood that just because they lived there, they could be injured or killed. I prayed that these good people, my gracious hosts, be protected from the darkness which surrounded their beautiful land and that the light I saw shining so clearly through them guide them through all this to the ultimate goal.

I also knew that I was there to witness, even to the small extent I could, what people have to go through, then understand and bear witness to what I had seen. As an American, one is taught to avoid dangerous situations like this at all costs when traveling abroad, but I am indebted to the Creator that He permitted me to be there and to share the danger and difficulty with my relatives in the human family. If we are not with the people who are suffering, feeling even a little of what they feel, how can we truly understand the human condition, experiencing it as our own condition?

Although it was no doubt dangerous to visit their land, under those circumstances, for me to share that experience with the people of Kashmir was a blessing I cannot forget, a knowledge that has been embedded in my heart. One of the most important gifts of traveling through the world on the spiritual journey is the ever-deepening realization and experience that all lives are interconnected. We are all embodiments of the one creation made by the One Creator. In respect to the absolute oneness of our Source and Ultimate Reality, we come to realize that every being that we meet is a manifestation of this sacred truth.

Whatever God, the Divine Guide, has willed me to see, that is the story I have to tell. It is my profound hope and dream that somehow, through telling the stories of the beautiful beings I have met along the way, I will, God willing, find some means of helping and supporting them, so beautifully and nobly did they welcome and receive me.

After our somewhat perilous trip through unknown danger, we arrived at their house, which was so large and full of rooms and people that I could not immediately make sense of it. One room was filled mostly with the elders, some rooms with mostly children of various ages, one room was the active kitchen, and one was a vast cathedral-like room in an attic with rays of light descending into it—the showroom where rugs and tapestries were stored.

As in all the Sufi houses we have visited in our travels, Issa disappeared and was assimilated into the local life. In the days that followed, when looking for four-and-a-half-year-old Issa, I would find him happily ensconced and merged in the activities of one or another of these rooms, blissfully intermingled and entertained, as though this was all a delightful show put on for him. He would usually be in someone's arms, hugging or wrestling with someone, as though he had been born there and always lived there.

Since traveling in the way of God has played such an enlightening role in my life, I could not but wish to share this with my child, and I am very grateful that he had the opportunity, as his world view was forming, to know and experience his intimate connection with these people and many other members of the human family.

The awareness of the universal family is one that I began to learn about in my father's house. From that point on, I have always had a community awareness. I have always known that the "family" was not nuclear, but universal, inclusive, and, in fact, the "family of man." The houses of the lovers of God are like this. This is the manifestation of the way.

Another sign of holistic community and the natural manifestation of the human family that we discovered again and again in our travels, as we did in this house of many chambers, is that the children and the elders are always together. The elderly are given the respect due to their age, experience, and accumulated wisdom, and they are integral to the fabric of the family, thus transmitting their knowledge to the generations that follow them in a way that is absolutely natural and holistic. Issa knew this and that is why I often found him in their arms.

Another place to which he gravitated was the third floor room, the vast vaulted room on the top of the house into which rays of light descended in a spectral pattern. When I could not find him elsewhere, I would go up, and often find him there sitting alone, silent, transfixed, with rays of soft light falling upon him. Filled with tapestries, carpets and light, it was the room where we most often prayed and also where we did our business.

The whole experience was like a manifest dream. I had dreamt all of this and now I was living it. Our gracious host had given us a very cozy room, one which was almost entirely filled with a huge bed. When I drew the curtains and looked outside, I was completely transported to another time, another dimension of being.

The view was mesmerizing, an ancient scene I knew I had seen before somewhere in my consciousness—the ancient wooden buildings in front of snow-covered mountains, people walking by from absolutely another epoch than contemporary mall traffic; all this I remembered, had longed for and had now found my way back to. The entire situation filled my heart with peace, yet, at the same time, with a kind of intense longing and excitement. I looked out at that scene and did not know in which world I really existed. I was deeply inclined to go outside and throw myself into that other existence, but, for a time, strongly resisted.

We went to sleep in the cozy room, and were awakened before dawn by the beautiful sounds pouring through the valley from minaret to minaret. In all Muslim lands, when the call to prayer goes out, it echoes and resounds from minaret to minaret to minaret. All time and space, one's heart and soul, are enveloped by this resounding echo. From hilltop to hilltop, all sounds and energies are inter-communicating, ricocheting, relaying the same message—calling us to remember our Lord.

Having lived in and traveled through many Muslim lands, I had become accustomed to this beautiful resonance filling mountains and valleys at the times of prayer. But pre-dawn, in the mystic vale of Kashmir, the resonance of the sound filling the valley was beyond extraordinary. Broadcasting from all the minarets, echoing from one to the next, was not only the call to prayer, but extended profound *zikr*, remembrance of God, one after the next, the words we love most, the words we were inspired by our Sheikhs to say, the words that express the love in our hearts for and from the One of Infinite Splendor, the Most Kind and Loving One who created us, echoing throughout this elevated valley. We felt as though the prayers of our innermost heart were resounding throughout this realm.

I also realized at this moment that whatever political oppression had imposed itself upon this land and people, could not silence or inhibit the power of their prayer.

After some days of retreat, in which we discovered these and other mysteries of Kashmir within our souls, our hosts told us that they wanted to take us out to meet the artisans who make the tapestries and to show us the beauty of Kashmir.

So, we ventured forth into an ancient world of extraordinary sights and sounds, a valley of crystal lakes, hand-carved wooden buildings and houseboats bordering the lakes and floating upon them, a land of terraced hills, and fruit orchards surrounded by huge snow peaks. The air had a crystalline clarity and was filled with the aromatic odors of fires burning everywhere.

There is a Kashmiri custom in which each person carries a basket of coals inside his or her beautifully embroidered garment. When you meet someone on a path, if you are not already carrying such a basket, the other person will give theirs to you. This is their way of greeting each other and sharing the warmth.

Our hosts took us on a tour of the town of Srinagar, past the intricately carved houseboats, to a small boat docked at the shore of Dal Lake in which we were to ride across the lake.

Our journey across the vast lake was bittersweet. We learned that we were the first visitors to ride in this boat in many months. Since very few people were able even to get into the country, the tourist industry had plummeted, and these ferrymen had no people to transport, no way to make a living. They told us that some of them had even resorted to eating poisonous roots because they could not cope with the hopelessness of their situation. Our lovely trip across the lake was undermined by this awareness.

Then, our hosts continued the tour of the land with its celestial gardens and orchards and crystal lakes surrounded by the towering snowy peaks which frame the picture that is the beautiful valley. We passed through the marketplace and met the merchants in their colorful old stalls. I was deeply touched at their beauty, refinement, and intelligence. Even the children there seemed to speak many languages.

Our tour culminated at an ancient mosque. I was guided to a carved wooden deck outside where I was to pray. It was built of dark rich wood, which had been prayed on so many times that it had become as soft as velvet, smooth and cool. Going down in prostration, I wished never to get up again. So much light, understanding and love flowed into me, as I remained prostrated there. I felt that, within the prostration, within the surrender, within the love, a door opened, and knowledge was given.

From the moment I had embraced Islam, or I could say, more accurately, from the time that Islam embraced me, I was moved and inspired, such that, whatever small amount of understanding or knowledge came to me, I wanted to share it, whatever life-giving water was poured into my cup, I wanted to share it with those who might be thirsting. So, it had been very natural to teach, that is, to share the knowledge about prayer, Arabic, the Sufi way, the way of true Islam.

It was at this moment in the blessed vale of Kashmir that I was told that the words I had been speaking were not *mine*. They were the words of God, the words of the Creator, Most Gracious and Merciful, Most Loving and Kind, that He had given to me to give to others, so that all of us may turn again to Him. This understanding came to me while I was prostrating on that dark, cool, ancient wood.

When I sat up at the end of the prayer and turned to my right, I saw that sitting next to me was a very elderly, holy woman. She was there as a witness and participant in this divine encounter.

With that final message, our time in the holy valley of Kashmir had come to an end. The snows were coming with force, and we had to fly out before we were snowed in for the winter. As we were leaving, we were told that there were many Sufis in the mountains whom we should meet. I knew that I would have to come back, *insh'Allah*, and find them.

17

Mecca, Medina, and the Mountain of Light
Saudi Arabia, 1996

Behold! We gave the site to Abraham of the House, saying: "Ascribe nothing as partner unto Me, and sanctify My House for those who compass it round or stand up, or prostrate themselves. And proclaim unto humankind the pilgrimage.

The Holy Qur'an 22:26

"Precious children, jeweled lights of my eyes, within you there is a house just for God. That is the Ka'bah. That is paradise. All the prophets, all the good ones from this world and the world of souls are there within it, praying and glorifying God...The sounds of their constant zikr, their salaams, and salutations on the Prophet, the call to prayer, and their prayers are always heard."

Sheikh Bawa Muhaiyaddeen

There are certain places to which one cannot go without an invitation. The Holy House of Allah in Mecca is such a place. I had been a Muslim for twenty-two years, hoping very much to make the journey to Mecca and Medina, but the invitation did not come until the destined time, the time when Allah willed to send it. He leads to His light whom He wills, when He wills, as He wills.

In my case, I was standing in the shoe room of the Fellowship, waiting to use the phone when I happened to see a little casting notice for a play that was going to be presented at the Fellowship. It was being directed by my dear friend Abd'al Hayy, with whom

I had shared so much of the adventure of "rite of passage" theatre in the sixties.

One of the characters in the play was a representation of the great Sufi saint, Rabi'a Al-Adawiyyah. The little note was a sign for me. I was seized by the sense that I had to play that part. I called and discovered that it had already been cast. They had been going to ask me to play it but thought I was too busy to have time for the rehearsals. So, they had given it to another person. The rehearsals were well under way.

It had been thirty years since Abd'al Hayy and I last worked together in the Floating Lotus Magic Opera Company. Now this opportunity had surfaced, and I told Abd'al Hayy and his wife, my beloved friend Malika, that they should be aware, at least, that I was ready if they needed me. Within a few days, they called to say that the woman playing the part had suddenly dropped out for various reasons and so they needed me.

I did not have much time to learn the part and integrate with the total flow of the company and the play, but the character and what she said were so deeply relevant to my being that they caused me to enter another world, that is, a totally different state of awareness.

One line that she said and that I related to profoundly was "Lovers are with their beloveds now, two by two by two, but I, unseen by all of them, am alone, Allah, with You."

The play dramatized the legendary story of Rabi'a, in which since she was unable to go to the Ka'bah on pilgrimage, the Ka'bah came to her. As the Ka'bah approaches her, she says the words that all pilgrims say on encountering the Holy House:

> "*I am here, O Lord , I am here.*
> *I am here, You have no partner, I am here!*
> *Surely all praise and blessings are Yours and dominion.*
> *There is no one who is Your partner.*"

As I spoke these lines, it was a case of art inspiring life, of art and life becoming one in the moment of truth. At the very moment that I spoke the words on the stage, I knew that this was not an act in a play—the words were the absolute truth of my being. I was saying them sincerely to the One to Whom they must be expressed. This was my invitation to make the journey, and I must go as soon as possible.

It was mid October. I inquired without delay and discovered that a group of pilgrims from the Fellowship was traveling to Mecca on *'umra* (the lesser—non-obligatory—pilgrimage) in December. Suddenly, it became absolutely clear that Issa and I would be amongst them. With lightning speed, since the Divine willed it, all of the details of preparation fell into place.

With fifty other people, many families with children, we set out on the first stage of our pilgrimage, the journey to the airport. There were televisions on the bus, on which we watched the movie Muhammad, Messenger of God. I had watched this movie many times with Bawa (ra) in his room in Sri Lanka. Now, the Sheikh was guiding us into a new dimension, walking in the footsteps of the Messenger. This movement would galvanize and transform the rest of my life.

We spent a few hours at JFK airport. There were many kids in our group and Issa thoroughly enjoyed himself as he is inclined to do. I found a spot in the airport and prayed freely and joyously, knowing that the journey was sacred and that all the world was a mosque or place of worship.

With this intention and abundant energy, we flew. Arriving in Saudi Arabia's capital, Riyadh, we found that, passing through the gate was not so easy. The guardian at the gate, inspecting my passport, noted that I was married. Where was my husband? How could this be? How could a mother and a child travel without a man? As I mentioned earlier, after Bawa's passing, I had increasingly felt that the marriage was lacking vital force for me. I had asked Kabeer for a divorce. The process took about five years to finalize, but by this time, we were separated, and he had given me a note that Issa and I had his permission to travel.

After a few minutes of confusion, the guide of our group turned up with the paper signed by Kabeer, giving us permission to make this journey. He explained the situation in Arabic for several minutes, and finally we were allowed to pass. This was a sobering experience we often encountered in Saudi Arabia, this attitude of the "gatekeepers." It contrasted with the bliss of our immersion in the light—the wide-open space of our journey—the dimension, which is not and could never be controlled or restricted by men.

Having made it through the gate, we began our journey into the desert. Like most things on the pilgrimage, the encounter with the land in Saudi Arabia is extremely powerful and intense. There are vast expanses of desert and areas of the earth where immense volcanic activity has taken place. One experiences directly that the land and the people of God have undergone great ordeals here. It is not a breezy tropical paradise, but a land of ultimate encounter.

One can sense powerfully how the pilgrims, gathering on the plains of Arafat under the scorching sun, are living on earth before they die, the mystery of the souls rising up on the Day of Judgment, the Day of Reckoning. The passages in the Qur'an that describe the Day of Judgment and what will inevitably come to pass are so powerful it makes sense that they were revealed in a landscape like this, which is absolutely unyielding, which does not give comfort or solace in itself, but forces one to turn in a direction other than the earth for things that people in other lands have in abundance and take for granted, such as water, vegetation, coolness, and shade.

Our trip through this desert went on for hours and hours in a bus packed with men, women, and many children. The children were amazingly quiet and submitted to the entire process, and in peace. The blessing in the intention of our pilgrimage was carrying us along and everyone was behaving differently than they would on any other kind of trip.

We finally arrived, after many hours of traveling through the volcanic expanse, in the proximity of Medina. Having traveled through the night, we arrived in Medina, the city of the Prophet,

Medina al-Munawwara, the city of lights, just before the dawn, or *fajr* prayer. We went to our room to bathe, and were cleansed and refreshed in time to hear the call to prayer echoing from the minaret, flooding the city of the Prophet Muhammad (saw) as it called the faithful to assemble.

I looked out the window and from above, the veils and robes of the women and men, mostly white, were merging one into the next in what appeared to be a stream of light flowing down the road. It appeared to me to be a vision of the people of paradise being transported as a current of light to the throne of God. We watched this pure and radiant river flowing so beautifully toward the mosque, and then we went down and became immersed in it.

Beautiful breezes were blowing as we were carried along toward a complex of illuminated buildings, which were bathed in and emanating turquoise light. The towering, commanding structures were surrounded by a vast expanse of shining marble, which shimmered like crystal.

Along with the sea of believers with which we had merged, we were gliding along on the marble toward the mosques when suddenly my prayer beads, a set of bright turquoise crystal beads, broke apart and sped across the marble in every direction, like luminous tears. That was the end of my life as I knew it, and the beginning of the next cycle, as the Lord was revealing in this city of lights.

Issa went with some of the men into the mosque where the men assemble, and I went into the women's mosque. The interior of the mosque was even more amazing than the exterior. Being within it was like being within a jewel of infinite dimensions with infinite passageways.

I had certainly seen many postcards of Medina showing a corridor of doorways within doorways. What one has no way of knowing by looking at those postcards is that the passageways extend in many directions. Whatever way you turn, you see a passageway leading in a different direction, into a different dimension.

To begin with, I wondered how, architecturally, this could have been done. I felt that these passageways had a significance that I could not begin to understand. They were a sign of the vast mysteries, interior and exterior journeys, that one could make in the discovery of the wonders contained in the House of God.

Having entered the mosque and adjusted my eyes to the light, I found my place within the sisterhood. There were rows upon rows of sisters from everywhere, tiny babies to ancient women, assembled beautifully in clusters in their native dress. I found my place, not only as a female, in this great gathering of women, but even more than that, I found my place in the vast assembly as a servant of God.

There was a great sense of unity in the midst of tremendous diversity. Everyone, it seemed, was moving together in submission to divine harmony. However individual a person might think she is, in the midst of the vast inspired divine movement, these individual characteristics were absorbed like bubbles in the ocean. One does not lose the bubble, but gains the ocean.

After the prayers, I reunited with Issa and we glided back to the hotel. The next days in Medina were timeless. I do not know how long we were there, but only that the beauty and sweetness of the Prophet Muhammad (saw) and the presence of God, filled all time and space.

This was Medina, the city where the Holy Prophet (saw) and his community went to seek refuge when they were exiled from Mecca because their belief in the One God threatened those who controlled Mecca at that time and whose livelihood, prestige, and position, depended upon the people worshipping many gods, many idols.

This was the Medina where the Prophet (saw) built the new community, founded upon the principles of the unity and absolute sovereignty of the One Creator of all, and the equality in the fundamental rights of all of His creations. It was the place where this inspired community of believing people developed in piety and love for God, receiving the wealth of the divine revelations, memorizing them, and then manifesting them in actions.

All of the divine mysteries and truths, which had taken place here were somehow alive in this blessed realm, accentuated by the remembrance, in the hearts of the worshippers assembled, of the words and events which had been revealed here.

Sensing this accumulated grace and blessing, we were flowing along in the state of love, worship, and oneness, with almost no ripples on the surface of the infinite sea.

This sense of the continuity of undisturbed peace was interrupted by one trial. At every time of prayer, I let Issa go with some of the men we were traveling with into the men's mosque. Then, one day, the time of prayer arrived and we could find no one to accompany him. He very much wanted to go by himself. I was hesitant. We had always prayed together, but now he was nine.

I could not take him with me and also did not want to deprive him of the chance to enter into that wondrous space and pray. I had to put the matter in God's hand and let him go. He went in and, after prayers, much to my maternal relief, promptly appeared in the place he was supposed to meet me.

The next day, however, he went in, but when the prayers were over, did not appear in the designated spot. I sat there waiting and waiting to see his beautiful, sweet face, his form, but he did not appear. This was agonizing. It was a test of faith, and, it seemed, I failed.

I waited and waited, but to no avail. Finally, completely stricken with concern, I got up and went back to the hotel and sat on a bench, bemoaning my plight. Where could he be? In what situation could he be? I knew that he was in the place of God, but had I failed in my responsibility to him in letting him go? The sense of concern was overwhelming my heart and even my body, when, suddenly, he walked in the door. I have no idea how he found his way, but here he was! My precious boy! The one entrusted to me!

Of course Issa was going to come back, was, in fact on his way back, but I understood in that eternal moment of his absence, the immeasurable importance of the responsibility entrusted to me, and I beseeched God to enable me to fulfill the trust. It also helped me to experience the anguish of those parents whose children are lost and do not return.

Having passed through that trial, we were ready to continue our journey and draw nearer to the One who created us, the One who had given us to each other as a trust, and placed us together as pilgrims on His path.

We had prayed for a timeless time in the cool oasis of Medina, the turquoise-emerald jewel, and now our pilgrim caravan returned to the vast desert, barren of almost everything but the blessings of the revelation which had descended upon it and oil within it, which had brought the betterment and also the corruption of the inhabitants of this land.

As the bus pulled out onto the road, I felt the immense magnetism of the Ka'bah. We were traveling with many people who had already been to Mecca and seemed to know what to expect. For me, however, Mecca, the Ka'bah, was something utterly unknown, an immense mystery that was very powerfully pulling us toward it. It pulled us through the black night, through the desert of black rock, through our own personal veils and fears towards its mysterious presence. We traveled in this way through the night.

We entered in the depth of the night. This revealed to us, as we entered Mecca, that the Ka'bah never sleeps. As we approached the hotel where we were to stay, we drove through a tunnel formed of volcanic rock and it was clear we had entered the sacred space. We got off the bus, performed our ablutions, and then passed, all together, through a gateway with very high walls leading into the sacred grounds, which surround the Ka'bah. The walls were immensely thick and high and our group of about fifty entered the holy precinct with great force, singing loudly all together the prayers designated for us to say as we were making that passage.

Immediately, in the middle of the night, we were inundated with light. The Ka'bah is always illuminated, filled with prayer and enveloped by prayer. Being a symbol of the unity of the Divine

Presence and the focal point of worshipful intention for all those in whom the light of Islam has dawned, it is like a heart that is constantly beating with the heartbeat of the prayers flowing into and out of it, penetrating throughout all time and space.

For this mysterious symbolic manifestation there is no night or day. There is no cessation in the turning of the cosmic sea of praise and worship that flows around it, or in the flow of the bloodstream—the divine remembrance—passing into and out of that heart.

Whatever else may take place in the world of Islam, there is no separation between men and women or children in the movement circulating around the Ka'bah, the earthly manifestation of the throne of God. Like blood cells clustering in the bloodstream or heavenly bodies traveling together in the galaxies, different groups of people, united as families, tribes, or spiritual orders, move together as units, each reciting in its own way the words Allah has given to humankind, through which He wishes to be remembered in this holy place.

Issa and I were traveling with a group of truly good friends and acquaintances, and yet, I felt deeply at that moment, the longing to be with the most intimate companions of our soul. In that brilliantly illuminated space, exposed to the gaze of God with no hiding my state, I felt strangely alone, filled with the profound longing for the soul's mate and innermost companions. I knew that I was not ready, not *completely* present. This was an introduction, a preparation, an opening of the door.

I was able to catch a glimpse of that powerful realm, but was not able to be completely present there, because my life was not ultimately in order and the inherent truth of it had not been revealed. I longed to and prayed to return to this powerful sacred domain in a state of readiness, of completeness, to return with the true eternal companions of my soul.

There are supplications we make with our tongues, with our hands, our thoughts, our intentions. This one arose involuntarily from the depth of my soul and being. Our prayers are not answered as we wish or when we wish, but they are heard, and everything that happens from that moment on is a response to the supplication. My soul spoke to my Creator in that moment in the midst of that powerful manifestation of His Presence, and from that moment on all my life has been a revealing or an unveiling of how that prayer is being fulfilled.

Allah says in the Qur'an: "And when My servants question you concerning Me, then surely I am nigh. I answer the prayer of the supplicant when he cries unto Me. So let them hear My call and let them trust in Me, in order that they may be led aright" (The Holy Qur'an 2:186). That moment was a glimpse of the fulfillment, a vision of all souls, hearing the call and inspired by the trust, gathering in the Presence of God, in the Light of God, in His Love, His Radiance, His Mercy. All of us, all humanity, turning around the Light of our Lord, were being drawn into that Light, to be consumed by it. At least we had the taste.

After we made *tawaf* (circumambulated around the Ka'bah) seven times, we went to the *Spring of Mercy* to make our ablutions in the water of *zamzam*. This abundant wellspring of God's mercy, which appeared in the middle of the most barren desert, is the symbol and embodiment of the response of the One Most Merciful to our prayers and supplications.

It was in order to discover and receive this plenitude—the water of life—not only for themselves, but for all lives, that Hagar (ra), the second wife of Prophet Abraham (as), and their son Ishmael (as) were sent into the most barren of lands with nothing but faith to sustain them.

I was considering deeply the overwhelming hardship and challenge faced by the mother left in the midst of that most barren of deserts, running from one hilltop to the other, in search of that water necessary to save her child's life. How utterly profound was the trial faced by that mother and her child and even more amazing was the solution provided by the One Most Merciful to the grave plight of His creations, who were so intensely beseeching His aid.

Now, I was here, drinking this life-giving water, on the spiritual journey with my son, contemplating these deep sacred teachings. It may appear to us that we are abandoned in the desert from time to time in our life's journey, sometimes we reach the point of desperation and hopelessness.

But the difficulty and severity of the trial, we may come to realize, is the pressure that must be imposed upon our heart and faith to make the supplication arise, which is so profound and sincere that it brings forth the water of God's Mercy. There, in the midst of the desert in which we feel we have been deserted, when we come to the point of true prayer, true submission, the rain of God's grace pours down upon us and our cup is filled.

Imagine the miracle of an ever-flowing source of water appearing in the midst of the bleakest and most barren desert. That is the true miracle of God's grace that manifested for Hagar (ra) and Ishmael (as) between the hills of Safa and Marwah, yielding water that has continued to quench the thirst of pilgrims ever since. It is a great sign of hope for us all, reminding us that the endless Source is there and we can access this plenitude, which will satisfy all our hunger and thirst, all our needs, only through our deepest prayer.

Here I was, a single mother with my son, making the journey between the hills of Safa and Marwah, realizing that we were as much in need of the help of Allah as Hagar (ra) and her son had been. Hagar (ra) was a humble servant of her Lord, apparently abandoned in the desert with her small son, but how often, how deeply, and in what a blessed sense she is remembered, and solely because of the sincerity of her prayer and the miraculous way in which God answered her prayer.

It is by the sincerity of our prayer and supplication, that the value of our life and journey too will be determined. *We* cannot accomplish the purpose for which we came here. We need to turn to our Creator with all that we are and all that we have and ask Him to fulfill all of our needs, just as they did. In our daily prayers we say, *"You alone do we worship and You are our only help."*

Whatever we may be searching for, thirsting, hungering, or yearning for, our provision is with our God, the One who created us all. That is why the Ka'bah is a central focus for all the people who have come to know it. It is not simply a focal point of worship for Arabs or for those born Muslim. As the last of the long line of prophets (as) sent to earth with His message, the Prophet Muhammad (saw) was sent by God as a mercy to *all* the worlds.

When you are at the Ka'bah, you know this. You are enveloped by humanity, engulfed by all the tribes. It was when he came to the Ka'bah, that Malcolm X realized that Islam could never be claimed by people of one color. For, it is the path of the submission of all lives to the Source of all life.

Thus, the journey that we make in *tawaf*, the journey around the Ka'bah, is a journey we make with people of all nations, all tribes. All of us come to stand in the place where our father, Abraham (as) stood. We can see his immense footprints and almost feel that we are walking in them. He is the guide, example, and inspiration for all of us, an especially powerful role model for those of us who have grown up, called within by the power of the One God, in a world filled with idolatry.

He found the strength to follow and serve the One God, Allah *subhana wa ta'ala* with all of his being, no matter what the people were doing around him. This is also what we must do. He was unwilling to carry on the family business of idol selling, and so must we be. Having been guided by God to the *Haqq*, the Ultimate Truth, Abraham (as) fearlessly proclaimed it through everything that he did, and as many sacrifices as he had to endure to manifest the truth under all circumstances, for him, fire itself became cool.

Through the power of his faith, manifesting in constant submission to the Divine Call, Abraham became the Friend of God, and the perfect example, the *leader* for humanity:

"And when His Lord tried Ibrahim with His commands and He fulfilled them, He said 'Lo, I have appointed thee a leader for humankind'" (The Holy Qur'an 2:124). It was here in Mecca, close to

where the zamzam water sprang forth that Abraham and Ishmael were directed to build the House of God.

> *And Ibrahim said, "My Lord! Make safe this territory one of peace and security and preserve me, and my sons from worshipping idols. My Lord! The idols have indeed led astray many of humankind. But whoso follows me, he is verily of me, and whoso disobeys me still,*
>
> *"Thou art Forgiving, Most Merciful! Our Lord! I have made some of my offspring to dwell in a valley without cultivation, by Thy Sacred House. In order, O our Lord, that they may establish regular prayer, so incline some hearts of men toward them and provision them with Your bounties, so that they may be thankful."*
>
> The Holy Qur'an 14:35-37

Now, we who are making the *tawaf* are amongst those whom God wished to compass the House which has been sanctified by the Messenger (saw) who came as decreed to rebuild the Ka'bah with the light of revelation. Whatever may have been the tradition of our fathers, we stand in the presence of our Lord, and prostrate.

We are amongst those who have been purified by the Revelation brought by the Prophet Muhammad (saw), which was the completion of the message brought by all the prophets (as). Everything has come to pass as the Qur'an revealed. Such is the significance of our journey, and the journey of every one who has heard and responded to the call of Allah to make the pilgrimage to Mecca.

So many have responded, coming from all nations and all corners of the earth, that sometimes it is difficult even to make the *tawaf* because so many people are moving around the Ka'bah at the same time. This was a challenge for me as a single mother with a son, since in the midst of that ocean of humanity when the call to prayer came, Issa had to go pray with the men, and so he was not right at my side. He also looked so much like all the boys of Mecca, and even of the world. I placed on his head a shining golden cap, so that I could identify him in any crowd.

Still, it was very unsettling to let him go into that massive assembly, and I was stricken from time to time by attacks of anxiety, which were tempered and quelled only by my faith in God.

Then, very fortunately, we learned that we could go up a spiral staircase and pass through large classes of Meccan children learning Qur'an, to a balcony overlooking the Ka'bah, where men, women, and children in families and extended families can all pray together in a very peaceful and protected way. This discovery was a great blessing for us, and we regularly went there.

From the balcony, I was able to see the Ka'bah and all the activity surrounding it from a new perspective. I could see that the vast numbers of people gathered together at the time of prayer were assembled in perfect symmetry. This symmetry allowed more and more people to enter into the divine configuration, and yet, the symmetry was always perfect.

I thought that this beautiful configuration was a sign of the sanctification of Islam as the completion of all the stages of revelation, which preceded it. If we were to see an aerial view of any other gathering of people on earth, I do not believe that we would be able to see such symmetry and harmony, in which all the people assembled are bowing down to the One God who sent all the messengers (as), all the books, all true religions.

While we were praying on that peaceful balcony, Issa made friends with people, as he always does. One day, our dear friend Malik told me that Issa had made friends with one of the guards of the sacred precincts. The guard gave Issa a beautiful Qur'an and took him and Malik on a tour of the inner realms of the *haram*, the sacred grounds, including a journey in an elevator to the top of a minaret overlooking the Ka'bah. Thus, while other children his age were going up in roller coasters, Issa was blessed to rise up in a different vehicle blessed to do and see things that are not usually done and seen.

Our hotel was less than five minutes from the Ka'bah. We both knew how close we were to all the light that was shining there and neither of us could easily sleep. So, we would quietly get up, take the elevator down through the bookstore, and then walk out into the ocean of light that was circulating around the Ka'bah. On the night before my birthday, as we were heading towards that ocean of light, Issa bought me a Qur'an in the bookstore, one of the many great gifts I received from God on that birthday. How great was the gift of the light that we shared on that night!

As a mother and nine-year old son traveling together, however not everything was always totally clear between us. We did have our issues to work on. And we had some very interesting, serious talks in our hotel room and worked on some of the fundamental struggles of our relationship and life. Finally, we wrote a treaty, which dealt with everything we were going through in our life together and we signed it, with witnesses, on that sacred earth and in the presence of God.

From the time that we signed that document as a heartfelt expression of our commitment to God and to the betterment of our relationship, we see how deeply our life and journey have been clarified, guided, and blessed. Such are the wonderful results of traveling for the sake of God. I am especially grateful that I have been able to share this holy transformative journey with my child.

There are many dimensions of journeying for the sake of God, and one of them is that sometimes you must go through an almost insurmountable difficulty and yet still you continue to travel. Then, the difficulty leads to a spiritual opening. When we had been in Mecca for several days, I became extremely ill. For a few days, I could barely move.

During this time, I heard about several people who were planning to climb the Mountain of Light to the cave where the Prophet Muhammad (saw) went into seclusion and received the revelation of the Qur'an. I heard that it was a struggle for many people to climb the mountain. I wanted to climb the mountain and go to the cave very much, but I was very ill and thought it would be impossible for me to make the journey since at that point I could barely walk. The illness, I thought, was part of the purification of the pilgrimage, and I simply had to accept and endure it.

Then, when we were about to start on our second ʿumra (leaving the holy precincts temporarily in order to repeat pilgrimage rites) suddenly, a kind friend offered me medicine. I realized instantly that the medicine was from Allah, as well as the illness and so I took it. By the end of the ʿumra, I was amazingly well. Then I knew that I must climb the Mountain of Light, no matter what, *insh'Allah*!

I went with four old and dear friends in a car to the base of the mountain. Quickly, one could see that this was an extraordinary place. Even in the village below, there are incredible rock formations. I felt that the mountain itself was somehow ablaze with vital energy. It was also very rugged and challenging to climb. A fellow pilgrim had led me to think deeply about the devotion and strength of Khadijah (ra), the beloved wife of the Prophet Muhammad (saw), and how she climbed this mountain every day to bring him food. In light of her profound devotion and the service that she rendered to the Messenger (saw) and his mission, I began to climb.

I bear witness that, after a few steps, I made no effort at all. I was carried up the mountain, exerting no energy of my own. This carried me up to the top of the mountain very quickly, much faster than my friends were able to go. I know that this was not at all due to physical strength or training because I was not in shape at all and had only the day before been extremely sick and weak, barely able to walk.

It was a gift from God, the Most Merciful, showing me that the ascent to the sanctified place, where the revelation is given, is empowered solely by grace. Climbing that mountain, I knew that the power of Allah had taken me, and I had not gotten there by my strength at all.

Close to the place of the cave where the Prophet Muhammad (saw) had stayed, I waited for the others, feeling greatly exhilarated and liberated from the physical body, the limited mind, and the force of gravity. I had never in my life felt so extremely healthy and strong.

When they arrived, we walked together, approaching the holy cave. There was a large group of people assembled there, worshipping in a loud and energetic way. They completed their worship and then continued on their way, allowing us to enter the cave in complete silence, stillness, and peace. Once you are at the entrance and in the cave, everything else ceases to exist. All sounds of people are silenced.

In this tiny cave, where there is only enough room for one person to stand and one person to sit or bow down, there is only the sense of the presence of the Messenger (saw) immersed in the Presence of God. One is led to contemplate what took place here and the huge significance for all the universes of what occurred to one man, hidden from the sight of the world, in the privacy of this tiny cave. This tiny space is, as I understood it, the epicenter of sacred space, that place where God and man, Master and servant met and united, for the sake of bringing mercy to all the worlds.

As a child in elementary school, hearing the little that we did about the Prophet Muhammad (saw), all that I could envision was a man on a horse riding into battle with his turban flying in the wind. We did not hear or know about the man called by all *"Al-Amin"* ("the most honest and trustworthy"), who, perceiving the great darkness of idolatry, injustice, and cruelty enveloping the world around him, entered this cave and remained here, meditating, contemplating, and supplicating for years, as he was being prepared to receive the mantle of his prophethood.

We did not hear about this great mystery as we were growing up in America. Nor did we hear about how the Revelations of the Almighty descended upon him with such power that he was absolutely overwhelmed and profoundly shaken.

We did not hear about how the Revelations of which the Qur'an is composed descended upon the Messenger (saw) verse by verse, as he sat in this cave, or how he shared these with his

Companions (ra), so that each of them memorized and absorbed every verse of the Qur'an as it was revealed. One of those verses states, *"If We were to send down this Qur'an upon a mountain, the mountain would be ground to dust"* (The Holy Qur'an 59:21). So powerful it was! And yet this powerful Revelation descended upon a small but growing group of humble, vulnerable human beings, and with the strength that God gave them, they were able to endure it and to become living embodiments of the words that the Creator was revealing to them.

I did not hear about these things as I was growing up in Southern California, but the yearning for true knowledge was burning in my heart, and it would not let me rest anywhere, compelling me to travel from country to country, from mountain to valley, from shrine to shrine, cathedral to mosque, until finally I discovered this cave.

Many holy sites have monuments built upon them. Underneath the marble and all the embellishment is the earth where one of the prophets (as) or friends of God lived and prayed. Very often shrines have been constructed over the places they were buried, but nothing artificial, man-made, or modern has been built inside or around the cave where the Prophet Muhammad (saw) prayed. It is as it was when he sat there, when the power of the Revelation came upon him.

I felt the awesome honor and blessing to be praying upon the earth where he prayed, the exact spot. It was awesome because I sensed so strongly that he was with me, within me, and the same Lord that guided him to pray there also guided me to pray there.

As deeply inspiring as it was to go there, it is not the cave, which is important, but what took place there. This is what is to be celebrated and proclaimed, especially in light of the fact that it has been hidden from the view of so many human beings whose right it is to know the truth about their Creator and what He has revealed.

This book is my loving endeavor to share with the reader whatever I can of what has been shown to me, so that the right of every one of us to know His liberating Truth may be fulfilled. Every step in this journey has been motivated by this intention.

As God willed, so that I could draw closer to Him and come to know Him better, on that day I was carried by light into the light on the Mountain of Light. It was a pilgrimage to a place where there was nothing but purity and light, a shrine built and preserved for eternity by God.

I also bear witness, through the ever-continuing miracles of my life and journey, that the Messenger of Allah (saw), the servant of Allah, who was chosen in his purity to be the vehicle for the last revealed Message of Allah, is our beloved friend; the more we love him, invoke his presence, and long to be in his company, the closer we come to that radiant Light, the very same Light and Truth which guided and manifested through all the prophets (as) who came before him, the Light of Allah, which dispels all darkness, illuminating the path that leads directly to Him, the One of infinite Grace and Power.

18

Return to the Continent of Origin, Allahu Wahidun!

Between Senegal, West Africa, and the US, 1999–2001

Did We not open wide your heart and lift your heavy load from you
that was breaking your back?
And have We not exalted your remembrance?
Truly with difficulty (comes) ease,
Truly, with difficulty ease. So when the load is lifted, then rise up
and to your Lord, strive.

The Holy Qur'an 94:1–8

From the moment I made the supplication at the Ka'bah, I felt that I was being pulled through all of the layers in my being toward the light of the Messenger (saw), the light of God. I had caught a glimpse of it. But I needed to be purified, clarified, and deeply realigned, in order to become the true servant that God created me to be. I needed to find my place in the divine universe and the true companions of my soul with whom I could return to the House of Allah in completeness.

We can imagine the goal, even catch a glimpse of it, but to reach the destination is a very deep complex process. As the title of this book suggests, there are so many veils to penetrate. I have referred to them as *ten thousand* only as a figure of speech. Sufis often say that there are seventy-two thousand veils to be penetrated.

The reality is that the light within us, is covered up by many things, and to realize the true purpose for which we were created,

to become who we truly are, we need to be liberated from attachment to these attachments. The divinely guided journey is the
means by which we learn to let go, one by one, of each thing we
have become attached to other than our connection to the pure
light, which is the spark of the Divine within us.

I have seen that the veils are pierced, penetrated, and lifted in
different ways. On all the different levels of our experience in this
life, both the difficulties that we have to endure, and our release
from these difficulties, can become a means by which we are purified and brought closer to the reality of our true existence, that is
our relationship to the Reality, which is God.

Marriage, child birth, child raising, earning a living, simply
interacting with other people, caring for and serving the creations
of our Lord, and through all this, striving to be a sincere servant
of the Master of all—all of these can be annihilating and purifying
experiences that we may have to go through to get to the Goal.

Simply being alive in the time in which we live and experiencing, to any degree, the suffering that so many people are enduring,
is a deep test both of our faith, and our commitment to serve. But,
as the Qur'an tells us, "*Truly, with difficulty comes ease. Truly, with
difficulty comes ease*" Inshirah 94:5–6). This is a passage of the
Qur'an that explains so much about what all human beings must
go through in our life on this earth and in our journey to God.

Many of us recite this *surah* many times a day because of its
profound relevance and power to remind us of the intimate and
intrinsic relationship between difficulty and ease.

As these complex experiences unfold, one after the next, we
come to see that, whatever difficulty we may be facing, there is an
ease, mercy and blessing, that comes with it, if only, in surrendering to the Source of mercy, we can perceive and access it.

In contemplating the meaning of this *surah*, and the significance of this formula given to us by our Creator, we must reflect
upon the circumstances in which the *surah* was revealed and the
great difficulties endured by the Prophet Muhammad (saw) and

his companions (ra), which they endured solely for the sake of God and the manifestation of His will on earth.

The Prophet Muhammad (saw) was sitting in the Cave of Hira, when the Divine Command was addressed to him through the mediation of the Angel Gabriel: *"Iqra! Read!"* Muhammad (saw) was unlettered and could not read. He was being asked to read and recite, receive, behold, witness the Divine Revelation as it was being transmitted to him.

On the first occasion, the power was so immense that he went to his wife Khadijah (ra) totally shaken. and asked to be covered by a blanket to calm him, so utterly powerful and overwhelming was the experience. From the very beginning, his task was immensely difficult, as was the task of all the prophets (as), to deliver to a humanity unwilling to listen, the message that God willed to send to His creatures.

What they had to endure of hardship in fulfilling the mission bestowed upon them by the Creator is far beyond our capacity to know or understand. But we know that they accepted whatever was given to them in a state of submission to the One who had decreed them to go through all this, and it was through this state of profound surrender to the Divine Decree, that all the difficulties they endured led them to the highest victory and success, that highest level of victory for a creation, which is to accomplish what the Creator wills it to do. This *success* cannot be attained without the journey through many different kinds of difficulties.

So, following the prophets (as), who are our guides, and the examples God has given us of the way a true human being should be, we each realize that we *must* go through difficulties in our search for the truth and in carrying that truth if we find it. This is clearly stated in the Holy Qur'an, when Allah *subhana wa ta'ala* asks us:

> *Or do you think that you shall enter the Garden without such (trials) as came to those who passed away before you? They encountered suffering and adversity, and were so shaken in spirit that even the Messenger*

and those of faith who were with him cried: "When (will come) the help of God." Ah! Verily, the help of God is (always) near."

The Holy Qur'an 2:214

This, I believe, is a crucially important passage of the Qur'an. It tells us, first, that we cannot reach paradise, the garden of nearness to our Lord, without undergoing hardship and adversity, and then that even the Holy Prophet (saw) and his Companions (ra), the most noble and blessed of all the creations, in the midst of what was decreed for them to go through, cried for the help of Allah. And, finally, Allah gives us the key, the solution to every problem when He reminds us that His help is always near.

We need to become aware, no matter what we are going through, that He, who has the solution for all our problems, is always unfathomably near. The difficulty is simply something that we have to go through so that we may come to realize, through calling the One that is always present, that His help is always near.

Consider all the hardship, oppression and plagues endured by the Children of Israel in Egypt, and then behold how the Holy One parted for them the sea, enabling them to walk through on dry ground while Pharoah and all his people drowned. Surely in this situation as in all, He revealed that along with the difficulty, on the path that leads to Him, comes the ease.

The utility, for the seeker of nearness to the Lord, of difficulties encountered along the way, is that they are indeed the context in which we turn to God for help. To this end, it seems that each one of us has a unique configuration of tests and trials to go through as we are journeying to our Lord. But no matter what difficulty may be given to us to experience and endure in the way of God, Allah Most Merciful has told us that there is an easing, an opening, an expansion or liberation and a blessing and teaching that comes with it.

However intense the contraction, it is not a permanent state, but will give way in due time to the next stage of expansion, the next stage of growth, the next door opening into the next step of our journey. It is a reward from our Lord, of mercy and knowledge, for each sacrifice that we make, each difficulty that we endure for the sake of drawing closer to Him.

And when we arrive at that opening and the pressure of the trial is released, as the burden is lifted from our back, with all the energy that has been liberated from the difficulty, the Qur'an tells us, we must stand in the presence of our Lord, and strive to rise in the celebration of His praise.

It is not possible for me, or for anyone telling the story of their life and journey in the way of God, to describe the number of times such a passage has taken place or the repercussions and the blessings and gifts that emerge from this process of labor, this process of dying and being resurrected by the grace of Allah. When we give birth to a child, the pain is as intense as we can bear, but not more.

Allah tells us in the Qur'an, *"We do not give to the soul a burden greater than it has the capacity to bear"* (The Holy Qur'an 7:42). Whatever it may be it is not greater than we can bear. But, sometimes, it does seem to be as great as we can bear. It is great because it pushes us beyond our limits, beyond our fears, prejudices, conceptions, and attachments. When you are in the midst of labor (as in the process of dying), you do not worry about what you look like or what people think or say about you. You are busy. You are completely involved in the process until it comes to completion, and the fruit for which you have been laboring is manifest.

Being able to bear the pain of childbirth earns for us the reward of the beautiful baby that comes out of that labor. Being able to bear the pain of child raising, if we do this in the way of God, earns us the reward of seeing a beautiful human being emerge.

As we continue to travel in the way of God, we come to realize that we are the child and the beautiful human being that is emerging, but nothing can happen without the labor! In order to be born truly, to be born again as a true human being, we have to die, again and again, so that everything within us that is not truly consecrated to the work of the Eternal passes away. The process of growth, evolution, and transformation inevitably demands deep change.

The Qur'an tells us that surely what is coming is greater than anything we have known before: *"Assuredly what comes after will be better for you than what has gone before"* (The Holy Qur'an 93:4). God willing that we are traveling on the path that leads directly to Him, we will realize what these words really mean. As we travel towards that end, we must continuously let go of what we have previously known and unconsciously become attached to, in order to reach or attain the greater reality that we are journeying towards. This requires true fearlessness, trust, and willingness to surrender to the ultimate Guide who is leading us through all the stages of our development.

Sheikh Abdoulaye Dieye (ra), I believe, came into my life to teach me about this and to stimulate the process of my purification. He guided me in a direction in which I had to face many challenges and psychological hardships, ultimately enabling me to become who I truly am.

He exposed to me the shadow world of unworthiness, fear, doubt, and pain, so that these very tendencies within me, all based upon illusion, could be dispelled. He came to break the earth, so plants and flowers could grow in it. He appeared in my life as a catalyst because I *needed* to continue to grow.

From the moment on December 8, 1986, when Bawa Muhaiyaddeen (ra) left this world, I had remained in a holding pattern, honoring the practices he had established, such as the inner *zikr*, the outer *zikr*, and also the formal prayer. I continued to work on the editing of books, as he had asked me to do. I had the child, Issa Muhaiyaddeen Kabeer, about whom he had spoken to me so many times before Issa was born, and then I proceeded to travel around the world with him.

All of this was good, but there was a sense in which, without being in relationship with a living teacher, I was not progressing and transforming as dynamically as possible. So, God placed in my way, another catalytic force to propel the seeker through the veils towards the Goal.

A few years after the passing of Sheikh Bawa Muhaiyaddeen (ra), I met Sheikh Dieye (ra) from Senegal, West Africa at a Sufi Symposium in San Francisco. He was one of the presenters at the conference. I met him in the suite we had organized to serve food to the participants in the conference.

Immediately, he spoke to me about Senegal and invited me to come, which I did a few months later. Then he expressed interest in Bawa (ra), and said that he would like to come with some of his disciples to Philadelphia. I invited them to stay in our house which was, then, as it always had been, a refuge for wayfarers on the path.

The Sheikh and several of his disciples, most of whom were from islands in the Indian Ocean, were happy to accept the invitation. It is always an honor and blessing to receive guests *fisabillilah*, in the way of God. Seeing the disciples camped out all around the house made me feel that this was what the house was all about.

Upon his arrival in Philadelphia, Sheikh Dieye (ra) said to me that he had come to pour water on seeds planted by Bawa Muhaiyaddeen (ra). It did seem that he poured water upon the earth within me in which the seeds were planted, and also turned the soil, so that it could be aerated and receive the water.

He knew things about me that I did not tell him. He acknowledged the potential within me to serve God and indicated to me that he could and would develop that potential. That was what interested me in this relationship—the possibility that he could help me to develop my potential as a servant of God. I wanted most deeply to continue to develop in the capacity to truly serve, and I hoped that, in whatever way, this connection could help me to progress.

The Sheikh frequently expressed what he was teaching through diagrams. I mentioned once that I wondered why, although I had been married, I had not found my true mate. He drew a picture of a pot covered with a lid. He said that I had such a large pot it was difficult to find a lid large enough to fit it.

The image he had drawn made a deep impression upon me. But as time went on, I attributed to it a different significance. It seemed to be an illustration of the transformative process I was undergoing in the presence of the Sheikh. The covered pot was a crucible in which an alchemical transformation was taking place. It was as though, throughout the work which unfolded between us, he had placed a cover on the pot, which was my process, and fire below, causing whatever was in the pot continuously to boil.

From the time I met Sheikh Dieye (ra) until he left this world, suddenly, at the age of sixty-three, I traveled with him and whatever small group of disciples was traveling with him frequently. This was definitely a journey through worlds which demanded, most of all, spiritual and emotional stamina. His own life was often threatened by various extreme health conditions. Nevertheless, regardless of any illness or condition, he traveled ceaselessly with the intention of accomplishing his mission.

He was like a candle burning at both ends and blazing in the middle. The intensity of this energy was contagious and activated a similar intensity within me. This is why I say that for me, traveling and working with him was like being in a crucible, whose lid was almost never lifted.

Wherever we were in the world, in whatever colorful locale or gathering, he corrected me, exposing faults and limitations. They might be faults I thought I had or faults I thought I didn't have. It did not really matter. Simply, whatever within me needed to be purified, was, by the process, constantly being addressed and cleansed. Once again, the attachments, illusions, and impurities were burning, while the gold, the pure essence of truth, was being cleaned and purified.

This training, in cutting the attachment to the ego, the illusory identity, purifying the sincere servant within to serve purely, was so difficult and intense at the hands of Sheikh Abdoulaye Dieye (ra) that sometimes I imagined longingly how simple it would be to just get up and walk out of whatever house we were in and back into the "free" world, where I would not have to continue to endure this process of continual annihilation. But, in reality, I was, for all the time that I knew him until I was released during the last week, undergoing a kind of profound psychological surgery on the operating table, and I could not get up and go anywhere until the operation was done.

Once in a while, he gave me a clue and a sense of hope, the sense of a light at the end of the long, dark tunnel, by saying very quietly to me in the middle of the trial, "I am only doing this to perfect you." Such messages gave me the strength to endure the very difficult process of purification and transformation.

Along with all the difficult contractions, there were two deep gifts of expansion which Sheikh Dieye (ra) also gave to me. He guided me back to Africa, the great continent of our origin, and, he introduced me to the teaching and the noble example of Sheikh Ahmadu Bamba (ra), the Sheikh of his Sheikh, and one of Africa's great Sufi Masters.

I had come to experience the mysteries of Islam and the Sufi path in many countries of the world, stage by stage and step by step. Knowledge is always revealed in stages. In Afghanistan I saw the beautiful vision, as the buses stopped in the middle of the desert, of all of the passengers getting out and laying their mats out in the desert to pray. That vision continued to evolve and deepen throughout my life and journey.

I saw the joyous family praying and playing joyously together all night in the garden under the starry sky in Mashad, and I beheld people of light pouring out of the mosque in that holy city.

I saw the ancient grandfather, Sidi Sheikh Abdul Muttalib, his wife and disciples bowing down in the cave adjoining the tomb of Ash-Shibli, the great Sufi Master, and then, suddenly and naturally, I too bowed down and became a part of the congregation. This is the organic process of embracing Islam.... entering into the reality of Islam.

First, you see an image, which slowly attracts you profoundly. Although it may be the first time you have seen it, this image, like the people spreading out their prayer mats in the middle of the desert, stirs up a deep sense of nostalgia and longing within you.

Although it is apparently the first time you have seen it, this image reminds you of something you have known before in your distant past, something within you that you are longing intensely to reconnect with and reclaim.

You are, at first, like a person on the shore of a great ocean, contemplating its beauty, and then you jump in, you become immersed, you become a part of and inseparable from that beauty.

Like that vast ocean is the assembly of the believers, called the *ummah*. Though there are impurities within the people in the *ummah*, the ocean itself, the assembly of souls gathered to worship the Creator, is pure.

From the moment of entering into the *ummah*, the community of true believers, I have continued to travel around the world, finding that this assembly, this gathering of the believers joined together to praise and worship the One and only Creator, is taking place everywhere, in all corners of the world.

The Creator has told us that the whole world is our mosque, the place in which we bow down to Him, and *"Whithersoever you turn, there is the Face of God"* (The Holy Qur'an 2:115). And this is what I have observed taking place everywhere the journey has led me. It is a universal reality totally transcending any cultural differences.

As we continue to travel on the way that leads from God to God, with each real step more knowledge and understanding is given to us about the path we are traveling on. In every country, in every village, in every mosque, in every assembly of the faithful, and in the presence of every Sheikh, I received more knowledge and more understanding of the meaning and experience of Islam and the path of *Tasawwuf*, the Sufi path. Then, to get the very essence of the teaching, I was guided to *Africa*!

Since the time that I first went to Africa, specifically to Senegal, West Africa, I have been drawn back eleven more times. What ultimately drew me there so many times is a great mystery that I have been compelled, from the first moment I set foot upon this land, to penetrate, and, stage by stage, come to understand.

Nothing in the landscapes of Senegal is so interesting and beautiful as to cause me to return so many times. So, why was I compelled to return again and again?

What was compelling, irresistibly magnetic, was the knowledge of the Divine, the gems and treasures of Divine Knowledge, the mystical dimensions of Islam, that lie beneath the surface in that vast desert in West Africa. It is also compelling because of the open heart of the people, and the uniquely powerful way in which the *zikr*, remembrance of Allah is pouring through that open heart and spreading throughout the land.

The first time I went to Senegal was in the month of May. I went with Issa to commemorate the *Maggal*, the exile of Sheikh Ahmadu Bamba (ra). For the followers of Sheikh Ahmadu Bamba (ra), the most important event in the life of the Sheikh is the time when he entered into an extended period of exile (ultimately thirty-three years) imposed upon him by French Colonialists.

It is not the time when he was liberated from this oppression that is celebrated, but his entering into the trial. The exile and all the tribulations that he endured on the path of God for the sake of God were for Sheikh Ahmadu Bamba (ra), as he said, the source of blessing, and that blessing is what is celebrated.

Our intention to learn about the life of Sheikh Ahmadu Bamba (ra), and all those who endure hardship for the sake of serving and drawing closer to God, brought us also some difficulty, and with the difficulty, as always, came the blessing.

We arrived at three in the morning, the time we always arrived and parted from Senegal. We were greeted, by Sheikh Dieye's driver, Sheikh Babu. Since there was not enough room in the car, Issa went first and I followed on the next trip. As soon as he arrived at the Sheikh's house, Issa was offered a tall glass of water, which he readily drank, being very thirsty after the journey. That was the beginning of his trial.

I was picked up several minutes later, and as the wind from the desert blew in through the car window, I felt the great peace of coming *home* again. Sheikh Dieye's house was about fifteen minutes from the airport, enough time to begin to get acclimatized to the land, the air, the energy. I went into the mode of attunement and knew that in some way I had certainly been here before.

As the Sheikh was an architect, his house was very thoughtfully designed and very spacious with a minimum of furniture. I went to pray in the appropriate corner of the large prayer and assembly room, and I felt and heard the resonance of prayer pouring through me, and filling all the worlds. I remembered praying in the *zawwiyah* (prayer room) on the Mount of Olives and in so many other empty rooms filled with light. I was so happy to be in the place of prayer, in a room filled not with furniture but with the sound of prayer.

The next morning, extremely early, everyone was awake, preparing to make the pilgrimage to Touba, the city founded by Sheikh Ahmadu Bamba (ra) as a spiritual center in which the teachings he had been transmitting could be manifested. Issa and I were in the back of the Sheikh's car in a kind of hatchback where we could fit only by lying upon each other. We traveled for many hours like this. Although we were packed in and squeezed, we were comfortable simply to be traveling together in the way of God.

The journey to Touba is extraordinary because on one single road there are so many cars, trucks, and buses packed with people, often standing for hours on the sides and roofs of these vehicles. All of these heavily laden vehicles, making the pilgrimage all at the same time.

That so many people travel, in any way possible, often under great physical duress, to get to Touba, is a sign of the deep impact that Sheikh Ahmadu Bamba (as) had upon the people of Senegal. He, who had been so greatly tried and had transformed every difficulty into ease and victory for the sake of God, became a beacon of light and a symbol of hope for people suffering and struggling in so many ways.

For the hope that he represented to transform their difficulties into the light of grace, a great many people are willing to undergo hardship to make the pilgrimage to Touba. The road leading to Touba in the time of the *Maggal* is so packed, it is almost impossible to move, a massive traffic jam on the way to God.

Sheikh Babu, however, was tremendously creative, fearless, and resourceful, and we soon learned that driving with him was often very much off the beaten path and paved road. So, when the cars were all lined up on the paved road, we often left the road entirely and drove over hill and vale, venturing across the natural terrain.

We arrived late at night in the countryside surrounding Touba and were received very beautifully and sweetly by many people making *zikr*, disciples of the Sheikh who had been preparing and waiting for hours to surround his car and welcome him to Touba, with love and honor.

On the pilgrimage to places of power in the presence of people of light, Touba is one of the power points, one of the centers of mystical energy, a place consecrated from its conception by Sheikh Ahmadu Bamba (ra), who invoked with its name the Tree of Touba, a tree planted by God in Paradise and referred to on Sufi literature. As Ibn Sirrin wrote in *The Interpretation of Dreams*:

> "When a man dreams that he is sitting under the tree of touba, he gains the best of both worlds, since God has said, 'For them is blessedness and a beautiful place of return' (The Holy Qur'an 13:29). If he finds himself in its gardens, he gains faithfulness and perfection of religion. If he eats its fruits, knowledge equivalent to the fruits he has tasted will be given to him. Equally, if he drinks from its water, its wine and its milk, he will be given wisdom, knowledge and riches."

It was to this mystical ideal that Sheikh Ahmadu Bamba (ra) dedicated the city he built, intending and beseeching God that the sincere seekers who made the pilgrimage to it would gain such benefits. Issa and I had now arrived at this station in our pilgrimage, ready to learn what God wished to reveal to us.

The procession moved to an enclave of tents set up specifically for this holy occasion. With the beautiful *zikr* surrounding us, we went to sleep for a short while under the tents and woke up with the sun burning so intensely we could barely move. I have never experienced such heat before or since.

The heat was so strong, we were barely able to sit up.

We were literally pressed to the ground. When we were able to barely get up and walk to the ablution area, we found only a tiny trickle of running water. Yet, this holy place, hotter than anything I could imagine, had been an oasis of cool refuge for Sheikh Ahmadu Bamba (ra) when he had finally arrived here after so many years of exile.

The heat of Touba, along with the water, which he had drunk immediately upon arriving, now made Issa very sick. He went to visit the Sheikh in his tent and immediately released the contents of his stomach on the Sheikh's bed. The Sheikh accepted this graciously, had the bed cleaned, and kept Issa near him. He later said that this was an initiation for Issa, in which he vomited up and released many of the veils and difficulties of his past, preparing for the next, wide-open dimension of his life, the new page.

Our arrival in Africa was, for both of us, the opening of the door into a very significant process and spiritual homecoming. Issa has returned to Africa five times so far. In the summer of 2003, when he was fifteen, he went alone to pursue his study of the Qur'an and experienced another rite of passage, this one almost on his own.

When he arrived at the airport in Senegal, for some reason he was not able to find his ride. Since he had the address of the school, he simply found a taxi and got there on his own.

On his return trip, when he arrived at the airport in Paris, again no one was there to meet him. He waited for a day and a half at Orly Airport, without doubting his destiny or losing the peace and light of the Qur'an that he had gained. When he was finally found, those searching for him said that he was sitting, patiently, with no sign of stress or distress, like a little Sufi Master. So, that was a sign of the progress on the journey of his soul, he had made, from the time he first arrived in Africa.

My own relationship with Africa remains a great and deep mystery to me, but it is a mystery, which is slowly and surely being unveiled. It is the mystery of the attraction of Adam (as) and Eve (ra), the black and the white, the East and the West, the apparent polarities powerfully attracted to each other by the power of absolute Oneness.

It is not only an individual quest, but the quest of humanity, the creation of the Creator Most Merciful, for reconciliation and union. This movement toward ultimate integration and unity, spiritually, humanly, and globally, along with the intention for healing the wounds of separation, is what compelled me, one born ostensibly white, to go to Africa so many times.

Sheikh Abdoulaye Dieye (ra) was not my ultimate guide in the path of reconciliation, healing, and union. He was a catalyst for my process of growth, a teacher and friend on the way, an expander of my horizons. One major way in which he did that was by inviting me to come to Africa.

He said that he had come to Philadelphia to pour water on the seeds planted by Bawa Muhaiyaddeen (ra). The teaching of Bawa's that he activated most for me was *"You must love all lives as your own."*

All the lives that I must love are not in the Fellowship house, they are not in my house, or the house next door, or the house down the street. A fundamental blessing of meeting the Sheikh was that in traveling with him, and then continuing to travel with his successor, Sheikh Aly, I met so many people and came to love so many more lives as my own. In this way, the Sheikhs did water the seed that Bawa had planted in my heart and made this love and knowledge grow.

Sheikh Dieye (ra) was a member of the Senegalese Parliament and also a candidate for the Presidency of Senegal. Several times, I had the very interesting experience of traveling with him and a group of disciples on the campaign trail. That was a fantastic experience, that is completely different than anything we, in the west, could imagine, a totally different kind of campaigning.

Wherever we went, into whatever town, village, or area of bush, great numbers of children came running and surrounded the Sheikh's car, exclaiming *"Allahu Wahidun! Allahu Wahidun!" "God is One! God is One!"* They were the Sheikh's supporters. Large groups of children and some adults would run alongside his car for many blocks, exclaiming *"Allahu Wahidun!"* This is what he was called everywhere; his own name was never used.

One day he said, "We are going to a political rally. Get ready." As we were traveling, I was trying to visualize what kind of rally it would be, based upon my past experience of political rallies. We drove for hours and went deep into the bush. There was nothing like a street sign anywhere, no sign of any kind indicating where we were. There was only the desert and the bush.

Once in a while, a horse-drawn cart would appear in the desert and our driver would ask the driver of the cart for directions. I thought to myself, "What kind of rally is this?" Thinking that many people would be gathering together from many different places, I wondered how they could even find this place.

We went from unmarked desert into thick bush. The car was surrounded, by the dense bush. Finally, we arrived in a clearing at a tiny village and all got out. We went into a small house and met with some of the Sheikh's people. We all greeted each other. Then, we went outside again and were told that the meeting was about to begin. Several straw mats were laid out under a tree and every-one sat down. A beautiful newborn baby was placed in my lap.

One mat was filled only with children. In fact, the majority of people at this "rally" were scantily clothed children. The Sheikh addressed his discourse to them. He was speaking in Wolof, so I could not understand what he said. But I saw that he was speaking to the little children, and they were applauding his points, respond-ing with great enthusiasm.

When his discourse, or campaign speech, was completed, he turned to me and said in French, *"The whole world has forgotten these children. You must not forget them."* In this sentence was the essence of the teaching that was given throughout the journeys and the kind of experience we had.

This message so deeply affected me. Both before and after I heard these words spoken, I have intensely wished to help the children of the world, the needy and indigent. When I had returned to America after this trip, I went to the Friends Meeting at the Quaker School Issa was attending.

When I told this story to those gathered in the assembly, they too were moved and within a week, many blankets and clothes were gathered to send to those children in Africa. This was so easy to do: to transfer even a tiny amount of the excess of resources that we have here to people who have so little and appreciate everything so much. I hope and pray that in my lifetime, I may not forget the lives in need, but may serve as a conduit through which aid is delivered.

My travels throughout Africa continuously inspired a deeper and deeper sense of love and connectedness with living beings. From one village to the next, one gathering to the next, I met countless African children, many of whom had never seen a "white" person before. All of them wanted to touch my hand, as I wanted to touch theirs and hug them. All of them were people I could not forget.

They are all our children, and whenever I hear or see on a bumper sticker the slogan, "God Bless America," I can only affirm with all my heart what I truly believe, *"God bless the world. God bless all the worlds that He has created out of His love and His light."*

I had always intuitively known these truths, the truth of the oneness and interconnectedness of all people but being in Africa deepened the knowledge and experience. When you are in the middle of a desert in a large gathering of children who have almost nothing, but are shining with light and love and joy, the consumer world, with all its glitters and attractions, all the things that you have personally owned or wished to have, fades away into the distance like a mirage, an illusion with no reality.

The reality that you see and feel, taste and experience, is that you are one with all beings, all of these children are your own, all lives are your own. When you hold these children in your arms and feel the warmth of their bodies and their hearts, you know that politics, power, and possessions have no intrinsic reality or benefit. What does have reality and importance amongst the things we encounter in the world is the preciousness of every living being that we meet. They are all uniquely precious and intrinsically valuable, being created by the One of Infinite value, power, and grace, and He has created nothing in vain.

Those who, throughout the ages, truly believe in, seek, gain, and wield political and mercantile power cannot afford to consider the value and preciousness of all living beings. As much as they speak about God and in the name of God, they are servants of the force whose express goal is to destroy the beauty and truth and unity of God's holy creation.

But the messengers of God (as), the people of God, those truly submitted to the only true Power, have come to earth again and again, appearing in every time and to the people of every nation, to purify the places of purity and protect and guide the pure of heart. As Jesus (as) did, they throw the money lenders out of the holy places and ask for the children, the pure of heart, to come forward.

They are the people who serve only God and speak only as God guides them to speak. Never do they speak as the corrupt leaders of the world guide them to speak. Sheikh Ahmadu Bamba (ra), who rose up out of the soil of Africa at the end of the nineteenth century to fight against the forces of oppression and corruption with the light of unwavering faith, was such a person.

Following the example of the Prophet Muhammad (saw), the last of the long line of messengers (as), with deep love and scrupulous dedication, he, along with other great servants of the One, living in Africa at this time, brought the light of the pure teaching of the One God, to the African people and, ultimately the world. This was the second gift of expansion given to me by Sheikh Abdoulaye Dieye (as), which he gave me simultaneously with the gift of return to Africa.

19

Walking in the Footsteps of the Friends of God

Dakar, Gabon, Lambarene, and Mayumba, 2000

Ye have indeed in the Messenger of Allah a beautiful pattern (of conduct) for any one whose hope is in Allah and the Final Day, and who engages much in the praise of Allah.

The Holy Qur'an 33:21

For many weeks, I had seen the word *Gabon* popping up in French e-mails being sent to us by organizers of an historic pilgrimage to be made by a group of people including Sheikh Mourtada (ra), the son of Sheikh Ahmadu Bamba (ra), for the first time in many years to a remote island in equatorial Africa called Mayumba, as well as to other locations in the region where Sheikh Ahmadu Bamba (ra) had spent many years in exile imposed upon him by the French Colonialists. This proposed event sounded to me like something very formal and "official," and therefore not too compelling to my independent nature.

Then, the word *walking* appeared—walking in the footsteps of the Sheikh. This definitely drew me. I felt these messages pulling on my feet.

By the grace of God, I had been blessed to pray in the cave where the Prophet Muhammad (saw) received the revelation of the Holy Qur'an. I had prayed in the gardens of Gethsemane, where Jesus (as) had prayed with his disciples, and walked along the paths

from the Mount of Olives to Bethany, where I sensed that he had
walked. On my first trip to Senegal, I had prayed in the prison cell
where Sheikh Ahmadu Bamba (ra) had been imprisoned. Because
all of these experiences had affected me so much, when I saw the
words "*walk* where he walked," I was moved to go.

Why is this? It is because I know that this life is a sacred journey, a pilgrimage leading to greater knowledge and experience of
the Divine, and, therefore, when, by the decree of God, the way
opens to walk in the footsteps of the people of light, automatically
my feet will go there.

Every day, many times a day, in the *salat*, we who are Muslims
say,

> *In the Name of God, the Merciful, the Compassionate*
> *All Praise to God, the Lord of all the worlds*
> *The Merciful, the Compassionate*
> *Master of the Day of Judgment*
> *You alone do we worship*
> *And to You alone do we turn for aid.*
> *Lead us on the Straight Path.*
> *The Path of those upon whom Your grace has fallen,*
> *Not of those upon whom Your wrath has fallen*
> *Nor of those who have gone astray.*
>
> The Holy Qur'an 1:1–7

The people of light are those upon whom God's grace is perpetually falling, those whose entire existence is a pilgrimage, those whose
sole intention is to worship God alone, those who turn to Him alone
for help. They are those who do not go astray. Therefore, they are
our guides, our *imams*, and our intention is always to follow them.

From the time that I learned *Surat'ul-Fatiha*, and even long
before that, I knew that I wanted to travel in their company and to
go the way that they were going. It was not to worship them, to
say how great they were, or to celebrate the miracles that occurred
through them, but to *go* the way that they were going, to follow the
Path that they were following.

This is the real reason that we went on the journey to Gabon and to other places where Sheikh Ahmadu Bamba (ra) had spent many years in exile and endured many trials for the sake of God and the love of His Messenger (saw). My purpose for going to these places was to access and develop within myself the qualities that I perceived in him, such as profound faith, determination, fearlessness, acceptance and contentment with the Divine Decree. These were all divinely inspired qualities, which enabled the Sheikh to live through the tribulations he experienced with ever-increasing faith and joy.

What does it mean to walk in the footsteps of the *awliya*, the *friends* of God? For me, it does not mean to wear a photograph of the teacher around your neck and thereby define yourself. Nor does it mean to create a tight, close-knit community, like a fortress, that will protect the teachings of the teacher.

The Truth can be protected and preserved only by the Truth. The *friends* of God, the beings of light that we stand behind and walk with, are those immersed in the unlimited ocean of divine consciousness. The only way we can really follow them is to dissolve in that ocean of God's Truth as they have, through God's grace and His guidance.

This is not an organization we can join and then claim that we are great because we are members of it. The transformation, the process of purification, dissolution, immersion, and merging does not occur quickly or easily; we have to persevere in the journey and go through many stages and stations, *insh'Allah*, to reach it.

I was guided, at this time, to walk in the footsteps of Sheikh Ahmadu Bamba (ra), not to worship him, or to serve his family, or to become a member of any exclusive group, but to study profoundly how he lived, how he stood directly behind the Messenger of Allah (saw), and how he served God with great dedication, following the example of the Prophet Muhammad (saw).

The history of his life is significant because in the course of fulfilling his mission Sheikh Ahmadu Bamba (ra) was faced with

extreme hardships and tests, all of which he transformed into vic-
tories for the sake of God.

I had been studying the life of Sheikh Ahmadu Bamba (ra)
and learned that he was a devout child born of a very pious mother and erudite father, who was also a religious leader, serving the
King. The young Ahmadu Bamba amazed those around him with
his knowledge, his nobility of character, sense of ethics and justice
and detachment.

He rapidly surpassed all his fellow students, as well as his teachers, in Qur'anic studies, and mastered of the Sufi orders predomi-
nant in Senegal, the *Qadiriyyah*, the *Tijaniyyah*, and the *Shadhiliyyah*,
until, as he expressed it in many *qasida*s (praise poems), he was
standing directly behind the Prophet Muhammad (saw).

Being empowered by the light and the presence of the Prophet
(saw), he accepted and submitted to no other authority than the
authority of God. Thus, he could not be controlled by worldly
powers and for this reason he became a threat to the authorities of
the world, especially the French Colonialists, the imperial force of
that time that was controlling and oppressing Senegal. It was not
only his own state of liberation that threatened the colonial forces
which were oppressing his country and his people, but the power
of God within him that could liberate others.

Sheikh Ahmadu Bamba (ra) had profound love for the Prophet
Muhammad (saw). It was by this love that he was elevated so quickly and powerfully out of the framework of this world. It was also
through his nearness to the Prophet (saw) and his pure devotion to
God that he had to endure many trials. These tests were apparently
imposed by the colonial forces, who wished to destroy the threat he
posed to them, but at the same time, they became the means of his
spiritual ascent.

We had been learning about the inspiring story of the life of
Sheikh Ahmadu Bamba (ra) from Sheikh Abdoulaye Dieye (ra)
who was now requesting our participation in the pilgrimage that
would take us to the places where the Sheikh endured some of the
many tests. Now, in response to this invitation to deepen our

knowledge and experience of the spiritual journey, two friends, Nasiha and Jariatullah, and I flew to Dakar.

When we arrived at the airport, however, we discovered that our flight had been cancelled and we did not know when the next plane would be operating. The pilgrimage had begun... this was the stage of acceptance—surrender to the Will of God. We remained in the hot, dirty, disorganized airport for nine hours waiting to discover what we were to do next.

This was a time in which to purify our intention and focus our inner prayer, with really nothing else happening, a time in which to realize that the journey to God is not what we expect or wish it to be. It is what it is, a school in which we are formed and developed, in which we grow in understanding in proportion to our submission to the Divine Will, which is manifesting through exactly what is happening.

Finally, after nine hours of being suspended in this state, we were released from the airport and given vouchers to stay in a hotel for the next few days until the next plane might leave for Gabon. We took a taxi to the hotel, which was quite a lovely one, surrounded by a beautiful garden of exotic trees on the shore of the ocean, a breath of earthly paradise after our confinement in the hot and dirty airport. This, in itself, was a gift from God, a reminder of His beneficence and confirmation of His words, *"Truly, with difficulty comes ease."*

A few days later, we went to the airport, the plane was running, and we flew to Gabon. We were greeted at the airport in Gabon like celebrities, the American pilgrims who had traveled so far to make this historic pilgrimage and then could not get a plane. Everyone had been waiting for us. There were cameras everywhere and flashing lights. It was strange indeed for pilgrims on an inner journey of the dissolution of the self, to be received like movie stars.

We met with Sheikh Dieye (ra) and the assembled disciples in the morning. Immediately, he spoke to me and asked me to tell the story of my life how I had embraced Islam, and what I understood about the "women of God." Then, he told me to prepare to speak to a huge assembly that evening. It was a gathering dedicat-

ed to the women of God, Jariatullah, the mother of Sheikh
Ahmadu Bamba (ra), Maryam, the mother of Jesus (as), and other
blessed women, may God be pleased with them all.

He mentioned a long list of fascinating topics and told me to
prepare a talk about them and have it ready as soon as possible. I
was floored. I went into a room and wrote and wrote and wrote
about all the things he mentioned, all relating to women on the
spiritual path. I was simply overwhelmed by the assignment and
the fact that I would soon have to address a huge audience on
such a huge subject, but I was doing my best to hang in.

With my raggedy pile of papers, I went to see the Sheikh. He
was working with a number of people. In the middle of all this, he
had me read my speech to him, which he kept questioning and
cutting back. By the end of the expansion and contraction of that
speech, I did not have a clue what I would say or how to make it
through that particular test.

At this point we were told that one of the many descendants
of Sheikh Ahmadu Bamba (ra) was offering us his house to stay
in. So, we were all transported from the hotel over to that house.
We had been given a house for the remainder of our stay here.
What a gift, I thought!

When we entered the house, I discovered that it was a different kind of a gift than I expected. It was absolutely filthy, cock-
roaches and all. Jariatullah and I thought of the clean hotel and
wished we could run back.

When I saw how the more seasoned *murid*s approached the
situation, however, I realized that lesson was the real gift. They
did not hesitate for a moment, but simply dug in to the cleaning
process. The value of the situation and location was its capacity to
be transformed. Only after everyone had worked together for several hours, did we have the house that we would live in and receive
so many guests in for the next several days.

In the evening, dressed all in "pilgrimage whites," we were
transported to a huge tent. Dressed in the whiteness of the purity
of the path, I felt tiny in the immense, regal gathering, but also

empowered with the grace given to us by God to focus the energy of that beautiful assembly.

Nasiha very sweetly sang a few verses from the *qasida*, called *Sindidi*, that Sheikh Ahmadu Bamba (ra) wrote for his mother, Maryam Boussou (ra), and the people in the audience were overwhelmed with joy. I spoke then about the women of God. I looked out over the vast field of human beings and beheld a great sea of love and grace, and I was sitting in the center of it.

After all the writing and rewriting of that speech, the most important thing was not the words that were spoken, but the experience of being in the centre of that gathering of energy, that assembly of love, dedicated to the women of God.

I was one of three white women in this ocean of brilliant black, this immense garden of exquisitely beautiful flowers. What was most overwhelming about the experience was the sweetness and the power of the love directed toward us and focused upon us.

At that moment, I was struck profoundly by the awareness of a contrast. We had arrived in the heart of Africa and were accorded the warmest welcome and deep respect. We were given the place of honor and became the focal point of a great amount of love. If only our African brothers and sisters arriving in our "civilized" land could have been given such love, honor, and respect, instead of being chained, enslaved, raped, and lynched!

The awareness of this deep imbalance and injustice has brought forth within my heart many questions, which are not easily answered. A great debt needs to be paid and a deep wound healed in the body of humanity. As I travel back and forth between America and Africa again and again, I ask the Divine Healer to reveal to me whatever small part I may play in healing this wound through the very love and oneness that is given so unconditionally in Africa, the land of our origin.

The next morning, we set out on the pilgrimage. There were many red vans filled with pilgrims setting off in a column on a winding road heading into the lush equatorial jungle. The vegetation in this part of the world around the equator is spellbinding.

Imagine the most dense, intricate vegetation that could be found in a rain forest anywhere else, and then multiply it many times over. There are layers upon layers of ferns and other leaves, banana plants, palms and other wondrous trees. As we drove deeper and deeper into the jungle, it was as though we were entering a new universe, blazing with the vitality of organic life.

In our caravan of red vans passing through the vibrant green jungle, we traveled for several hours. Beautiful *qasida*s by Sheikh Ahmadu Bamba (ra) were sung throughout the journey. Although we were from opposite sides of the earth, there was nothing but unity and love amongst all the travelers as we focused on the journey of the Sheikh, intending to follow the way he had cut through these jungles, with the power of his illumined faith.

But while we had the luxury of riding in vans, driving along paved roads, he had *walked* through those jungles and been exposed to continual dangers, challenges, and profound tests. It was the power of the light of his faith, his God-consciousness (*taqwa*) that had carried him through all difficulties. He was unimpaired—on the contrary, spiritually strengthened—by every challenge he faced and surpassed. In this sense, he is an excellent role model for all of us who are facing challenges and tests. Further, we must never forget that it was the Prophet Muhammad (saw) who was the inspiration for all that the Sheikh did and was, just as he is the primary example for us all.

What amazed and inspired me most about the *qasida*s that the Sheikh wrote in the midst of his tribulations in exile, was that these experiences, oppressive as they may have been for another, were celebrated by him. All that he wished to express, no matter what was happening, was great contentment and gratitude to the Lord.

How much more amazing, that is, wondrously inspiring then, is the revelation of the Holy Qur'an, which came through the vehicle of the Prophet Muhammad (saw), even as he and his Companions (ra) were being so thoroughly and continuously tried.

Our caravan arrived in Lambarene, the village where Sheikh Ahmadu Bamba (ra) landed when he was exiled to this region by the French. We sat on the shore of the sea, where the boat in which he traveled had docked. We prayed, recited the Qur'an and the *qasidas*, and contemplated what had taken place here.

Sheikh Ahmadu Bamba (ra) followed the example of the prophets (as), specifically the Prophet Muhammad (saw), who endured for the sake of God and the transmission of His message, difficulties and hardships that we cannot imagine.

Our hardships do not compare to theirs, but they are the ones that God has given us to face, those upon which our own judgment rests. To follow these great men, our *imams*, to the best of our ability, we have to face our challenges and tests as they did, penetrating whatever darkness we may encounter with a heart empowered and illumined by faith in the All-Powerful Lord. It is not our strength, but the strength of our connection to the Power, which heals the sick and gives life to the dead, which carries us through, test after test.

This is what those guided by the light of the One Most Radiant have come to realize. And this is what gives us all the strength to transform any hardship to ease. Having contemplated the trials which the Sheikh had endured here, all of which, it seemed, strengthened his faith, we got back into the caravan of vans and returned, on the winding roads that had brought us here, reaching our little house late at night.

The next morning, we went with all our fellow pilgrims to a very small airport from which we flew, in a tiny plane, to the island of Mayumba. When the plane landed on the island, we were greeted by a wondrous sight and given an amazing reception. It appeared that the whole population of this tiny island had assembled in an immense circle on the tarmac to welcome us.

Each segment of the circle was dressed in a different beautiful indigenous clothing style, each group singing a different song, performing a dance, or making another unique offering as a way of truly welcoming us and honoring the memory of Sheikh Ahmadu Bamba (ra) and the wondrous events, which had occurred when he was here.

I felt that we were being received as royalty and that they were royalty also, as we made our way around the great circle greeting each of them. When I came to the end of the circle, I saw Sheikh Dieye (ra) standing under a small overhang, and went to stand next to him. He was in a state of intense joy, speaking about the great mysteries of this island Mayumba and what had happened here.

He explained that, here, on the island of Mayumba, Sheikh Ahmadu Bamba (ra) had been exiled for years. The French Colonialists had sent the Sheikh here, certain that he would die, as had the other prisoners they had sent here. Every night, the waves rose up and flooded the island, so that almost all of the people who had been sent here were drowned.

But Sheikh Ahmadu Bamba (ra) was not one of them. As he described in his *qasidas*, he spoke the powerful words of God to the waves and they submitted to the power of God, and were subdued.

Many miracles have been attributed to Sheikh Ahmadu Bamba, (ra) by those who honor his memory. What happened is only truly known by God, who was the real Witness of these events. But I believe certainly that the true miracle that manifested in his life, which gave him the ability to do whatever he did, was the Holy Qur'an and the love of Allah and His Messenger (saw). All of the *qasidas* he wrote unconditionally testify to this profound truth. All who follow him should thus follow what he followed. May we all be guided on the Path that is Straight, protected from ever going astray.

Of the array of gifts that he had to share with those he met along the way, that which I believe was most loved by Sheikh Dieye (ra) was his love and respect for Sheikh Ahmadu Bamba (ra), his teaching and the way in which he became the example of the teaching. This was the strongest transmission I received from him in the time allotted for us to know each other.

The last time I saw Sheikh Dieye (ra) was on a trip through Southern California, which was focused on the Inner Directions Conference in La Jolla. I remember this last week with a depth of feeling, because it *was* the last week. Once again, I am struck by the importance of realizing the preciousness of every life that we encounter. We have no idea how long we will have to come to know, understand, and love each being sent to us on our path, before that being returns, often suddenly and without warning, to the Source.

At the same time, even as we begin to appreciate and sense the preciousness and magnitude of every life that we encounter on our journey, every teacher and friend who appears on our path, we cannot get attached to any form, precisely because, at any moment, that form can disappear.

It is, thus, very important to realize, as one after the next of the friends and teachers Allah has willed us to meet on our journey to Him, returns back to Him, that Allah, Alone, is our only Friend that lives forever, our only *Beloved,* who never dies and never leaves us. And it is His Teaching, His Guidance, and His Acceptance, none other, that we truly seek and need.

From time to time, Allah places, in our path, a person who has a certain amount of information to give us, which will help us to proceed in our journey. Then that person, as all lives must do, returns to the Lord, in exactly the time and the way decreed by God.

There is nothing we can do about this, but surrender to the Decree of Allah. We must, certainly, pray for the soul as it makes its journey beyond this world. And then, let us look, see, pay attention: What information did he or she give us? What legacy did they leave us that will clearly guide and illuminate our own journey back to our Lord?

These were understandings I became more deeply and intuitively aware of during the last week I spent with Sheikh Dieye (ra). It was an intense week because the soul of the Sheikh was already transitioning, and, the sense of the "hand" of God upon us was very strong.

One wall of the apartment was glass overlooking nothing but the ocean. It seemed as though the ocean, alternately very peaceful and very turbulent, always full of light, was in the room. Just as the waters surrounding the island of Mayumba were subdued and illuminated by the words of God, which had been addressed to them, I prayed that these waves, too, within and without us sub-mit and be illuminated by the powerful truth of our Lord.

Sheikh Dieye (ra) was transported, speaking intensely, often almost transfixed. I was translating most of the time. The Sheikh was kind, respectful, and caring to me. He spoke to me about the time we had spent and the work we had done together and expressed his gratitude for all that I had done. I felt that my journey with him had come to a place of peace and clarity and light. The struggle was over.

And this, I sensed, was a result of the intense therapy I had passed through in his company. The Sheikh had been simply mir-roring the very deep process I had to go through in the time I had to journey with him before he left this world.

It was a therapeutic process of learning to accept everything that unfolds on the path of God, learning to accept ourselves as we are, without avoiding anything, accessing what we hide in the depths of our being, and bringing it forth so that, exposed in the light of day and submitted to the mercy and grace of God, every-thing within us can be healed, transformed, and illuminated.

Only by fearlessly accepting the very things within ourselves, and others that disturb us most can we begin to be healed, trans-formed, and liberated. I am indebted to Sheikh Abdoulaye Dieye (ra) for encouraging me to do this.

The Sheikh left this world on March 21, 2002. We heard that a car in which he had been traveling had been in an accident and that the others in the car, were minorly injured, but he was the least injured. The next day came the shocking news that, as a result of an aneurism in his brain, which had been triggered by the acci-dent, Sheikh Abdoulaye Dieye (ra) had passed away. The legacy he left is in the heart of each person that he touched. I can bear witness only to the gifts and lessons that I received. Of the true meaning of all things, Allah alone is the Knower:

> So Glory be to Him in whose Hand is the dominion of all things and to Him will ye all be brought back.

The Holy Qur'an 36:83

20

The Therapy of Liberation,
A Journey of Consecration

Senegal, Mauritania, Morocco, Mauritius, 2003

And on earth there are signs [of God's existence, visible] to all who
are endowed with inner certainty, just as [there are signs thereof]
within your own selves: can you not, then, see?

The Holy Qur'an 51:20–21

Sheikh Dieye (ra) did not leave this world without having prepared a successor. For many years he had been training Sheikh Aly N'Daw, who was also born in Senegal, but was eventually sent by Sheikh Dieye (ra) to Reunion Island in the Indian Ocean to build a spiritual community there. Sheikh Aly also traveled extensively, following the example of Sheikh Dieye (ra). While Sheikh Dieye (ra) was alive, Sheikh Aly, his successor in training, manifested in the humblest way.

When Sheikh Dieye (ra) and the disciples first stayed in my house, Sheikh Aly came too, but while Sheikh Dieye (ra) stayed on a bed upstairs, Sheikh Aly stayed on the floor downstairs. He attracted no attention to himself, but was extremely kind to everyone, a very warm and loving friend to us all.

Following the passing of Sheikh Dieye (ra) I had the blessing of traveling with Sheikh Aly and a small group of disciples to various parts of the world. Throughout these journeys, teachings, which flowed as effortlessly as the breath, contributed to my basic understanding of the integration of spiritual teaching within the experience of life. This began with a healing process that he has called the *"therapy of liberation."* Explaining this therapy and why it is needed by those on the path to God, he said,

"The therapy of liberation is a way to help people, through the experience they have had, to find their way back to God. The focus is on the transformation, not the elimination, of any aspect of the personality. The question is how to transform. It is based upon our very own life experiences, and comes through the exercise of forgiving, as opposed to judging and finding fault. This is the transformation that God refers to in the Qur'an, when, again and again, He invites us to pardon. When you look closely, you see that whatever teaching God is giving in the Qur'an, at the end of it all, He comes back to this idea of forgiveness. The aim of this work is to help people grasp the idea that they can transform themselves. Whatever is happening, it can be controlled and must be transformed.

"At what moment do idols become established in our heart? How does this happen? At puberty, the child starts becoming judgmental about what he sees his parents doing. It is at this moment that the child opens himself to problems, because he has started to judge. How did pride arise in Iblis? It is because Iblis judged Adam, and, from this, sprang pride. Where did jealousy spring from? It came because Iblis judged God in His creation of Adam. So this is the danger in judging. We continue to judge and to judge and to judge until today. Perhaps, even when we came here today, we were engaged in this important task of judging what others were doing and saying.

"It is not a surprise at all that we have problems now, and that these problems have become, in fact, our life's priority. As long as this is not resolved, we will never be able to assume our role as the servant of God. We will not be able to truly assume the position that the Lord has created us for, that of His true representative on earth.

"So, how do we put an end to this? It is by the prayer of asking for forgiveness. Why must we do this? Because, the Lord did not create anyone in vain.

"Each one of us can be an instrument of the Divine Will.

"All of this leads us back to the teachings of the Prophet, our Master Muhammad. And this is what allows us to give religion its true value, its true dimension.

"As has been stated in a hadith of the Prophet, 'All humanity constitutes a single family, and the one who is most loved by God is the one who is most useful to this family.' The Prophet showed us this when he delivered the last sermon. Everyone was there to bear witness that he had fulfilled his mission and that, in fact, he was the most useful person to humanity.

"We see that all of this is related to service. The state of being a slave, or servant of God, revolves around service and also around love. So, in this way, we come to understand that our relationship with God is linked with the relationship that we have with others, and the relationship that we have with the Master himself. And the contract that we have with the Master is thus linked with the original contract that exists between ourselves and God."

Sheikh Aly taught that in order for each of us to become healed and transformed in such a way as to become a true representative of God on earth, we need spiritual formation.

"This formation unfolds little by little. Our character is thus formed to the end that we become the instruments of God. And the formation is nothing other than the way in which we arrive at the state in which our heart is pure, loving, and completely concentrated upon the Lord. One arrives at this state by participating in these various activities.

"Because from the time God called Muhammad (saw) to be a Prophet, it was within the call that God formed his character. And it was thus that he became the Seal of the Prophets.

"When he met people who didn't like what he did, the Lord told him what to do, how to behave. When he met people who were opposed to his mission and plotted against him, the Lord told him how he should behave. The Lord said: Pardon them and forget, until the decision of your Lord intervenes.

"Thus it is through these encounters that the formation of each person occurs. So the work on the terrain, in the field, is very important and we must know that it is in the middle of the situations of life itself that our formation unfolds. And separating ourselves from others is not the way that has been indicated.

"In each situation, there is a behavior that the Lord has shown. And that behavior is zikr (remembrance of God). There is the external zikr in which we gather together in a group and sing together, but there is also the internal zikr, or remembrance, which arises in

the middle of all these different situations and guides us to the right
conduct.

"The Prophet (saw) met certain people in his life. The goal of some
of the people was different than the goal of the Prophet (saw). What
did the Lord say to him? He did not tell him to throw these people out,
but to treat them in a very beautiful way, so that tomorrow, they
could return. And this will make it easy for them to return to God.

"We arrive at this nobility of conduct, we see this nobility of con-
duct in the work that we have to do."

The example of the Holy Prophet (saw) interacting with all
those that he encountered on his path and the fact that the teachings of the Qur'an were revealed in the very midst of these interactions is a constant reminder that the exercise of living and interacting with other beings is a sacred exercise. It is a continual test to
see if, in the midst of the challenges and vicissitudes we must inevitably face in our daily lives, we are able to put into practice the
realizations we are gaining deep within.

Traveling with the Sheikh was always the context for learning
about healing and becoming liberated from debilitating patterns.
It was always the context for the formation of character, with the
goal that each one of us would develop truly noble conduct, and
with the completion of our formation, become a true representative of God on earth.

As humble and hidden as Sheikh Aly was when his Sheikh was
alive, as soon as Sheikh Dieye (ra) had departed from this world
and the responsibility fell upon Sheikh Aly to carry on the work, he
manifested his strength. Immediately, he called together all the disciples who could come to gather in Senegal for the next *Maggal* to
visit the city of Touba, to visit the tomb of Sheikh Dieye (ra), and
to travel together to Mauritania to visit the tomb of Sheikh Sidi
Ahmad Ismouhu Deymani (ra), the disciple of Sheikh Ahmadu
Bamba (ra) and the Sheikh of Sheikh Dieye (ra).

When Sheikh Aly and many of the disciples arrived at the airport at three o'clock in the morning, "perpetual Senegal airport
time," Sheikh Aly himself picked up almost every piece of luggage

and loaded it onto a luggage cart. I saw that his sleeves were rolled up and he was going to serve the disciples, not wait to be served.

The next morning we were told that we were all going to a memorial for Sheikh Dieye (ra), which was being held in a huge hall in a newly built cultural center five minutes from the Sheikh's house. With almost no notice, I was informed that I was to speak. I had brought some photographs of the Sheikh's visits to America, mostly of him embracing children, expanded to a large size. I took them to the gathering. I really did not have anything prepared to say ... just a feeling in the heart.

The huge auditorium was packed with illustrious people of Senegal, including many dignitaries. For me to speak correctly to this assembly in French, having nothing prepared, was truly a spiritual challenge. I knew that there was no way that I could do it by myself, and I was completely dependent upon God to use me as an instrument.

When I was called up onto the stage and went up to the podium, I felt like I was walking into the wide, open space without any plan of what I was going to say. Invoking the grace of Allah, I recited *Surat'ul-Fatiha,* the opening chapter of the Holy Qur'an. The power of the *Fatiha* filled the auditorium. I felt that it was the grace of God that was resonating throughout the hall and through the hearts of the people. So I did not have to speak myself. That was immense relief!

I then held up the pictures to show how the Sheikh, throughout his travels, had embraced children. I spoke in French but felt that *I* was not speaking; the words, activated by the power of the *Fatiha*, were pouring through me. The heart was communicating with the heart. I saw many people in the audience weeping, it seemed, not with sadness, but because their hearts were moved. The power that I felt was manifesting was from God alone. It was the awareness of the divine love, the divine embrace, that moved the audience to tears.

Then we went on a journey to many places we had visited with the Sheikh. As well as those places of power and peace in Senegal that we had visited often and now visited again on our pilgrimage, this time we crossed the river on a barge, and entered the land of Mauritania. We were greeted on the barge by tall, princely men, all dressed in white robes with light blue outer garments similar to togas that rolled up on their shoulders like wings. They were extremely kind and extended to us the warmest welcome.

It was dusk as we crossed the river, and the water was dark and glittering. Our gracious guides led us to a configuration of beautiful, hand-embroidered tents, under which we assembled, were graciously welcomed by the local Sheikh and the whole village, which had assembled in the tent, singing and dancing their traditional songs and dances and reciting poetry in praise of the Prophet Muhammad (saw). After this beautiful welcome in the amazing tent, we sat in the remembrance of God, in *zikr* and prayer throughout the night.

For me, it was a night of deep memories. I had the profound sense of having sat through nights of *zikr* and remembrance, in tents such as these before. The tents were immense, chambers upon chambers of billowing hand-embroidered cloth. I could not imagine how many hours went into the creation of this beautiful cloth.

Of his exile to Mauritania, Sheikh Ahmadu Bamba (ra) had said that it was a journey of consecration, and that was the feeling I had in the tent that night. We were on a journey of consecration.

Whereas Gabon, to which Sheikh Ahmadu Bamba (ra) had been first exiled, was a spiritual wilderness, Mauritania, to which he was exiled later, was a land whose people had been prepared to receive spiritual teaching, through generations of development. It is a land of spiritual elevation, of deep Qur'anic study and training. Sitting in the illuminated tent, I felt the presence of Sheikh Ahmadu Bamba (ra) and other great African Sheikhs gathering in huge billowing tents such as these. I felt the power of the teaching and transmission that had taken place.

Outside the tents, large campfires were burning, and the desert sky was brilliant and cool. I slipped out of the tent from time to time during the night, so that I could experience the beauty and the vibration of the land, itself, and of the desert sky.

Once outside the tent, I came across a group of boys from the village. Their large, beautiful eyes were glowing. They spoke to me about their Qur'anic studies, and I saw the light of the Qur'an shining through their faces, their comportment, and their words. Every time that I meet children who are developing in this way, shining with the clarity and peace of the prophetic way, uncorrupted by the rampant chaos of the modern, misguided world, I believe that there is hope and blessing flowing from a *divine plan*.

The Holy Qur'an, like all of the revealed scriptures describes to us the end of the world, but that is not the end of our story. In a saying of the Holy Prophet, God says, *"My Mercy precedes My wrath."* Allah tells us again and again, for those who obey His commandments, pray regularly and do righteous deeds, there will be gardens with rivers flowing beneath, wherein they shall have no fear, nor shall they grieve. To find this kind of peace and security in this world and the next, we need to study the words that Allah has sent to us and to make them the reality of our life.

So, when I meet, anywhere in the world, children like those I met in Mauritania, I feel that there is real hope and a real future for those of humankind who truly turn to the Creator for guidance that becomes the very substance of their life.

The next morning, in the beautiful, cool light of the dawn, I sat outside the tent on the blessed earth of that village, and recited *Surah Ya Sin* and *Surat'ul-Waaqia* for the people of this consecrated land, may the consecration ever continue, as the light of the Qur'an is passed down as a living legacy to generations to come.

Then, after sharing breakfast with all, we set out on a pilgrimage to the tomb of Sheikh Sidi Ahmed Ismouhu Deymani, the Sheikh of Sheikh Dieye. We traveled for hours through the desert and mountainous terrain. It was a rugged drive and many of the brothers were squeezed together, standing up in the trucks as they bounced along the very rocky trails. Such are the rigors of traveling for the sake of God and every sincere effort and sacrifice made for the sake of God brings with it a hidden reward.

From time to time, we would stop at an oasis in the desert and drink at a watering hole. At one of these oases, a great number of camels, donkeys, and other animals were also drinking. The higher we went up into the barren, rocky desert, the more animals we found assembled at the watering holes. I was amazed to see so very many animals of all sorts gathered together in perfect peace.

So peaceful were the gatherings of beings at these oases that even the presence of many people and trucks could not disturb them. I noticed especially one long row of donkeys, standing in a perfect line with each donkey resting its head on the back of the donkey in front of it.

What a beautiful vision of the natural condition of creatures living together in harmony and balance! It was one of the signs from God on the path, transmitting an understanding about how human beings, too, could travel and live together in harmonious interdependence and peace.

We traveled further and further up into the wild mountainous desert. At another oasis where we stopped in our rocky ascent, I received another message. I heard, "Speak. Tell the story. Tell people about the things you have seen and experienced."

I had the sense that I was to go to places like colleges and organizations and speak about my experiences in Africa and throughout the world, talk about the experience of being united with African people and people of all the world. I heard in the depth of my heart this message to speak to people, wherever their ears were open, about this ongoing pilgrimage on which all differences, such as those of race, color, and culture, are completely dissolved in the oneness of the Creator and the oneness of the human family.

When we had traveled very far into the desert, we finally arrived at the tomb of Sheikh Sidi Ahmad (ra), and prayed there that the work of Allah, through all of us, be fulfilled. The tomb, so many hours into absolute desert wilderness, was well hidden from the world, one of those secret places that is just what it is, with no external artifice at all adorning it. We had traveled so far to find this holy spot, which was truly only seen by the "eyes" of God.

The next morning, we were more than graciously received in another tent by the descendants of Sheikh Sidi Ahmad, and then we returned on the ferry to Senegal.

When our collective pilgrimage was completed, and all those who had come together from countries around the world left to return home, I was drawn magnetically to Morocco, which is actually on the opposite side of Mauritania from Senegal.

I went to Morocco ostensibly to investigate business possibilities, but, in reality, there was a much deeper reason I had to go there, and that was a stage of the pilgrimage. Just as West Africa was a part and reflection of the mysteries of the soul, so was North Africa another dimension. In the architecture, the art, and the mysticism of Morocco, I felt there were keys to my awakening that I needed to find.

Morocco is a place flourishing with art and beauty. Even the airport is an artifact of beautiful tile-work. As I witnessed the spectacle of exquisite artistry, the question posed itself: what inspired these people to be so creative? This creativity was a mirror, and I saw, in the walls of beautiful tile mosaics, a reflection of my life and journey, which is, itself, like every life, a mosaic composed of many amazing tiles, arranged in an amazing way.

May we each be able to perceive the configuration of the mosaic of our life, appreciate its beauty, and decode the meanings encoded in the complex arrangement of tiles.

We landed in Casablanca but, then, began to drive through the rolling hills and gardens, the beautiful verdant landscape to the ancient city of Fez. Fez is a city where great Sufis have gathered throughout the centuries, and the prayers of all who have gathered there to pray and receive knowledge of the Divine still are tangibly present.

So that is why I, too, like multitudes of others, had to come here, so that my prayers, supplications, and contemplations, inspired by this accumulation of blessed energy, could unite with theirs, that is, unite with the One to whom all supplication is addressed in a place where He had been deeply remembered.

The journey to places of power in the presence of the people of light is one in which every place that you visit and every person that you meet along the way is a mirror to your soul and once you have seen and experienced this, it becomes a part of you.

When people ask me, *"Where do you come from?"* the answer is: *"From all the places that I have been."* What we each are is a composite of all the people and places that we have visited and deeply embraced. Such is the mosaic of tiles of which our life is composed. And these are the experiences in which the story of our soul is told.

And now it was, in the city of Fez, that the mystery of the soul, and its timeless story, was revealing its multiple dimensions. I want to describe this beautiful, ancient city, because it is a place that I would like the reader to visit, as we travel together on the journey of self-discovery.

The old city of Fez, is encircled, by huge walls, within which is a fantastic beehive of creativity. Everywhere, in every nook and cranny of the outer edge of the old city, artisans are humming. They are making fine grillwork, pottery, embroidery, leatherwork, woodcarving, hand-painted furniture, and practically every other craft one could imagine. The outer circumference of the old city is one extended multi-media craft workshop, which, with so much woodwork going on, smells like a shrine filled with freshly ground sandalwood and cedar.

On the next level, going in, in concentric circles, from the studios where this plethora of crafts is being created, one finds the colorful, also fragrant shops, where the crafts are being sold.

In the center of the configuration of the holy city of Fez, is the illuminated, sanctified space of the *Kairouine Mosque*, in the center of which is a beautiful courtyard, in the center of which is an ever flowing fountain.

All of the beautiful, intricate tiled doorways into the immense mosque are thus leading into the empty illuminated space in the center, which is filled with prayer, and in the center of that space is the fountain, which, for me, was a symbol of the abundance of the Divine provision that is always flowing.

With the open, sanctified space of the mosque in the center of the city, all that is taking place around it seemed to me to be blessed and balanced. I felt that the configuration of the city was inspired, and also I very much sensed the spiritual presence of the *awliya*, the friends of God, that had lived and prayed here throughout the centuries.

When I saw people gathering in circles in the bright open space in the center of the mosque courtyard, I felt, "The great ones have assembled here; the great Sufis have gathered together here. The lovers of God have celebrated His Praise abundantly here. And I felt that I was sitting with them, all of us united in the love of the Divine, in the light of the open space in the middle of the Kairouine Mosque.

The Holy Qur'an tells us of those who have died in the way of Allah that they are alive, though we see them not. They are present in the Presence of the One, who they love, the Inspirer, the Teacher of all, the Living, the Eternal. The great Sufis who gathered here are eternally present as long as the Beloved is loved here.

In earlier times, such as the times of the great Sheikh, Sheikh'ul Akbar, Muhyd'din Ibn al Arabi, so many more people lived in the awareness of the Divine, gathering in holy places like this and sharing the divine mysteries. As the stories of his life tell us, his journey through life was profoundly mystical, greatly blessed. Wherever he went outwardly and inwardly, he met and deeply interacted with the *awliya*, the illuminated ones.

From those times to today, the spiritual landscape has changed. And what was abundantly revealed in the time of the Sheikh'ul Akbar is now hidden.

Today, even in this holy city of Fez, the majority of people are gathering in the cafes to smoke more, it seems, than in the mosques to pray. The people of our time, around the world, are gathering at sports events, gathering at nightclubs. But who is gathering as the great Sufis did here to share knowledge of the Divine, always increasing in themselves and one another consciousness (*taqwa*) of Him?

"Please count us among them," I beseeched the Everliving One as I sat in the illuminated courtyard of this ancient mosque, where so many great souls had prayed. Please count us among them!

The next stop on the journey of the soul in pursuit of *taqwa* (consciousness of God) was the island of Mauritius. I went there the following summer with Issa, as soon as he was finished with his school year. We went to visit there with many people of the community of Sheikh Dieye (ra) who we met when they came to stay in our house, and who we had met again and again in Senegal. Now we were going to get to know our friends even better, by staying and praying with them in their homes.

The airport in Mauritius was, like the airport in Morocco, full of light. You know as soon as you enter the airport that you have arrived in a wonderful place. It was completely decorated with murals and other works of beautiful, whimsical art. Right away, as soon as you have landed and set foot in the land, you feel that you have arrived in a country with a *heart*!

Reuniting with dear friends, we got into the car and began to drive into the lush, fertile terrain, the verdant fields and hills, great mountains, marvelous waterfalls, palm trees and exotic tropical vegetation.

But, as lovely as the island of Mauritius is, we had not come as tourists on a holiday. We had come to gain more knowledge and understanding of the way of God, and, in accordance with our intention, the gift that we received there was greater in its beauty than the most beautiful landscape. This gift was to perceive the beauty of the circle of the believers and then experience how the circle *works*.

There are many families in the spiritual circle activated by Sheikh Dieye and Sheikh Aly around the Island of Mauritius. Our trip was arranged so that we would not stay with a single family, but would travel from home to home and thus become closer to everyone.

What I noticed immediately in every home, was that there were big piles of highly activated and much used prayer beads. This was another sign of the activated remembrance of God, that touched and inspired my heart.

In the home of my dear friend Ruqayyah, where we stayed the longest, the community gathered almost every day and prayed extensively for everyone in need. In addition to a large dinner served to the poor and needy every week, these prayers were going on continuously for people in the community itself.

This is the way to build real spiritual community, I deeply felt. We must not judge or gossip about each other, but pray for each other, not superficially, but deeply. To pray with deep focus and intention for another is a very effective way of implementing the practice of forgiving and dispelling judgment. The more you pray for someone, the less you will be likely to judge that person, and the more likely you will be to truly intend the best for that person.

It was the regular, daily practice of this community to pray for each other, whatever the need may be. So, if someone lost a job, or had to take an important test, or was ill, or getting married, or going into labor, or needed prayers for any other reason, the whole community would pray extensively for him or her.

For example, they would say *Bismillahirrahmanirrahim, In the Name of God, Most Merciful, Most Compassionate*, invoking the Mercy and Compassion of the Creator 16,000 times for that specific purpose. I felt that this was a wonderful way of thinking about each other, holding each other's best interests in our hearts, and supplicating the Creator on behalf of this person.

During our stay in Mauritius, a tragic accident occurred which brought to light the importance of the circle of prayer even more deeply and poignantly. A young girl, who was a part of the community, was, shortly after she was engaged, to be married, in an automobile accident with several other girls. For a week, she was in intensive care, and then, by the Decree of Allah, she passed away, may Allah bless her journey back to Him and also give His comfort to her family.

The week that this child was in the hospital was the week that we happened to be in Mauritius, traveling from family to family, house to house. The prayer circle was activated everywhere. Even in houses filled with young children, everywhere the prayer beads were moving. Everyone, including the young children, were engaged, more than in anything else, in praying for those families in their difficulty.

I, as a traveler, there to learn as deeply as possible about the life of the community and how the circle works, was blessed to participate, again and again, in the circle of prayer, as well as to go to the hospital and sit with the grieving mother. How can I convey the experience of sitting on a wooden bench next to that dear woman and embracing her, as she had to pass through an inconceivably profound trial.

A few days later, the child passed and we gathered with the large extended family to honor her life and pray for the journey of her soul, as well as to express our deep solidarity with those who were suffering so deeply the loss. As sad as this gathering was, it was also inspiring, because the power of the prayer, the power of the solidarity of the community, the power of the human family, itself, was also undeniably evident.

All of this was the deep gift that Allah gave to us on our pilgrimage and learning journey on the island of Mauritius. As I and two of the sisters were riding together on a bus back from the funeral prayers, we looked up into the sky and saw a huge, brilliantly clear rainbow descending vertically directly from heaven to earth. It was a sign of the direct descent of God's Mercy to the earth, confirming acceptance of the beautiful teaching we had learned in our time here, of the importance for each and every one of us to deeply care and pray for one another.

21

Repel What Is Evil With What Is Better. Travelling to Places in Peril on a Mission of Healing, Solidarity, and Peace

India, Nepal, Bangladesh, Pakistan, Kashmir, 2003, 2004

And your Lord shall give to you and you shall be satisfied. Did He not find you an orphan and provide refuge? And did He not find you astray and guide you? And did He not find you without means and provide sustenance? So as for the orphan—do not oppress him. And as for the beggar—do not drive him away. And as for the grace of your Lord—proclaim it.

The Holy Qur'an 93:5–11

At the end of 2003, Sheikh Aly told me that he was planning to go on a mission of peace and solidarity to India and several surrounding countries, and was searching for those inspired to come. With so many valuable and meaningful memories of traveling *fisabilillah*, how could I really refuse the call? Each time that *providence* presents to us the opportunity, how can we refuse to grow?

Since I had been for so many years doing business with Kashmir, I could also add this dimension to the journey, and so, it was clear that this was the next step in my pilgrimage. *This mission of peace and solidarity* was to be undertaken by a small group: Sheikh Aly, three of the women we had stayed with on the island of Mauritius, and myself. It was very well organized, by Djamila, who had been doing graduate work in the field of social work and had come to know people in different countries who were dedicated to helping others. To her list of contacts I added mine, and so God provided us with a beautiful itinerary of visiting people committed to the cause of doing good in many countries.

Almost every place that we went to was imperiled in one way or another, the people were enduring trials, and the situation was dangerous. Sheikh Aly was never deterred by news of the difficulty or danger in a region. When we were warned that we could be approaching a situation of conflict or danger, he said that that was a place, which was in need of peace and so we must not avoid it but must go there and bring peace. He said that if there was difficulty, that was *why* we must go there.

Our journey to India was a continuous witnessing of the transformation of darkness into light. We saw people, oppressed and tried, who were so filled with the light of hope and commitment that it seemed they were able to achieve anything. In every country, in every village and city where we traveled, we found the righteous ones activated by the power of God to change the world around them, people inspired to give with all their heart, not expecting anything in return.

We visited places and people assaulted by political oppression, poverty, and strife, but what we found in every crucible was *gold*: the transformative power of love. It is by the love of God that we are brought back from death into life, and it is His compassion implanted in the hearts of His servants that inspires them to bring hope and life to those who might die without it.

We began our journey in Lucknow at the City Montessori School, a wonderful school which is dedicated to peace, nonviolence, and unity founded by Jagdish and Bharti Gandhi. This school began with five students in one family and now, with twenty-seven thousand students, it is the largest school in the Guinness Book of World Records. As large as it has become, the school remains passionately dedicated to manifesting these noble principles.

The students in this unusual school have created an international congress of world governments, to set an example of real justice for the adults in the world. In response to their many extraordinary efforts, these students were awarded the peace prize by UNESCO in 2002. So with this beautiful vision of what people of any age can do to change the world, we began our journey.

On all of the buildings of the school are engraved teachings of universal truth, such as a quote of Baha'ullah: *"The world is but one country and mankind its citizens. Every child is potentially the light of the world."* So, where there was nothing, a small city has been created, with twenty-seven thousand students, each of whom is potentially the light of the world. Every one of those students going out into the world may become the catalyst for another school of peace, non-violence, and unity.

Next, we went to a leper colony in the countryside. There, in emerald fields well cultivated by the leper community, the Sheikh embraced the people. It was a vision of light, not one of hopeless despair. The women of the community, dressed in beautiful saris, were working in the fields, and the men were sitting in clusters, upright, with a kind of stillness and purity and grace. I saw in those emerald fields not fear and misery but peace and dignity in the people, the light of submission, and that light dispelled so many preconceptions, stigmas and fears I had been unconsciously harboring about our brothers and sisters who are afflicted with leprosy.

Back in the city of Lucknow, we met with a group of children who had been living on the street but who are now living in a shelter with a very loving priest. Each boy showed us, smiling from ear to ear, with great joy and pride, his bedroll and the rice that the boys had just cooked. For they who previously had nothing, those small things inspired so much pride, contentment and joy.

Then, we went into the countryside and met with a group of poor children who had been left behind by the Indian educational system, until a small group of kind and loving people created a school for them. We met with these rescued children in their stone schoolhouse, and shared with them their joy at being given the chance to learn.

The same compassionate caring people guided by Dr. Sumita Gandhi who had organized this school, had also created a system of literacy that enabled people to read and write in six months, and this system was spreading around the world.

Next, we went to Kathmandu, Nepal. There we were hosted by Som, who was in charge of four orphanages. We visited one of the orphanages where a great many children were sheltered together in an extremely warm and loving environment. There was a sense of solidarity and real fellowship in this home. We could feel that the power of love had created a real experience of extended family, so that the children were saved from isolation and despair by the sense of belonging, the joy of having a warm and loving home and a great family.

This brought to my mind and heart the many passages in the Qur'an in which we are instructed that the treatment of orphans, as well as of the needy and the destitute, is of paramount importance. As He tells us in the Holy Qur'an:

> They ask you what they should spend. Say, "Whatever you spend on good (let it be first) on your parents, and your near kin, and the orphans, and the destitute and the wayfarers." And whatever good you do, surely God knows.

The Holy Qur'an 2:215

In light of the importance of the welfare of orphans, as well as the destitute and needy, revealed to us by our Lord, we needed to visit the orphanage, to take these children and those lovingly helping them into our hearts and prayers, as this mission of solidarity continued to unfold.

After taking us to visit the children in the orphanage, Som took us on a walk around Kathmandu. This was very significant for me. I was retracing the original steps of my journey. I was back again at the burning ghats, where I had sat and meditated thirty years before, but now I saw things in a totally different way. I was walking along the same well-worn paths, past the same ancient buildings as I had passed in the beginning of my quest for the Master and the way of God, but now I was walking with the Sheikh, and others, appreciating, with deep gratitude, all that God had revealed to me of His path since I last walked here.

Som took us to the shrine of Bodhinath, which I had circumambulated in my early journey, and as we were walking around it, behind two young girls who were making their circumambulation in prostrations, Sheikh Aly said to me, "You have completed the circle. You have come back to where you started and the circle of your life is complete. Now you are ready to rise."

At that moment, I had the real experience of the circle turning back into itself, so that the beginning and the end were merged in the continuum. I knew intuitively and spiritually that a totally new dimension of the journey was going to be revealed, but I did not know how, when, or in what context. This was a clear message and spiritual premonition, which was totally accurate.

After Nepal, we went to Bangladesh. In the town of Tangueil (pronounced "Tanguy") we were hosted by a dedicated person named Tuhin Islam, who works for an organization committed to transforming the condition of every sector of disadvantaged children in the community, including children of ethnic minorities, child laborers, and the children of prostitutes.

Shortly after we arrived, he took us on a tour to meet with these children in so many different shacks and rooms where they had been assembled to be educated and trained so they might have a real chance to make something of their lives.

The most troubling place on the tour was a brothel which was a village in itself, consisting of about three thousand women and children. It was deeply shocking and saddening to me to see to what degree the principles, laws, and safeguards offered by the One Most Merciful, had been abandoned in the formation of this sad village.

And yet we saw these very principles of mercy and righteous-
ness, manifesting through those who went in to help and rescue the
souls from that tragic fate. We walked down the long lanes of this
village and saw our young sisters, our aunts, and mothers lined up,
their faces masked with bizarre makeup, endless lines of young girls
gazing into stark emptiness. We saw the rooms where they live and
work, the beds under which their children have been growing up.
Imagine the miserable plight of a child growing up under the bed
of his mother as she engages in her daily and nightly work.

The project aims to save the children and their mothers too, if
they are willing and able to become liberated from their patterns.
For the children, who truly wish to be free, a large home has been
built in the countryside where they are educated in every way.
They are removed from that space beneath their mothers' beds
that was the only home they have had, and transported to a beautiful estate in the countryside built for them.

There, many children are being educated academically, reli-
giously, and culturally. In addition to all academic subjects, they
are being trained in cottage industries, agricultural skills, martial
arts, and traditional arts.

Most importantly they are given the opportunity to become
rehabilitated from those patterns into which they were born, and
live a productive free life. In contemplating the blessing granted to
the children to become free of their inherited oppression, we prayed
that we too might be liberated by the grace of God Most Merciful
from the legacies, which have been imprisoning us.

We were invited to spend a day at the children's home. It was
so lovely there. Most beautiful of all were the children themselves.
We prayed with them, played with them, and saw the bright large
rooms where they live. During the day we saw them practicing
karate, and in the evening they performed for us a marvelous, very
professional program of traditional Indian dance. As we were finally leaving, walking to the van, ten or so children were holding
onto each of my hands and I to theirs.

My primary instinct was to stay with the children. I felt that my body and heart were merged with them and I could never leave them. I experienced again the exhortation, "You must love all lives as your own." Each child that I saw was a reflection of both the child within me and the child I could have borne.

Meeting, caring for, and embracing all the children we met, and at the same time, accepting and embracing the child within myself, I found that the journey was continuously educational, deeply touching, and therapeutic in many ways. I was very grateful to be witnessing, in the midst of an often heartless world, the power of love and compassion made absolutely manifest.

The next morning the director of all the programs, Mr. Hamid, took us out to the fields, which had been cultivated by his organization. The produce from the fields funds all the projects, including two hospitals where all the people in the community can get health care for free or for almost nothing.

Mr. Hamid told us he wanted to take us to the source and inspiration for all this, that which had motivated him to work for the sake of God and His creation without cease. "It must be your mother!" I said.

We followed a little winding path into the jungle and came at last to a light-filled village shack. There we met, sitting on a large bed, Mr. Hamid's mother. Her hands, her face, her fragrance, and her vibration were like those of the venerable Sheikhs I have been so blessed to meet along the way.

When we left her presence, I wanted nothing but to return and stay with her longer. But that was not possible. A few months later, she departed from this world, leaving a great and growing legacy.

Before completing this remembrance of the selfless, noble servants of the Merciful that I was blessed to meet in Bangladesh, I would like to contemplate and celebrate the wonderful work of Muhammad Yunus, a native of this beautiful land. What he, himself has done in creating the Grameen Bank, an extensive structure of micro-credit banking, is proof that every human being is capable, with the grace of God, to make an immense difference in transforming the condition of his fellow beings.

He began his experiment with micro-credit banking observing a group of very poor people who were forced into a corrupt system based on usury, because they had no other way to get the funding to develop their small businesses. Because they were poor and had no collateral, they were unable to get funding from any bank.

When he counted up all the money that these people needed to pursue their goals, it was a total of twenty-seven dollars! For only twenty-seven dollars, this group of people who could not get this money from any established banking system was forced into usury, a practice hated by the One Most Merciful.

Muhammad Yunus, acting on behalf of the Merciful, gave this group of people the twenty-seven dollars that they needed to develop their businesses. This worked very well, and he continued to help other groups of people like this.

Thus he began his practice of micro-credit banking, which now, thirty years later, is empowering more than seven million people, mostly women, to fund their businesses and take care of their families, rising up out of the depths of hopeless poverty to become truly independent and successful. This is a miracle of God's Grace made manifest in absolutely tangible action.

As much as we see that the land of Bangladesh has had to endure of intense poverty along with so many natural disasters and their aftermaths, let us consider the greatness of spirit, which has manifested there: How the most extreme poverty has been transformed into abundance and great success.

This is indeed a tremendous inspiration for every one of us and a message for the entire world. Certainly we cannot each help seven million other fellow beings on the planet, but every person that we can help, every loving thought and action truly counts. May we each search for the many ways that we can do this.

As we were driving away from Tangueil, into the lush landscape of Bangladesh, rich with rice paddy fields, both blessed and deeply tried by the abundance of water, tears flowed from my eyes in streams. What overwhelmed me most deeply was the comprehension of how much capacity one person has to help another. And the acts of true charity are yet greater and more exalted when they are addressed to those most helpless and most deeply in need.

All of this was the manifested teaching of the Messenger (saw) of Allah and of all the prophets (as) who preceded him, the teaching of Allah, the One Creator who sent them all. As our Creator, Most Merciful, tells us in the Qur'an, *"Repel evil with what is better."* He tells us that good works and good words lead directly to Him:

> *And whose speech is better than one who calls others to Allah and does good deeds, and says, "Surely I am among the willingly surrendered ones)." Good and evil deeds are not equal. Repel evil with what is better. You will see that the one with whom you had enmity will become, as it were, your dearest friend.*

> The Holy Qur'an 41:33–34

Whatever difficulty, whatever evil we, or our fellow beings face, with the Grace of God, may we not be discouraged, frightened, or upset, but may we repel it with what is better. The light from one small candle can illuminate a huge dark room. This is the divine teaching that we saw manifesting in action, everywhere that we went.

Imagine what would happen to the condition of the world, the human condition, if we all followed this divine advice? Such an approach taken by one after another of the inhabitants of this planet, would, person by person, extinguish the fire fueling all the conflicts, all the wars, all the pacts of revenge!

This, as simple as it is, is the most powerful teaching. May every one of us who hears and comprehends this message from our Creator, discover the way to implement it in the multiple contexts of our life. Let us start with ourselves, take these words to heart, and see how they transform the situations we encounter in our life!

Next we were led to Lahore, Pakistan, to the shrine of Al-Hujwiri, who was known as Data Ganj Baksh, the bestower of treasure. He had written the great Sufi book, *Kashf al-Mahjub,* or

"The Revelation of the Mystery." It was one of the first Sufi books I had ever read. Early in my development, I had read this book, and it had a profound impact upon me.

The first words that we read and hear about the reality of God and the path that leads to God are so profoundly beautiful to the soul, because they are like its first food, its first life-giving water.

They are not simply words on a page; they are our vital connection to another realm. So, they are precious and beloved to us, like valuable gems we find on a road that came from another *world*! We have no idea where they came from or how they got there, but we feel that they have special meaning for us, and although we do not really know what they mean, we keep them near us, feeling that they are a sign of great treasures, we are destined to receive.

Al-Hujwiri's book was like that for me when it came into my hands in my late teens. To this day, I remember the feeling of holding my well-worn copy in my hand and of carrying it with me everywhere. It was a link to the unseen, containing clues relating to my real purpose in life.

I cannot remember when that precious book fell *out* of my hand. But, somewhere, in the course of traveling I had lost the book amidst all the vicissitudes of my life, and had not seen it again all these years until this moment when, in the library below the mosque, we were handed the book written by the saint who was buried here. It was like mysteriously finding again a love letter that I had lost thirty years before. It was not the letter that was so precious to me but the One who sent it, the One who had been with me forever and was ever continuing to send His messages and the signs of His Presence, His boundless Love.

This was another sign that the circle was coming to completion. Subtly, in the midst of all the outer events, I was witnessing: the deepest supplications for divine knowledge, which had been made throughout my life, from the time when I first set out on the journey of the soul, were guiding me powerfully towards the Goal.

In the beginning, the One of Infinite Grace *called*, making me know that the purpose of my life was to journey in quest of His Truth. Now, as the veils were lifted, I was coming *home* to realize the beautiful completeness of the message He had been sending from beginning to end, and the end was, in fact, *endless*. Further, I bear witness, the power of what was coming was infinitely greater than anything I could have imagined or asked for.

The sense of the presence of the Beloved and the power of His Love, was very real as we stood in the library beneath the shrine of the great Sufi saint. I felt that, step-by-step, I was being drawn closer to the understanding of the divine plan for my life and the lives of others.

We called it a *journey of peace*, and truly this was the goal, but I realized as I traveled, that, to get closer to that goal, I had to wage a war (of clarity, wisdom, and inner strength) with those elements within me that were still *not* at peace, which truly had to be exposed and healed.

The journey was like a rite of passage. At every stage, in every country, I had to pass through some kind of deep illness, physical, emotional, and spiritual. As much as I was learning from our beautiful meetings with the people of the world, I was also being tested and purified.

This was often dramatically demonstrated. One day, for example, I was stricken with a fever and could not move for a few hours. When I got up and took my laptop out of its carrying case, I found that the screen was shattered. This reflected something that was shattered in myself. I had to accept all the pain and trauma I experienced, in order to finally release it, before I could be liberated from the circle of the life I knew to rise up to meet and embrace what was ultimately destined for me to realize on the journey to my Lord.

It was through accepting my own pain, limitation and joy that I could feel the pain, limitation, and joy of everyone that we met, and, through the power of humility, and submission, pray for the redemption, healing, and liberation of all. Every'child released from the terrible prison where she had lived beneath her mother's bed was myself. Every leper sitting upright in the courtyard with his brothers and sisters and accepting his destiny courageously and peacefully was a manifestation of myself.

The joy of every orphan finding a home and brothers and sisters to live and grow up with was my joy. Each of the young boys proud to have a bed roll and rice that he had cooked was also expressing the joy and gratitude I felt to have exactly what I had been given, that joy of having made it through so many challenges and difficulties, and still being alive to take the next step!

Deeply, I was experiencing those lives as my own, my life and love also mysteriously reflecting theirs. That was why we were drawn together and did not want to separate. These were the teachings I needed to learn on my journey toward peace, solidarity, and liberation.

This is, I believe, part of what Gautama Buddha learned when he left the opulent palace of his father, the king, and went into the streets of the world, to encounter and learn about the many dimensions of the suffering of the human condition. Traveling on the path, we experience that liberation and union with the ultimate Reality does not come without suffering.

From conscious suffering arises compassion, which leads to deep contemplation of the oneness and interconnectedness of all life, and this inspires the yearning to serve in the process of transformation and liberation. This is the understanding and energy that leads us to accomplish real change in ourselves, as well as in the conditions of the world around us. There is not one problem that we face that cannot ultimately become fuel in the process of personal and global transformation. Bu we must turn in the right direction to get the answer to all of our problems and the cure for all our diseases.

In order that we could learn more about this process, and participate more deeply in it, as the final step in our mission of peace, we went to Kashmir, there to unite with a community of people who had been gaining mastery, for so many years, in the art of responding to what is evil with what is better.

As I mentioned in the earlier chapter dedicated to these noble people, what amazed us most about them is that whatever hardship they had to endure, such as years of occupation, danger and oppression, their *zikr* (remembrance of God), their faith, illumined intelligence, and boundless generosity always seemed to increase, becoming deeper and stronger, no matter what adversity they had to face.

The believers are asked in the Qur'an if they think they will enter paradise without being tested as those before them were tested. Certainly the noble believers of Kashmir understand this *ayat* deeply. For so many years, they have been tested in so many ways.

And every time I return to their beautiful land, I find that they are more kind, generous, positive and faithful. I pray that all of the sincere people of this land (and all lands) be rewarded for their steadfast faith in Allah, which they have manifested under all conditions and that all their needs may be satisfied in a paradise much greater and more enduring than anything they may have lost.

Descending once again through the radiant skies and then the magnificent snow peaks crowning the Vale of Kashmir, my heart was deeply moved by all that I had experienced and all that I knew of this land and its people. I felt, certainly that I was coming home again to one of the places on earth that I love most and pray for most deeply.

We were welcomed, upon landing, with great love, sweetness, and, as usual, immense hospitality, by Yousuf and Nedeem Shah, my dear friends, who had been supplying me, for many years, with tapestries. From the moment that we arrived at the airport, we felt that our Kashmiri hosts rolled out a beautiful tapestry beneath our feet and it was that which we walked upon, throughout our stay in Kashmir. In truth, it was their love, generosity and respect unfolded before us, upon which we journeyed through their land.

The first day, they had arranged for us to stay in a rustic hotel overlooking Dal Lake, with rugs and tapestries everywhere, a very Kashmiri kind of lodge. This was the beginning of winter in Kashmir, very, very cold, and there was a metal drum filled with fire in the Sheikh's room, around which we sat through the night, singing a beautiful *zikr*. It was another ancient, eternal night in which the *zikr* sang itself and resonated throughout the universe.

The next day we were transported in small boats to an exquisite, hand-carved houseboat with beautiful stained-glass windows and handmade adornments of every kind, moored in the middle of the lake. There, encompassed by peace and beauty, we stayed for the rest of our visit. We would travel back and forth to land in small boats.

While on land, we went on a journey from mosque to mosque, the great mystic mosques of Kashmir, mosques high in the snow-covered mountains, majestic mosques on the lakes. I saw, experienced, and felt the way in which the Creator was being praised in this elevated land and understood that this deep worship and love of the Creator was what was giving these people the strength of spirit to respond to darkness with light.

Everywhere we went, we were connected, heartfully and soulfully, with the people. I longed to speak with them, to deeply support them, and to understand their real story.

Then Yousuf arranged a meeting at his house. He said he had only invited members of his family, but the large room where we all gathered was packed with extraordinary, venerable, light-filled people of all ages, from very young children to elders, all of whom were members of Yousuf Shah's family.

Sheikh Aly gave the last discourse I heard him deliver, and it brought his teachings for me to completion. He began by addressing the congregation, saying,

> *"It is a very great pleasure to be in Kashmir amongst you. We have been introduced to this part of the world only through the media and through books of geography. We have heard that the people here are fighting a war and we have heard about the actions of the gov-*

ernment of India. We knew that there were many Muslims living here. And even though we were not here, we were very moved because we knew that our Muslim brothers were here in this part of the world. And we felt concern about what was happening in this part of the world. We felt that your suffering was our suffering."

I appreciated this introduction very much. I realized again what I have experienced so many times in my journey—that what we hear or see in the media can never convey to us fully the reality of the lives of people. *The news is heartless.* Thousands of people in a region undergoing one kind of oppression or disaster or another, are dismissed in thirty seconds.

That is why it is a great blessing to travel, to live with people and see how they live and in what ways they are facing and surmounting their difficulties as well as begin to comprehend their pain and their struggle.

By coming to know the people of the world one by one, we realize the preciousness of every life, and then seek for any way that we can truly share with that living being. This is one way that the great disorder of the world can begin to be corrected. In regard to the sharing of knowledge, we had come to Kashmir on our journey of peace and liberation certainly as much to learn as to teach.

Then, Sheikh Aly spoke about Islam in the life of the Prophet (saw) and the journey of the Prophet (saw) from Mecca to Medina. The discourse was simple and direct, targeting the very essence of the point of spiritual transformation that I had been coming to understand with greater and greater certainty.

"When we reflect again upon the shahadah, the profession of faith, La ilaha ill'Allah, we see that it means that there is no god but God, no divinities but God. And we see that the struggle of Muhammad in Mecca was a confrontation between God and all the 'divinities,' a confrontation between the Creator of the universe and all the idols, the weaknesses, the vices that the people were attached to.

"We must not forget that the mission of the Prophet (saw) was to take the people from the darkness and lead them to the light. When we make the shahadah, we say that there is no god but God. The

*ilaha is not God, only God is eternal, everlasting. The entire mes-
sage of Islam is how to move from the ilaha to only God. And all of
the work that the Prophet did was to purify the Ka'bah of all the
idols within it, consecrating it to God, the One God. This was not
only the transformation of the Ka'bah. It was a complete transformation of the population.*

*"To leave Mecca also meant to leave the qualities of the Meccan
people. At this time, the Meccans did not believe in one God. The
values of the society were tribal values, racial values, cultural values,
values according to wealth. In that culture, according to these values, from the time of your birth, your destiny was fixed.*

*"But, in Medina, the Lord gave the Rasul (saw) a place to put
into practice that message that he was spreading. And, in this place
where he was spreading the message, he taught other human values.*

*"It is very important to see the way in which the Meccan people
accepted to leave Mecca and go to Medina. The Prophet showed
them the concept of freedom in the choice that they made to leave
Mecca and go to Medina.*

*"We have to make the choice to leave all the vices in our heart to
go to God. So, the message of God is, first of all, a message, which
gives us our freedom, a message, which liberates us.*

*"Thus, at every stage of our life, in every situation, God teaches
the meaning of taqwa, or God-consciousness. And, in this context,
we see the difference between the society of Mecca and the society of
Medina. The society in Mecca, with all the idols in the hearts of the
people and all their problems was the manifestation of la ilaha
(there is no god) and the society in Medina was the manifestation of
ill'Allah (except the One and Only God). So, we have to move from
one state to the other."*

Once again, the message was absolutely clear. We must move
from one state to the other, from worshipping and serving anything other than God to worshipping God Alone. Although the
Prophet Muhammad (saw), proposed this choice to all those
around him fourteen hundred years ago, as did all of the prophets
(as) before him, the Truth is eternal, and exactly the same choice
is being proposed to us today.

As all of the prophets (as) have told us, we cannot serve two
masters. We cannot serve that master to whom we have been

enslaved through all our attachments, accumulated sins, and illusions, and, at the same time serve the one and only God, our Liberator.

We must make the choice, make the total paradigm shift. We cannot serve our fear, pain, unworthiness, anger, arrogance, pride, desire, attachment to worldly wealth and power, and all the countless idols with which we have packed our inner Ka'bah, our innermost heart, and, at the same time, be free to worship our Lord, the Unique One, celebrate His Praise and enjoy His eternal peace with all our heart and soul. This was the choice put before me at this stage of my journey.

In reality, there was no choice, only the powerful imperative, "Surrender into the Bountiful Source! Let go of the past! Trust completely! Clear the Ka'bah, the heart, completely, so that it may be filled only with the Light, the Power, and the Grace of God!" This was the final message that Sheikh Aly, as my Sheikh, had to give me, before passing me on.

Having returned from Kashmir, we accompanied Sheikh Aly to the airport in New Delhi and watched him, smiling and waving, disappear into the crowd. I sensed at the time that I was truly waving goodbye. And although I have spoken to him a few times, I have not seen him again. Many useful and beautiful teachings, experiences, and understandings had been shared, and yet I had to continue to travel on. As he had indicated to me, walking into the unfoldment of my destiny, I was to rise to discover the next unfathomable dimension of the journey.

One week after I returned home from the trip to India, a few hours after we had honored, by reciting *Surah Ya Sin*, the passing of Kabeer's holy mother, Maimunna Ummah, who had left this world at age ninety-three, I was stricken with pain from one side to the other, pain, which did not cease, no matter which way I turned.

When an attack of such unabated intensity occurs, unlike anything you have ever felt before, you have no idea what is happening.

The experience goes beyond any point of reference that you have. I could not imagine what was happening or what to do about it.

My friend Sara standing next to my bed and tuning in to my condition, said, "You had better go to the hospital." My brain was not functioning enough to think of that. But I understood that what she said was right, and, with the help of the people in the house, made it to the Emergency Room.

There, I waited for, what seemed, an interminable time for a room. The intense pain did not at all abate until finally I was given a bed in a small room. It was only, when I lay down on the bed, that I was able truly to let go and let Allah and the doctors take over. From that moment on, the peace came and covered me like a blanket, and the pain was irrelevant.

At about three in the morning, after test results were back, I was diagnosed with acute appendicitis, which can be very serious, and even lethal, if it is not diagnosed and treated in time. By the grace and protection of Allah, the appendicitis did not become acute until I had returned home from the dangerously rough and rugged route, (we were often so many miles away from any hospitals or any health care systems that we could have known about) and I was now five minutes away from our local hospital. This acute condition was clearly the culmination of all that I had been suffering on the trip ripening into its full intensity here.

The appendicitis was diagnosed at three in the morning, and at the time of the *fajr* (early morning) prayer my appendix was removed through laproscopic surgery. I remained in the hospital for a few days more and then was released.

But I was not really well. Deeply something was not quite right. When I returned to the hospital to see the doctor for a check up, it seemed that not all the material had been removed, and a large abscess had formed. He ordered more tests, and the next day I was readmitted, urgently, to the hospital.

The second hospital stay was profound. Hooked up to tubes and subject to invasive procedures which occurred throughout the day and night, intravenously fed powerful antibiotics which had, for me, extreme side effects, with nurses and doctors passing through so quickly and impersonally, they barely had time to say hello, much less give a healing prayer or caress, I began to experience the painful plight of the many members of our human family: brothers and sisters, aunts, uncles, and children, everywhere, who are confined, as prisoners to hospital beds, from which, many of them may never again get up.

As much as I possibly could, I felt them and the very difficult life that they must endure, and as difficult as that was, I then began to sense the pain of those who could not even get to the hospitals to get help and were suffering in so many places and ways.

These people, too, are lives that are a part of this story.

All the people suffering in hospital beds, in their own beds, and in the streets, mountains, or valleys where they may lay, are a part of this story, because this is not only the story of one person's journey; it is interconnected with the journey of all creations in search of the meaning of existence and return to the Source.

And we cannot reach the goal without sacrifice, suffering, purification, transformation, and our inevitable meeting with death. I had spent only several difficult days in the hospital. What about the people who spend weeks and months, and even die in the hospital?

Most sincerely we pray that wherever our fellow beings are, they may receive comfort and solace in the presence of their Lord, the comfort of His presence in whatever difficulties they are facing, as at the time of the transition from this life, peace and salvation in His Eternal Existence in the life to come.

The room in which I stayed to receive this teaching in the hospital was two doors down from the hospice room, where our brothers and sisters are sent to die. It was not yet my time to go to that room, to make that journey yet.

But I had to come to this room two doors down to make a passage, profoundly to give up my life as I had known it.

As I left the hospital room and walked slowly out of the hospital, I had to consider deeply that I had been blessed to leave alive,
and with the gift of life, came the responsibility to fulfill this life's
potential, that potential that Allah created it to fulfill. Every step
and every breath remaining were, by His Grace, another chance to
gain and deepen knowledge of His Path, to serve and surrender
more deeply, to receive and surrender to true guidance, to send real
provision to the hereafter, and draw closer to the Goal.

22

In the Time Allotted Before, in the Blinking of an Eye, We Must Go. How Can We Reach the Goal?

– Out of the context of time and space –

To Allah we belong, and to Him is our return.

Baqara 2:156

Blessed is He in Whose hand is the Sovereignty, and, He is Able to do all things. Who hath created life and death that He may try you, which of you is best in conduct; and He is the Mighty, the Forgiving.

Mulk 67:1–2

I had been told that the circle of my life was complete and I was ready to rise to another real dimension in the journey to my Lord. Within a few weeks, I was in a hospital, connected to many tubes, two doors down from the room where terminal patients are sent to die. I had just returned from a mission of peace and solidarity in which I witnessed how noble and great are things that a human being, with the grace of God, has the capacity to do for others. I was experiencing, in difficulty and ease, the blessing in every step of the way. What was the message coming through all that was unfolding? And where was it leading?

As I walked slowly and tentatively out of the hospital room and down the long corridor, I knew that my life had been created, and also preserved, for a reason and a purpose.

A short while later, I was sent again to this hospital, this floor, this corridor, to the room two doors down, the hospice room, to recite *Surah Ya Sin* for a neighbor, who had just passed away.

By the Decree of Allah, her time in this world was up. She had not one more chance in this life, to say a prayer, think a noble thought or perform a loving deed; whatever of good and evil she was able to do in this life, the pen was lifted and the ink was dried.

But what about you and me, dear reader, and all the other beings who are still alive, still full of the potential, either to serve and worship the One Creator of all, or not? Consider the sacred opportunity that we have!

In the precious time remaining, what are we going to do? This is the great challenge posed to all the children of Adam (as). We are told that, on the Last Day when we are standing in judgment in the presence of our Lord, *every atom's weight of good will be seen, and every atom's weight of evil.*

We do not seem to realize the importance of what we are doing here, what choice, what challenge is being presented to us, every moment of our lives. If we did realize the ultimate importance, repercussion and result of every action, would we not want to make each action—and, as well, the thought and intention that lead to the action—really good? It would be very helpful to us now and in the future if we could consider deeply while we have the chance to improve: How can we become truly good, so that our scale, in judgment, will be heavy on the side of the good actions?

In the course of coming to understand what causes us to incline to goodness, we must also understand what could make us incline toward evil. And so let us consider what our Creator tells us about the contrasting dimensions of our human condition:

In the Holy Qur'an, Allah tells us:

> *Truly We created humankind (insan) in the most exalted form and then brought the human being down to the state of the lowest of the low.*
>
> Tin 95:4–5

Knowing that the time is limited in which we have to learn our deepest lessons here, let us contemplate these words of our Creator, seeking to understand what exalted form we were created in, and how we then descended to such a low state. Through understanding the way in which we were brought down, we can also understand the way in which we can rise, to attain the exalted station that He intended for us when He created us.

Having fallen through ignorance, and disobedience to the Divine Guidance, from the original state of grace, may we rise by means of divinely inspired knowledge and obedience.

With direction from the One who is the Knower of all, may we come to understand from what world we descended, to what world we came, and discover how, with His Mercy and clear Guidance we may rise in returning to our exalted Source.

One descent we made is to the earth itself, this world (*dunya*) of material, emotional, and mental density.

Before we came to incarnate in this dense world, we had existed in the world of souls, in realms of light, in proximity to and in remembrance of our Lord.

According to the words of the Holy Qur'an and hadith, in pre-existence, before we came into this world, there was a great assembly of the souls, gathered in the presence of God, and this assembly was addressed by Allah, *subhana wa ta'ala*, who said, "*Alastu bi Rabbikum?* Am I not your Lord?" In response to this, the souls expressed their recognition of the Sovereignty and Divinity of the Lord, pledging fidelity to Him alone.

Some of the souls, we have been told, made this response of affirmation more quickly and some took more time to affirm: "Yes, You are our Lord!" In accordance with the speed and certainty with which we responded to the question addressed to us by our Lord in *alam'ul arwah*, the world of souls, we came into this world with greater or lesser certainty about this knowledge and the affirmation of it.

We did not want to leave that world and come here, but we were told that we had to come here to learn certain lessons and, eventually be given an examination. The results we received in that examination would determine exactly where we would go from here, for, indeed, this world, itself, is a temporary stop on the journey to our Lord.

After we have been in this world for a while and become implanted or entrenched in this dense realm, we may or may not have any recollection of where we were before we came here.

To have forgotten this:

Where we came from, who we really are, and why we have really come to this world, is a cause of great confusion and suffering for us, wasted time, and misdirected thought and action. May we come to realize the truth before, suddenly, it is time to leave this world, and we have not accomplished the purpose for which we came here.

As a small child growing up in my mother's house, like many young children, I had the awareness of the other world, the other realm, and it was an extremely different reality than the world into which I had incarnated. This is why I wondered what I was doing here and felt deeply nostalgic, yearning for knowledge about the world from which I had come, and the mysteries of the Divine Source, which no one around me had the slightest knowledge about.

On the contrary, life here was organized on entirely different principles. The things that were being discussed and sought after were very different than the things that my soul yearned to know.

The questions I had, about the origin and end and real meaning of existence, could only be answered by one who had knowledge of these deep matters, and that was something that I would have to search for and find. The profound inner longing to make the journey in search of real knowledge was already activated within me as a child, so even at the age of twelve I received the mandate, written on a scroll: *"Seek, and the truth shall make you free."*

What does this mean? To "seek to be free" indicates clearly that we are in a prison from which we seek to be liberated. What is the nature of the prison in which we are apparently entrapped?

As we have all been encountering, consciously or unconsciously, throughout our journey through this life, it is a psychological prison that was constructed, layer by layer, veil by veil, from the time that we arrived on this earth and had to deal with the various trials appearing in the life of this world.

And the very unique challenges that we each face present us with the deepest, most difficult obstacles that we have to overcome, in order, ultimately to pass the test presented to us by the Divine Examiner, realizing the purpose for which we were created, the mission that we have to fulfill.

By facing these specific difficulties and challenges, we hopefully gain the discernment to know what is right from what is wrong, and develop the strength of character: faith, determination, and certitude, and also the tools that we need to transform darkness into light, ignorance into true knowledge.

We each have the capacity, or potential, to alchemically transform everything that is dark and heavy in our lives into gold, that is, into light. But we can do this, only with the grace of God, the power of God, and the guidance of a true Master, who is totally surrendered in the service of God and authorized to transmit the knowledge of Allah and of the journey that leads to Him.

As I did, many of us had a recollection of the beauty and light of the vast realm from which we had come, and in contrast to this was the tiny table at which I was now sitting, so small that even I, alone, did not fit.

I felt that my clothes were too small. They could in no way fit the vastness of the soul I sensed within. The part that I seemed to have to play, a part that, step by step, was formed by the accumulating veils, was an identity that was hiding the light of the soul, its origin, and its destination.

And thus, by the contrast of the identity I was assuming in the world and the truth of who I really was, a fundamental conflict emerged, and, in response to that conflict, a structure of limitations, composed of accumulated veils, was created, in which I became somehow imprisoned.

I speak to you, o heart and soul of the reader. Whatever prison, you and I may have consciously or unconsciously constructed around ourselves, reacting as we did to the sometimes stressful, hurtful, and

challenging circumstances of our unfolding life, that artificial structure is hiding from ourselves, the light of our true nature, that nature
which is inherently inclined to lovingly serve our Beloved Lord.

Let us make the intention, to find true guidance, exchange
falsehood for Truth, and thus find the way to deconstruct the prison walls, so, without a door or lock and key, we can dispel the illusions and be free, to become who we truly are—who the Creator
Most Merciful intended us to be.

For this we need tools, we need the blessing and the guidance
of the One who created us in the most exalted form. We need to ask,
to beseech Him that we may learn: What was the Divine Intention
when He created us, and how can His intention be fulfilled in us?

To come to know ourselves, so that we may know Him, is a
course of mysteries and challenges. It is a process of deeper and
deeper unveiling. One by one, each of the illusory identities that
we have acquired must be discarded, that is, recognized, as unreal.
To do this, we need to know the difference between what is unreal and what is real.

The statement in Arabic, which is witnessed—that is experienced—as the first pillar in Islam (*La illaha ill'Allah, Muhammmad
ar-Rasulillah*), if we understand its true meaning, will be our greatest aid. This statement bears witness that there is no reality other
than the Reality that is God (the One Creator of all) and that
Muhammad (saw) is the Messenger of Allah: the last of all the
prophets and messengers (as) who came before him.

This is the most powerful tool that we have been given by the
One who created us in the most exalted form. This realization is
the holy fire and the light for the alchemy of our transformation.
We must realize that nothing exists that nothing *truly* exists other
than the reality that is God. The true reality, the true nature of our
being is His treasure that He placed within us through which He
desired to be known.

> "I was a Hidden Treasure and loved to be known. Therefore I cre-
> ated the creation that I might be known."

Then what are these other multiple realities to which we have become attached and with which we have become identified—the fearful, depressed, ailing, arrogant, rebellious, jealous, lustful, angry, unbelieving aspects of the self which is inherently false, that is, illusory? These are the aspects of ourselves which, veiling the light of the Reality within us, need to become transparent, must be transformed. But how?

On the path of *Tasawwuf*, we learn of the stations of the self, heart, and soul, through which the seeker must pass on the journey of ultimate transformation.

All of these complex aspects of our being, which have been thriving on unrest, separate from the Source of Peace, are guided station by station to the Source of Peace and the other Divine Attributes. This is a deep spiritual science which is understood and can be implemented only by a true Sheikh.

Like this, is the journey of the seeker for the Divine Qualities guided by the Divine Guide, with the direction of the authorized teacher (Sheikh) until the *nafs* (self, soul) is totally surrendered, purified, and transformed.

This journey leads the nafs (self) finally to the stations of *nafs ul mutmainnah*, the soul at peace, *nafs- ur-radiah* (the content soul) *nafs'ul mardiah*, (the satisfied soul) and *nafs al kamil*, (the perfected soul). Such are the places, the stations, the realms that we pass through, with the Grace of God and the guidance of the Sheikh on the journey to our Lord.

It is when the transformation is complete, when the *nafs* (the self which is now at the level of the soul) has reached this station of true peace that it is invited by the Creator to enter the garden.

O Soul at Peace
Return to your Lord
Pleased and well-pleasing
Enter the ranks of My worshippers—
Enter the garden.

The Holy Qur'an 89:27–30

To even hear these words and imagine our Lord speaking them to the soul within us is amazing, inspiring of hope. But how, in truth, can we attain that eternal station of peace?

In this and many other passages in the Holy Qur'an, our Creator, Most Merciful, invites us to enter the garden.

> *And vie with one another to attain to your Sustainer's forgiveness and to a paradise as vast as the heavens and the earth, which has been readied for the God-conscious who spend [in His way] in time of plenty and in time of hardship, and hold in check their anger, and pardon their fellow men because God loves the doers of good; and who, when they have committed a shameful deed or have [otherwise] sinned against themselves, remember God and pray that their sins be forgiven—for who but God could forgive sins? And do not knowingly persist in doing whatever [wrong] they may have done. These it is who shall have as their reward forgiveness from their Sustainer, and gardens through which running waters flow, therein to abide: and how excellent a reward for those who labor!*

The Holy Qur'an 3:133–136

To become the truly righteous, those who are God-conscious (*muttaqun*), those who continuously forgive and seek forgiveness, and who are continuously giving of the bounties they have received— to become those who are thus invited to enter and dwell in the gardens of nearness to their Lord—we must understand how our original parents, Adam and Eve (as), fell from that state of grace.

Whatever caused them to fall from the state of paradisial innocence and purity, is exactly the same force that is dedicated to making us descend over and over again. Our Lord tells us again and again that Satan is our avowed enemy. And, we are told, we have no enemy but that primordial enemy who caused our parents to go astray.

In Surat'ul A'raf, Allah warns us:

> *O Children of Adam, do not let Satan seduce you, as he caused your parents to depart from the garden stripped of their garments exposed to their shame. Surely he sees you—he and his folk—from a place where you cannot see him. Surely We have made the evil ones to be allies of those who do not believe.*

The Holy Qur'an 7:27

The qualities and aspects of ourselves—those false identities to which we have become attached that cause us to surrender ourselves to anything other than the light and grace of God's Qualities—are, it would seem, allies of Satan and his folk. And they are waiting in ambush to catch us in their entrapments, as we are traveling on the journey, and deter us from our noble Goal.

This is what the *seducer* would have them do. For Satan has said, as the Qur'an tells us:

> *"Now that You have caused me to err, I shall lie in ambush for them along Your Straight Path. Then I shall fall upon them from before them and behind them and upon their right and upon their left. And You will not find most of them to be grateful."*
>
> The Holy Qur'an 7:16–17

Understanding the forces and tendencies within ourselves, which, allied with Satan, are lying in wait to ambush us, and learning how not to be entrapped by them, is an essential part of our therapy and cure.

We each have to fight the Great War (*Jihad al Akbar*) within ourselves against everything within us, which turns us away from the Divine Reality, which is our Source and End.

The inner war was called *Jihad al Akbar* by the Holy Prophet (saw), when he returned with his Companions (ra) from fighting a battle, at which time he told them that it was time to fight the greater war, *the war within*. From this we learn about the intensity and importance of the war that we have to fight within ourselves.

But how do we fight this war—not with guns and bombs, not with hatred and aggression. We need the Grace of God, skill, and subtle wisdom to see through, and thus overcome the ruses and tricks of the *tempter*, the *seducer*, the one who is our only enemy, no matter what form he is hiding behind.

The arrogance, unworthiness, fear, jealousy, sadness, anger, desire, pain, and so many other states of being we have become subconsciously identified with, are *fronts* behind which that force is operating, whose express purpose is to undermine our commitment to reach the Goal. We need to become aware of this, as we are engaged, moment-to-moment, in this battle against illusions within ourselves.

This war is fought with understanding, with love and forgiveness. It is a war of awakening and transformation (not of destruction) in which darkness is dispelled by light, and fear and hatred are dispelled by knowledge and love.

No doubt, every one of us who came from the vast pure realm of God's Presence into this world of limitation and testing has suffered different kinds of wounds. From the first days of our life here - especially in worlds where, often, money, power, sex, egotism, and brutal warfare are worshipped and pursued with much greater determination than the path of the True God - we began, in these early years, to hear words that were not true and suffer their impact upon us.

Can we begin to remember the moments in our childhood when falsehood, fear, and unworthiness were first injected into our hearts, pulling us away from the state of purity, trust, and submission that we had experienced as babies? Can we remember the shock of that encounter and the way that poison entered into our bloodstream?

That pain and fear and confusion which began to flow in our blood in our earliest years, may continue to subtly corrupt and undermine our awareness throughout our life, until, God willing, with the power of faith in the Truth and surrender to the Truth, with real spiritual guidance, we can truly dispel those subconscious tendencies which make us doubt ourselves, our Divine Source, and the sanctity of our existence.

We need to access and retrieve the state of grace we originally had, to find and reconnect with the purity of the inner child intact, the *believing soul*, somewhere living within ourselves. And, then we may be able to clearly see how that purity and fundamental trust became covered up, and almost completely hidden from view.

In Arabic, the word for covering up is *kufr*. Allah tells us that this is one of the most serious diseases in the heart of man. What, then, is humankind covering up? This word is most often used to describe the way in which so much of humanity has rejected and denied the message sent by God through His messengers (as) to illuminate and awaken the people. And what a great loss it has been for humankind to reject the great gift from God, and cover up the light of revelation with the darkness of ignorance!

But, the light, the reality, and message of Allah have also been placed within our hearts. The human heart, as it was created, by the Lord Most Merciful has a vast capacity. The words of Allah tell us: *"The heavens and the earth do not contain Me, but the heart of My faithful believer contains Me."*

Our Creator, in the very act of creating us, has placed within us, within this heart, Himself, His light, His treasure that He wished to be known. It is this light, this Divine Reality within us that becomes covered up in the course of our interactions in the world, until we may not even know that it is there!

As we faced, one by one, the challenges of becoming conditioned to life in this world, reacting to the shock of one after another, *perceived* attack, we built layers of protection over our heart to defend and protect it. And thus was the essential purity and trust in our hearts, veil by veil, covered up.

Allowing ourselves, to feel, again, the heart of that open child, we may be able to remember how, where, and when that child, the believing soul, withdrew and went into hiding and then, denial.

Now, as we are reviewing this material (our life story) we have the choice to make the paradigm shift. And we must do this if we want to be truly free.

Imagine if we could see goodness in the place of evil, truth in the place of falsehood, if we could see, with wisdom, the circumstances of the people who seemed to oppress us and forgive them, forgive ourselves, and become free of the endless cycle of aggression and oppression, moving from the world and paradigm of darkness into the world of light. That is how the therapy works.

When we become aware of the love and grace of our Creator that brought us into existence, this is the medicine that can heal whatever wounds we seem to have suffered in this temporary world that we have come to in order to be tested, purified, and transformed.

We need to see, with wisdom, that our Creator, who is the Best of Planners, determined that we should be born in such and such a place, with exactly the parents that we had. This was not an accident, but part of a plan.

All of the details—where we were born, under what circumstances, through what parents, where we grew up, what inspirations arose within our souls—all of these things are messages to us from our Lord, messages ultimately leading back to the One who created us, messages that we need to accept and come to understand.

There is a much greater plan at work, a much greater dimension to the story of our life than we can see, and that is why we need to access and imbibe the medicine (*Ash-Shifa'a*) of Allah's light and grace and mercy to penetrate the veils, showing us the way to heal our deep karmic illnesses.

Inspired and guided by this light of grace, wishing truly to understand and forgive, in the process of seeking the truth that would make me free, invoking the mercy and guidance of the One who had truly given me life, my real Sustainer and Nourisher, I turned with compassion toward my mother.

When I say that the table in my mother's house was so small that I felt that I couldn't fit, this means that I felt that somehow it seemed that there was no place for me in her world. My thoughts, understandings, feelings, and longings were not understood or valued by her in the context of *her world-view*.

This was the source of my tendency to feel that somehow I was *unworthy*. It is not that the worthiness wasn't there; it is only that she couldn't perceive it. Living within the world that she did, constrained as she was by her level of understanding, she simply could not see these things.

As an essential part of the healing, the forgiving and understanding, I realized, how important it was for me to thus see with the eyes of wisdom, love, and compassion, simply that she did not have the benefit of seeing all that I saw. She did not have access to the knowledge which, throughout my life was being revealed to me, and that is why she did not understand or appreciate who I was. Such was the nature and size of the limited table she set in her house, the limited state of her awareness and understanding.

My father and Sophie had a table that was very big, and usually surrounded by guests from everywhere. I felt very comfortable there, knowing that anyone might come to the door from anywhere, and they would be welcomed, just as I was, free to express my unfolding being. That was an expanded space, in which I was able to grow in the formative years.

So, this was a dynamic contrast, which formed me. These expanding and contracting influences created a dynamic tension; all of these forces were necessary to keep pushing the baby, the awakening soul, through the birth canal. And there would be no birth or movement without all of these energies and forces being activated.

There was also another table of which I was aware and from which I received the greatest nourishment, and that was an *unseen* table, the table of *divine provision*. It was at such a table, that Mary (Maryam, ra) was eating every time the Prophet Zacharaiah (as) came into the temple to bring her food.

And it is this continuous source of provision and love coming from the Source, that is, by far, the most powerful element in every stage of the healing and spiritual transformation. Therefore, at whatever table I am sitting, I am certain that the real provision is always coming only from Him, our sole Sustainer.

All of these dimensions of the *table* were significant in the forming of my character and the challenges I had to overcome. Since all of the elements are necessary and useful in one way or another, we must be truly grateful for each and every gift we are given on the path that leads us toward union with our Lord. By being truly grateful for everything that has been given to us, we defy Satan who said: *"And most of them are not grateful."*

Finally I saw, at the end of my mother's life, how the therapy was working. This was revealed in a very graphic way when I went to visit her in the last few weeks of her life. I had been told that she was very weak and could barely move. When I entered her apartment, she sat up, bolt upright, blazing with life.

She said, "I have been waiting for you! Where have you been?" She then spoke to me, it seemed, for twenty-four hours straight. She spoke to me only when no one else was in the room and was a completely different person when anyone else was around.

To others she may have appeared to be intolerant, cantankerous, impatient, and extremely paranoid. But then, when they left, she became like a rapturous radiant young girl, joyful, poetic, full of love, and very humorous.

There were certain things that she had to tell me and could not leave the world without, somehow, passing on to me. She said, "I have thought a lot about it and I have decided that *you* are the one that can carry on the work!"

I truly did not know what work she thought that was, that is what work she had been doing that was most important to her, which she wanted to pass on to *me*. Only as I am writing this now, do I begin to sense what she wanted to pass on to me. And that was love.

She had not discovered the love of God. We had several talks about this and it was something we could never agree upon, since it was an awareness that I had come into this world with, and one, which, until the end, did not apparently dawn within her.

And yet, she was impelled to transmit to me the legacy that she had for me. All that she could wish for me was the best of what she had, herself, experienced deeply. What she had experienced, which had the greatest meaning for her, was the love of her husband. This was the highly cherished treasure of her life, the greatest thing that she knew. And that, I believe, is what she wished to give me and what she wished me to carry on. (I did accept to carry on the *legacy of love*, but not in a way that she could have imagined or fathomed.)

Sitting on the television near her was a photograph of herself and Kenny, her husband, gazing at each other, smiling, with intense adoration. On the wall of her room that she was facing were beautiful photographs of my brothers and a painting of me, painted when I was about ten years old.

It was a very pensive portrait, which, I thought, looked thoughtful and somewhat sad. She looked at the painting and then looked at me, sitting close to her bed, and seemed astonished. "Who is this beautiful woman?" she asked. The pensive child had grown into another being, nourished by the love and guidance, the beautiful, all-merciful parenting of God, and this she clearly perceived in our last meeting.

This was the first time that I felt she truly saw me, that is, saw the essence of the divine beauty within me. And this moment, between us, was the moment of liberation. She said, "I have lived my life and it is complete. Now live yours! Do not make a memorial for me. Live your life completely! That will be your memorial to me."

I have no doubt that this is what she wanted: that I should live my life to its completeness. The significance and impact of her words—her intention for me, and the fulfillment of my life, went far beyond her comprehension.

From the beginning of my life to the end of hers, she wished for me and willed for me the gift of freedom to find the truth for myself, and the gift of courage to live by the truth I had discovered to the point of completion. In accordance with the true intention she held for me, I pray that all the blessings which have descended and will descend upon me in this quest for truth and completion, aid her and my father in their journeys in the next world.

As much of a blessing as it was to be seen, even a little by my mother as she was preparing to leave this world, her inability to see this until that time was also a gift to me, one of the most potent catalysts to my journey and growth.

Although the gift of freedom was given, the love that I yearned for so deeply from my mother was not given freely and easily. If it was, I may have been inclined to stay at home and take refuge in my mother's loving arms, in the loving warmth of her abode.

But the love that I truly sought could only be found through leaving my mother's home, and searching profoundly, sacrificing myself, again and again to gain it, stage after stage, in many places and many ways.

On the journey of the soul to attain its liberation, nothing occurs without sacrifice. At every stage of the way, we have to give up life as we knew it, to discover the wealth of treasure, the wealth of understanding that lies behind every closed door waiting to be opened.

When we begin to perceive the dynamism and inclusiveness of the path of self-realization, we see that everything, if we allow it to be, will be catalytic to our growth, and therefore, without any regret or dissatisfaction, we must thank our Lord, Most Generous, the only true Giver of all, for all that He has given to us to know and experience on the path, which is our life.

Because I could not find everything I was seeking at home, I found my home everywhere in the vast universe, and found that vast universe within myself.

From the moment that I was released from my mother's hold, released subconsciously by her, from her jurisdiction, I was the leaf carried by the wind of the Divine Will. Whether or not she could accept the "concept" of the Divine, from the time that I was very young, she had released me into the jurisdiction of the *Divine Hand*, by which I was guided for the rest of my life.

As I came to see and register the immensity of what I saw, I sent my parents parchment scrolls with burnt edges, upon which I had etched out ecstatic messages from all corners of the globe. One day, a large bagful of these messages that I had sent to my parents throughout the years came back to me. I poured them out of the bag and saw the mass of energy inscribed upon those pages.

I wondered if they had ever been read, and what my parents could possibly have thought about these strange messages if they had read them. I was like an explorer who, in traveling, had discovered *an entirely new world*.

It was only in the final moments with my parents that I felt that they may have begun to see what I had been seeing, in me, this moment with my mother in which, in her last request she bequeathed to me love, and a life fully lived, and, another very beautiful moment that I was blessed to share with my father.

Several years before he left this world, my father, Lennie, suffered a stroke while driving a car. Thus began the last phase of his life on earth. From that time on, he suffered a number of debilitating illnesses, until, at last, he was bedridden permanently.

At a certain point in this progression, he expressed a strong desire to go the *mazhar*, the shrine of Bawa Muhaiyaddeen (ra). Although he was ill and it was difficult to travel, he made it to Philadelphia, traveling with Sophie, and we all went to the *mazhar*. It was a beautiful sunny day. Lennie laid down on the ground in front of the *mazhar*, and went to sleep for quite awhile. When he woke up, he said that he had a wonderful rest, and seven years had been added on to his life.

The last seven years of Lennie's life were, in truth, a testament to love. During these last years, when Lennie could no longer get out of bed or even sit up by himself, Sophie took care of him with great love, peace, and happiness.

And this love, which she continuously manifested, this love, which always existed between them, was a legacy for me and for all who witnessed it. When he was no longer able to say anything else, still he could say, "I love you." I felt that this was a period in his life in which he was surrounded by peace and able to resolve within himself many things, even though he could not tell us about it.

Almost the last thing he did tell me, while he could speak, was a description of very deep dream. I had been sitting at his bedside reciting *Surah Ya Sin*, (the *surat* referred to as the *heart* of the Qur'an) which I had the blessing of reciting many, many times for him. After reciting the *surat*, I left the room. Several minutes later, I was called back in to the room by someone taking care of Lennie at that time, who said that Lennie had a dream that he wanted to tell me about.

Lennie told me that he dreamt that he was in heaven. First, he said, he was doing penance for things he had done in his life that were not clear.

Then, he said, there was a huge feast being served with delicious foods of all kinds. He told me that it was very, very beauti ful there. Also he saw many books there, written in many languages, and he could read them all. Those were the last words that my father really spoke to me.

It was wonderful for me to contemplate that my father, who introduced me to the outspread table, might be served a beautiful feast in paradise and also, that he might be nourished by the feast of divine knowledge there.

Now, both of my parents and several of my teachers and friends had left this world. And I knew that it was time for me, still living on earth, to take the baton, run the marathon, and, with the grace of God, fulfill whatever legacies had been bequeathed to me. I was in my late fifties, still truly a child at heart, but aware, intensely, of the passage of time, knowing that just as their time on earth had come to an end, so would mine.

> *By the time*
> *Surely man is in loss*
> *Except for those who have faith*
> *And do righteous deeds*
> *And encourage each other towards truth*
> *And encourage each other towards patience.*
>
> The Holy Qur'an 103:1–3

This time we have left on earth, in which to fulfill the purpose for which we were created and sent here, is profoundly precious. May we realize the importance of every moment and treat it with respect. Every remaining moment is the opportunity to serve our Lord with deeper and deeper sincerity. May that faith to which He is referring be awakened and established deeply within our hearts, and may that divinely inspired faith express itself in truly righteous deeds.

We are also instructed in this short, but immensely important message about the passage of time that we must encourage in each other truth and patience. In order not to be in a state of loss, as the time is passing by, we must encourage ourselves, and, one another, to drink, to imbibe knowledge from the wellspring of

Divine Truth and develop patience, steadfastness, and contentment with whatever the Divine decrees.

It is true patience and acceptance of the Divine Decree that dispels the anxiety which makes us feel, often even with desperation, that we are responsible to make things happen in the way that we think is best. Inevitably we will fail to achieve anything when driven by the anxiety born of lack of faith in what God wills.

Instead, we need to access the Truth and accept its decree in every situation in which we find ourselves. To have this deeply focused awareness and acceptance of the Divine Principle as it is manifesting in our life is the way in which we can avoid wasting or losing our time, but will, instead, find ourselves traveling, moment to moment, in the journey of ever greater nearness to our Lord.

We have no idea which moment of our life will be our last. So, let us make the maximum effort to use however many breaths remain, in the most beneficial and fruitful way, the way that is most pleasing to our Creator and most beneficial to His creation.

In order for us to gain understanding of the human condition and our life in the universe, the Qur'an tells us to travel the world and behold what has become of those who reject the truth. As powerful and indomitable as a civilization or a person may have appeared to be in the height of glory, we can see what has become of them all. Behold the ruins! Contemplate the graves! Surely nothing created lasts forever, and that *blast*, which transforms everything, comes in an instant without warning.

> *All it will take is one blast whereupon they are summoned before us.*
> The Holy Qur'an 36:53

I remember, as a child in school hearing about the destruction of Pompeii. I saw a picture of a stone table with dishes on it, on which the people had laid out their meal, not knowing that Mount Vesuvius would erupt the next moment, and their whole world would be destroyed, before they could eat the meal they had just prepared.

What we see on the news every day makes us know that the startling tale of the destruction of Pompeii is not only a legend of the past. Wherever we look in the contemporary world, we can see the signs, the proofs, that life on earth is impermanent and subject to destruction. Many of us, across the country and the world, witnessed the news that a huge apparently well-constructed bridge, without warning, crumbled into pieces. What does this tell us about the rest of the seemingly dependable infrastructure that we rely upon?

Just as I was in the process of completing this chapter, I saw, on the news, that Southern California, the land of my birth, was being consumed by fire. Fires, we could clearly see, were burning totally out of control throughout the land. So many beautiful homes, which had taken so much time and money and effort to build, were destroyed, one after the next, on a single day. Tragedy that this was, with so many people suffering the consequences of this disaster, what is this telling us?

And then we saw the floods once again sweeping across the landscape of Bangladesh, testing, again, the forbearance of these long-suffering people.

Now, as I continue to write, we behold profound difficulties striking the land and people of Burma.

We have also witnessed, in our very lifetime, man-made disasters, which stagger the human imagination, break the human heart, and stun the soul. In Darfour, Rwanda, Kenya, Somalia, Uganda, Tibet, Iraq, Afghanistan, Pakistan, and in many other lands, as in the streets of most American inner cities, we behold the great suffering, which has arisen as a result of untold abuses in a very uncivilized world, "civilizations" gone radically astray. Certainly we see in all of these situations the signs that man is, indeed, in a state of loss.

Witnessing all of this, we are led to deeply inquire: What is the underlying message of these cataclysmic events? And how, as we witness tragic merciless acts, taking place throughout the world, can we be amongst those who, accessing the Source of mercy, become conduits of that mercy and healing? We need to see, behind all these phenomena, signs from the Unseen and learn to see all that is unfolding with wisdom from the Divine.

Then, as we behold daily the continuous series of natural and man-made disasters, when we look with wisdom, we can see without doubt that there is nothing we can truly count on in this impermanent world. This is a very important concept to grasp.

The ephemeral world is, as we gaze upon it, crumbling, dissolving, and burning before our eyes. This perception, itself, is an invitation, a call to awakening. The signs of destruction manifesting all around us are messages urgently directing us to turn towards the Eternal.

> *All that is on earth will perish. But will abide (for ever) the Face of thy Lord, full of Majesty, Bounty and Honor.*
>
> The Holy Qur'an 55:26–27

The question is *how* do we shift our consciousness from identifying with the perishable to identifying with the Eternal?

As we behold that, in fact, the world is, in one place or another, breaking apart before our eyes, how do we detach from the destructible world and unite with the Eternal Source, That which never dies?

How, in the time allotted, can we make this shift of awareness? How can we detach from the perceptions and concepts promoted in this world and affirm our fidelity to the original covenant we made with our Lord? How can we—each and every one of us—find out what we came here to do, what assignments we have to fulfill, and then proceed to accomplish these tasks?

My journey through ten thousand veils was one in search of the answers to these fundamental questions. I came to see that, in the middle of the apparent chaos of the breakdown of this world, there is a way that leads to eternal peace. Our Beloved Lord, who created us out of His Love and His Mercy, has sent us with instructions, things to do and not to do.

We need to read that *manual*, understand these instructions, and follow these directives, so that we may come to know the One who sent them and live our lives in harmony with His will and in accomplishment of His will. This, in truth, is our way out of the conflict, crisis, and destruction that we see critically imperiling the world in which we are living, albeit temporarily.

Following the way that leads us to eternal peace, in Islam, there are steps prescribed, which guide us to levels of deepening understanding and experience. Based upon the principles clearly stated by the Creator in the divine message sent down, they are guidelines, which lead us on the path of self-transformation and realization and thus help us to solve the mystery of what we are doing here, before, in the blinking of an eye, it is time to leave.

The state of *islam* is the state of surrender, submission to the Divine Will. It is not a *religion* sent, for example to the Arab people; it is a state in which each one of us created by His merciful intention, comes to realize the Infinite Greatness and Sovereignty of the One who created us, and we surrender to Him in accordance with the guidance and the signs He has revealed, and is revealing to us. It is a structure built upon five pillars, each of which is a dimension of the practice of worship, realization, and charity enjoined upon us by our Creator, so that we may live a balanced, loving, and fruitful life.

The state of *iman* is a state of deep knowledge and faith. We come to see, with this resplendent inner knowledge, and experience the meaning, the inner life, of the commitment we have made. It is the inner state not only of faith, but of determination and certitude. We experience with certainty that we have chosen to affirm the best, what is most real and eternal in existence.

When we have attained this state, our faith is secure and we cannot turn back to faithlessness. This is something we come to know for ourselves, which greatly blesses and inspires our life and our journey.

But the knowledge and inspiration, which have come to us and are established in our heart must manifest in our actions. The state of *ihsan*, which comes from the word which means beauty, goodness, and perfection, is a state in which we manifest, through clear and consecrated action, the knowledge and faith that we have come to realize as travelers on God's path.

The state of *ihsan,* manifested as the path of *Tasawwuf,* the true Sufi path, is not simply the perfection of deeds; our actions will not be pure if our consciousness, feelings, thoughts and intentions are not pure.

And for the purification of all the dimensions of our being (*attaskiat'un-nafs*), for the profound inner journey of the unveiling of the heart and soul, we need, according to the path of *Tasawwuf,* the direction of the spiritual Guide, one who has attained the perfection of the state of *ihsan* and can clearly lead others, also, to the completion of the way.

I had, by the Grace of Allah, been blessed to set foot on the path and travel upon it, guided by blessed teachers, for many miles, and yet, I knew deeply, I was still in process, had not attained the goal, and more steps on the journey of the ultimate transformation were still ahead.

Having experienced the passage of my parents in a state of peace, my therapy was moving along. But, the essential question was burning, time was passing, and I was still not correctly aligned to be a representative of God in my designated place.

Both of my parents and all of my teachers had left me with a legacy of love, but how was I to fulfill it? And far greater than this was the legacy of love given to me and to all of us by our Creator when He created us. How was this potential to be fulfilled?

There was a key, essential element necessary for the fulfillment of my journey, which had not yet been revealed and manifested, my ultimate mirror and Guide to the inner realms.

I had seen, in a dream, that a man of light was approaching me. He was immense and powerful, liberated, bounding with energy, with black yet luminous skin and green light pouring through his eyes. He was altogether emanating light. He was eternally young and immensely creative.

He placed in my hands a book composed of three-dimensional visions, the history of all of existence. Then he said, "I am the one who has known you forever and loved you forever." And he embraced me completely, such that I dissolved completely in that embrace.

In the next part of the dream, I saw that shops had been created all around the world, the size and visibility of convenience stores, where people came, to be spiritually guided, inspired, and regenerated..... totally transformed. In reality, they were places of prayer and training. Written upon each of these way stations, were the words, written in multicolored flowers: "*ACT NOW!*"

This dream of the *man of light,* kept me going through all the years, all the mountains and valleys of intense, arduous travel. By visions like this, I was sustained through so many years of solitude, nourished by light and hope and faith in the ultimate fulfillment.

But now, as the second half of the dream indicated, was the time for real action, action that was the manifestation of that divine love, the time for bearing the fruit of the blessed tree.

The dream was significant both as a sustenance and encouragement to the heart and soul, revealing that, no matter what we have to go through, we will, God willing, reach the Goal, be embraced by the Beloved, dissolve in that embrace, and then become the manifestation in action of that love.

The being in the dream was not a human being but a *light being* coming to me with love from the Beloved Lord. It was an ocean of eternal love and knowledge that embraced the soul, the light within me, and in that meeting, that merger, *I was dissolved.*

In the Arabic language, this state or station is called *fana,* the annihilation, of the limited being. The drop dissolves in the Ocean. Only if our individual beings are dissolved in the vast Ocean of Divine Love, will we be able to assume our true responsibility on this earth, to transform both ourselves, and others, until we become purified and true servants, acting in every moment for the sake of the One Alone who is worthy of praise, the Most Loving, Merciful Lord of all.

For us to be freed from the limitations of our own "bubble" and merged in the ocean can in no way be determined by the bubble. Everything has been decreed, by the Divine Will, written on a preserved tablet before time existed. What was magnetizing and calling us from the beginning is that which we find, awaiting us, at the end.

In the beginningless beginning, thousands of years before anything had come into existence, the light of Muhammad (saw) was bowing in adoration before the Lord of Majesty and Glory. It was through this extended act of pure worship that all things came into existence, and that is why the natural inclination of all things is to worship and praise the One of Infinite Grace who created them.

Unfortunately, the majority of creations, especially those in human form who have the greatest capacity to worship the Lord, have lost contact with that natural state of love and praise. But the light of Muhammad (saw), which existed before anything else had been created, continues to exist and shine within us all, whether we realize it or not.

As we discover this light within us, which dispels the darkness, perpetually loving and serving the Creator of all, we come to know with ever-deepening certitude that this light is the source of our salvation and the means of our spiritual ascent.

With this ever-increasing knowledge growing within us, as much as we invoke, and welcome the light into our heart, we experience, with increasing clarity, the Divine Presence within our lives, within our beings. We realize what it is by what it does, how it transforms us, how it enables to see what we never saw—what we could not even imagine seeing before.

As this light, which we call *Nur Muhammadiyyah* continues to dispel the darkness and obscurity, veil by veil, within us, revealing to us the illuminated path that leads us to our Lord, we realize how hidden a mystery in our world is the truth about who Muhammad (saw) really was, and what he truly brought to humankind, and we consider, with amazement, how deceived and misguided are those who feel that they can make cartoons denigrating Muhammad, the most exalted of God's creation.

We understand that this is simply a result of centuries of profound misinformation and misguidance.

But the One of Infinite Mercy and Love leads to His Light whom He wills. And we deeply thank Him for blessing us to be amongst those He has guided to discover the Truth that is hidden like the *sun* behind the clouds. And since that brilliant *sun* has revealed to us even some of the rays of its divine splendor, we, too, bear witness to its illuminating radiance, along with all those who this light has illumined.

I speak to you, dear reader, not as one born Muslim, proud and defensive of my religion saying to you that *my religion* is better than *your religion*. No, I am writing to you only to share with you my experience of light dispelling darkness, the light of wisdom illuminating realm after realm, as the journey proceeds in the direction of its Goal.

When I was young and read the stories of those who set out on the spiritual journey, I was thrilled and amazed to contemplate that a human being could make such a journey, and, overcoming so many obstacles and ordeals, could reach the Divine destination. It was in this way that the *Unseen* caught my attention and laid claim to my life.

Now, what a wonder, so many years of traveling later, *I* am the person writing the story about the spiritual journey, and all of the obstacles and tests I had to face and overcome. Perhaps, God willing, someone reading this book will then be inspired to make the journey. That, indeed, would be another great wonder. It is in such a way that seeds, distributed by the wind, fall into fertile ground, souls are invited to return to their Lord, and the message is spread.

Wherever you may be in the course of your search, I encourage you, o traveler, to keep traveling. Seek true guidance, and never cease to yearn to attain the Goal. Know that surely, with difficulty comes ease, and the ease, which will sustain us through any difficulty we may have to face, is the love of the Creator, which created us and wills us ultimately to unite with His Infinite Bounty.

It was that Bountiful Grace that called and guided me. I set out knowing nothing about where I was going, impelled only by the deep instinct to seek for the path of Truth.

As I was moved from one place to the next, assuredly, I did not choose to go where I went, to see what I saw, or learn what I learned. I did not write the script for this rather amazing story; the itinerary of both the outer and the inner journey was revealed to me.

Even the writing of this book has been a most unusual experience in which the teachings—the points I am to share with you—come forth on the page. I do not choose what to write. I think about a certain day in my life, and everything seems to fade away except the teachings—the shining points of knowledge that were given on that day. So many things about my life I have forgotten, but this is what I truly remember—these points I have been sharing with you—these understandings, which unfolded for me along the way.

In sharing with you this array of points, I do not want to make you believe what I believe, but only for you to contemplate the possibilities!

When I say that I was guided by light from God, which led me through many realms, truly I did not know what to call it as it was guiding me. I came to know and then define it in accordance with my level of understanding at each stage of the journey.

When I arrived at the monastery, I experienced that the *man of light* whose presence I felt within was connected to the Prophet Jesus (as). In *El Khalil* the place of the *friend*, where the Prophet Abraham (as) and many members of his family are buried, I felt that the light within me was connected to the Prophet Abraham (as) and that I, too, was truly a member of his family.

Then, when I prayed on Mount Hira in the blessed cave where the Prophet Muhammad (saw) had meditated, prayed, and received the revelation of the Holy Qur'an, I understood and experienced that the light which had been guiding me through all the states and stations was the *Nur-Muhammadiyyah* , the light of the one who is praised because he is the one who is most deeply perpetually immersed in praise.

What was revealed stage by stage was not a comparison or competition between religions but one continuous revelation of the Divine Truth. There is only one Light—one Divine Reality that sent and guided all the prophets (as)—all the people of God. As the Holy Qur'an tells us:

> *The Messenger believeth in what has been revealed to him from his Lord, as do the men of faith. Each one believeth in Allah, His angels, His Books and His messengers. "We make no distinction (they say) between one and another of His messengers." And they say: "We hear and we obey. We seek Thy forgiveness our Lord, and to Thee is the end of all journeys."*

The Holy Qur'an 2:285

Bringing to completion all of the messages brought by all of the prophets and messengers (as) who came before, the Prophet Muhammad (saw) is called *Khatimil Nabiyyin*, the Seal of the Prophets. He was sent by the One Who sent all who came before him to complete the messages they brought, not to deny them.

This realization in itself is the key to a great paradigm shift for humanity. After so many centuries of bloodshed in the name of *"my religion is better than your religion,"* would it not be wonderful if we could realize that there are not *many* religions, but only a continuity of the Revelations of One Truth?

In the course of moving through the stages of understanding, this is what was revealed to me. This is what I came to realize with certainty. Having come to this realization by means that are beyond my own fathoming, I offer it to you. Please investigate this concept and see what you find, yourself.

23

The Circle Is Complete

The story continues, dear reader. Having come to realize, with certitude, that the Prophet Muhammad (saw) was the Last Prophet, who brought the completion of what was brought by all the prophets (as) who came before him, I deeply wanted to understand and experience what it was that he brought to us as the *Gift* from God.

To the best of my ability I studied the Message he was sent to bring from the Lord, following the commandments and avoiding what was forbidden, always yearning to understand more deeply what these words meant and what real bearing they had on my life. I had studied for years searching for the meanings of this Message— what the Creator was saying to us, His creations, and how to manifest the reality of these words in all the dimensions of my life.

I yearned to know the inner meanings of these words, and the secrets that they contained. I had read and heard about the profound mystical science which awakens the inner knowledge of the meanings of the Qur'an which would guide me directly to the One who sent this Message to His creation, but this knowledge was not yet awakened in me and I longed to reach that ocean and become immersed in it.

But where could I find it and how could I become immersed in this ocean of knowledge? It was like everything else which occurred, in my journey—not something I could do myself. It was a treasure held in the *hand* of the Most Merciful to be bestowed as He willed.

I came to discover, as the mystery of the divine plan was revealed, that this treasure—this ocean of knowledge which He willed me to enter—was the gift of the light of the Holy Prophet (saw) entrusted to me and other sincere seekers through his pure descendants and followers.

This was the manifestation of the divine plan. Beginning as it did in the house of *BaniIsrail*, by the Grace of the One Most Merciful, my journey was completed in the house of *Ahl'Bait*, the family of the Prophet Muhammad (saw). This was the completion of the circle mentioned earlier. And within the completion of the circle came the keys to spiritual ascent.

How did this manifest in time and space? Shortly before I went to India on the *mission of healing and peace*, I was guided to attend a conference celebrating the ascension of the Prophet (saw) held in Columbia, South Carolina. As soon as I saw a flier for this gathering, I had the deep sense that I must go and participate in it. There was no doubt about this. As ever, the *hand* of the Merciful One was moving me.

I boarded the train and felt, as the train gently rolled down the tracks, that I was being carried to the next dimension of understanding and knowing. I went to sleep and had a very beautiful dream. In the dream, I was told, *"Tomorrow, you will meet the people of paradise."*

I arrived in Columbia at three o'clock in the morning and was greeted by a wonderful person named Sheima who took me to her apartment to stay. Some hours later, the organizer of the conference, Zain, came to visit, since she was helping him with the organization of the conference. She introduced him to me. After he had spoken to me for several minutes and learned something about my journey, he asked me if I could please make a presentation at the conference. I said – of course, it would be my pleasure. I was inspired to speak about the subject *The Beauty of Islam*, not about architecture and art, but about the beauty in the heart and soul of the people who love and surrender to the One Most Loving and Most Beautiful. Although I had nothing at all prepared, the speech flowed like a river into its source. I was inspired, simply by looking into the beautiful faces of those who were listening, felt that I had always known them, and that these were, as the dream had foretold, people of paradise I was destined to meet. That was the night that I met Sheikh Harun Rashid Faye, who would be my guide to the inner realms, and his circle of companions, the *fuqara* of Monck's Corner.

Issa and I went to visit the Sheikh and his community in his mosque in Monck's Corner a little later. He made a prayer for us that touched us very deeply. I had the sense that he knew us, and our spiritual potential, in a profound way. He was extremely kind and loving to us and to everyone. With the community we sang beautiful songs of remembrance (*zikr*), which strongly evoked the love and the presence of the Holy Prophet (saw). So it was filled with love of Allah and His Prophet (saw) that I set out to drive on the night journey back to Philadelphia and sang the *zikr* the whole trip back.

A few days later I flew to India for the journey to places in peril described earlier. When Sheikh Aly said to me that the circle was complete, and I should prepare to rise, I sensed subtly and deeply the spiritual impact of our meeting with Sheikh Harun in South Carolina.

Shortly after emerging from the hospital the second time, walking, step by step, down the corridor with the knowledge that my life had been preserved with a purpose, I returned to South Carolina to speak at another conference and more importantly, to learn what that purpose was and how to fulfill it. The more time that we spent with Sheikh Harun and his community, the more certain both Issa and I were that he held in his hands the keys of divine knowledge that would open the doors of our spiritual awakening, enabling us to become truly activated inspired servants of the Divine.

As we watched the Sheikh in action every moment of the day serving and caring for everyone, teaching from such a deep level divine knowledge in its essence and, as well, in its application, we wanted to go to the source of what was really moving him, what gave him such tireless energy to give all that he had for the sake of God? By what means were the secrets of the spiritual path placed in his hands? What profound source of generosity enabled him to give this knowledge so profusely to those who surrounded him? By what blessed decree had he become, thus, an agent and vehicle through which the *Nur-muhammadiyyah* was shining, transforming all the lives it was blessing, including our own?

Unraveling the divine mystery, by turning to the source, I learned about the extraordinary house in Senegal, West Africa, in which Sheikh Harun grew up, a house totally dedicated, to the dissemination of divine knowledge, a house, which became a center of light and enlightenment for the countless numbers of people that frequented it.

I deeply felt that the divine treasure, the legacy of the Holy Prophet (saw) had been passed through the generations, by means of an unbroken chain, to the people of this house, whose blessed duty was to share it with the seekers of divine truth throughout the world.

I came to learn about how profoundly inspired were each of the beings, who were pillars of light in this dynamic divine work, the blessed mother of Sheikh Harun named Khadijatu Kubra (ra) who transmitted to countless beings the light of the Holy Qur'an, Sheikh Samba Gueye (ra), his grandfather who had made of his home a great center of learning and spiritual transformation, and Sheikh Moustafa Gueye Heydar (ra), his uncle and Sheikh who would mobilize his journey and his mission in Senegal and around the world.

Whatever was to come to pass that would transform the lives of myself and so many others began in this humble, deeply dedicated house, which was a repository of blessings, a treasury of the secret knowledge of Allah, *subhanawata'ala*.

Setting out on the quest, from Hollywood and then Berkeley California, how could I have imagined that I would finally arrive at this storehouse of the divine secrets and mysteries? It is a wonder to me even now, ever more so, as the gift of each teaching unfolds, but I know that, as God willed it, this is the knowledge that truly I had always sought, the knowledge, which had been magnetizing me from the start.

Sheikh Samba Gueye (ra) to whom this divine treasure had been passed down from one noble representative to the next, through forty-four generations from the Holy Prophet (saw) knew what powerful medicine, what powerful tools had been placed in his hands, and so, as he was guided, he made of his home a school of divine teachings that was filled with students day and night. The students in this school of light were seated in concentric circles, each circle receiving a different level of knowledge and training.

The Sheikh's daughter, his first-born, Khadijah (ra), and his son, Sheikh Mustafa (ra) were, as God willed it, at the epicenter of this transmission and transformation.

Khadijatu Kubra (ra) set the highest standard for women on the path to God. She was fully immersed in the light of the Holy Qur'an and transmitted that powerful light and blessing to all who she met, all who were blessed to receive the wonderful divine teaching that passed through her. Her son, Sheikh Harun (amongst many others greatly blessed by knowing her) never ceases to bear witness to the immense impact his mother's prayers and teachings had upon his life and work.

Her brother, Sheikh Mustafa (ra) also had an immense role to play in the transmission of the light of Muhammad (saw) to the sincere hearts and souls, wherever they were, who were seeking Divine Truth.

Sheikh Mustafa (ra) was pious and inspired from birth. He was one designated to receive the bounties of his Lord and to transmit these bounties to the creations, who were spiritually dwelling in dry, parched lands, awaiting the descent of the rain of grace.

Born into such an illustrious and blessed family, he was destined by Allah *subhanawata'ala* to receive the wealth of blessing and manifest it throughout his life.

As a young man, when other young men were drinking, dancing, and searching for women, Sheikh Mustafa (ra) went into seclusion in search of divine illumination (*ilham*) and guidance (*hidaya*). When he was seventeen years old, reading about the life of the Prophet (saw) he became overwhelmed, by the longing to see the Prophet (saw), and so he wrote:

> *O Allah! Answerer of all our prayers! O Allah!*
> *Grant us visitations from Al Mustafa (Prophet Muhammad)*
> *that will give us honor both in the unseen and manifest in the open*
> *for our eyes to see, O Allah! O Allah!*
> *Visit us (O Mustafa) out of your generosity with the best of all*
> *visits so that our hearts can be cured as well as our eyes, O Allah!*

In his twenty-third year, deep in seclusion in a village near the city of St. Luis, he was then visited by the Holy Prophet (saw) who placed in his hand the *wird* (a blessed series of prayers to be used every day in invocation) and a *tariqat* (school of *Tasawwuf*), which was to be called the *Mustafawiyya* or *Muhammadun Tariqat*.

At the age of twenty-three, Sheikh Mustafa (ra) was the youngest person ever to enter the *dairat'ul awliya* (the divine assembly of illuminated ones). The Sheikh (ra) lived a secluded life-style, very rarely going out, because his inner life was so utterly complete, full of the love of Allah (*subhanawata'ala*) and the light of His Messenger (saw).

Totally illuminated, intoxicated with the love of Allah, he never went out to advertise what it is that he had to offer to the seekers. But the true seekers, (from the most humble, to the leaders of lands) wherever they were, were magnetized by the light of the piety of his being and direct connection to the Divine, and so they came to see him, in his abode to receive the great gifts that the One of Infinite Mercy had to give through him.

And I, along with the other sincere seekers, was guided to this house, and this holy assembly—guided around the world so many times, from one station to the next, one level of understanding to the next, until, at last I reached the holy destination I had been seeking, with great hope and a secret inner knowledge, from the beginning.

By the Grace—the All-Powerful Will—of Allah, Most Merciful, Most Wise, were my steps guided, step-by-step, ultimately to this resplendent abode, this treasury of the Divine Secrets illuminated by the light of Muhammad (saw), known as the *Mustafawiyya Tariqat*, the way of Muhammad, a path of pure service, knowledge, exaltation and victory leading directly to the Divine.

> *The light of the most meritorious of humankind removed the veil from my eyes, so they could see the essence of the Prophet, during the state of witnessing in the unseen realm of the universe.*
>
> *He unveiled for me, secrets of the unseen and presented himself to me without a blemish, erasing sins and sorrow in his honorable circle.*
>
> *I was honored sitting therein as he chose me from amongst the many. He protected me from harm and taught me from his wisdoms.*
>
> *Praising him causes me to drink from the cup of his openings.*
>
> *From his existence I was conferred lights, like continuous rain.*
>
> *I attained that (spiritual) drinking point from those who were noble in their manners.*

That is what is desired and sought by those who are most firmly rooted on the path.

The guidance of the Prophet leads my way, unveiling my Lord for me. He does away with my faults, a station of eternal adornment.

He unveiled for me the secret of (spiritual) arrival as well as the knowledge of the hearts and of existence.

That is the gift from His pre-existent excellence that comes with (divine) witnessing.

His book is from Ar-Rahim, the Compassionate, and he is the agent for those who want to visit the beautiful garden.

O Allah! Give me the book (of my deeds) upon the Day of Reckoning with the Prophets and the Companions and every great triumph.

That would be the best of endings, having reward and completion and the attainment of the shade of the Prophet's cloud along with lasting goodness.

Grant us, by him, openings with salvation and piety and the achievement of brilliance with Mustafa as the example for character.

Grant us, by him and by Your noble countenance, enlightenment with our every glance, and profound bliss.

He will be the benefit of protection for the souls in the eyes of Al-Quddus (the Holy), allowing them to gain victory and the privilege of drinking from the cups (of love) on the Day when all peoples will stand for reckoning.

Sheikh Mustafa Gueye Heydar
Excerpts from Bahr'ul-Muhit,
The Vast Ocean

24

The Way of Muhammad, Mercy for All the Worlds

As Manifested in the Life and Community of Sheikh Harun Rashid Faye, My Guide to the Inner Realms

Light upon light.
Allah leads to His light whom He wills.
Allah speaks to humankind in parables.
And He is the Knower of all things.

The Holy Qur'an 24:35

As for those who fear their Lord unseen, for them is Forgiveness and a great Reward.
And whether ye hide your word or publish it, He certainly has (full) knowledge, of the secrets of (all) hearts.
Should He not know, He that created? And He is the One that understands the finest mysteries (and) is well-acquainted (with them).

The Holy Qur'an 67:12–14

With Him are the keys of the unseen; none knows them but He. He knows what is in land and sea; not a leaf falls, but He knows it. Not a grain in the deep darkness of the earth, not a thing green or dry but it is in a clear Book.

The Holy Qur'an 6:59

O Seeker of Truth! How amazing and overwhelming it is to contemplate and begin to truly grasp that God, our Beloved Lord, knows everything we are doing. He knows everything that is happening everywhere.

He is with us every moment of the day and night. He walks with us everywhere we go in search of Him. He hears every prayer we utter in the inmost depths of our heart and soul. For it is He who inspired and brought that prayer to life within us, the Lord of boundless Compassion and Love, the Eternal Guide, the unfathomably boundless Source of Divine Knowledge, that *Treasure* that willed to be known.

From the moment I received the message as a child, "*Seek, and the Truth shall make you free*," as much as I could, I dedicated myself to seeking that Truth.

And yet, how much more powerfully, did that Truth seek me. When we take one step toward the Bountiful Source, we are told, He takes (and has already taken) ten steps, a hundred steps, *a thousand steps* toward us, for how much infinitely greater are the steps of the Creator than ours.

And that is why I say *not* that I decided to move wherever I liked on the face of the earth, but, instead, only that I yearned for God, and I was *moved,* by His Power, and Grace, towards the wondrous Goal. I took one step, as it were, off the edge of a cliff and He enabled me to fly into the unknown realms.

I set out on a journey, having no idea where I was going, or what I was actually seeking, but it is He guided my steps on the journey leading certainly to Him. Where I was inspired to go and the places where I arrived were not determined by me but by One who knew me and the places I was destined to go far better than I knew myself or where the journey was leading me.

The Holy Qur'an tells us, "*Wherever you turn, there is the Face of God*" (The Holy Qur'an 2:115).

From the time we took our first steps, and learned to speak, He was there, but we did not know how to perceive and acknowledge His Presence. In one way or another, He kept calling, "Come closer, My dear servant, draw near!"

I heard that *call*, night and day, and that is why I say I felt that, like a magnet, He was seeking and pulling me. He is seeking us! Calling us! If only we could open our eyes and see, open the ears of our heart and hear, and then, gratefully, obey.

Through the veils I traveled, internally and externally, guided and propelled. What I found in the end, was, in fact, guiding me from the very beginning, but I did not know what it was, that magnet, that *light* shining, through all the veils.

It is the light shining at the end of the tunnel, and also at the beginning, and, truly, all the way through. However dark that tunnel we are passing through may appear to us to be, the light and power of our Creator is shining *within* us, sustaining us, empowering and directing our blood to circulate perfectly, our heart to beat, our eyes to see. Why are we not aware of this? Why are we not grateful for the wondrous gifts that every moment we are being given?

There are countless miracles of His Grace taking place at this very moment, and no matter what we think that *we* are going through, we must not overlook these wondrous signs of His Presence and Power, which are keeping us alive, sustaining us in every way, and subtly revealing to us the ways to return to our Source.

The great journey is long, intensive, and challenging. Along the way, we may get distracted, get caught up in a detail, and forget the great ideals, which motivated us to journey to our Lord. We may have a pain, a wound, a weakness, or illness and we become completely absorbed in and focused upon this dysfunction, this distress, this disease.

But as we focus only upon the dysfunction, the illness, this one area of blockage or distress, we are not conscious of all the billions of molecules and cells within us that are functioning perfectly, swimming along in perfect harmony, which by their very existence, as they flow in the divinely orchestrated dance, are proclaiming His Praise.

Although we may be sick in one part of our being, we are not aware of how well we truly are, not aware of that Power, that Love that is directing the divine dance of the billions of cells and molecules within us, just as It is directing the dance of the planets and stars in the galaxies above.

And He, the Best of Planners, will guide our steps, guide our thoughts and awareness if we allow Him to, just as He is flawlessly directing all of our molecules and cells. He will guide our spiritual evolution, bless and direct our journey to the degree that we place our life and direction in His all-powerful *Hand*.

We realize what an amazing story it is—this journey of our life—only when we begin to see with certainty, *What* is behind all the appearances, what Power is making everything move. This is what I have learned and I am learning from the story of my life.

It is not the story of me, the small leaf blown in the wind that is important, but what Wind blew this leaf, to what places, what stations it was blown, and for what purpose it was blown from one place to the next.

So many years of a life have passed by and I am now assessing all this, contemplating the countless signs. I have hoped and prayed that the story would have a happy ending, both for me and for you, o seeker of Truth. And I believe, God willing, that this journey does lead to an abode of eternal joy and peace, if only we hear the words of Truth, follow the way ordained for us by His love and grace, and gratefully obey.

We have been given a heavenly invitation, and we have the choice to accept or reject it.

What makes the ending happy is the acceptance of the Divine *gift*.

What Allah *subhana wa ta'ala* inspired me to seek for from the beginning, I saw manifesting before my eyes in the end.

The weathered traveler, having journeyed through so many deserts, up steep mountain slopes, across rivers and seas, and down into deep ravines, in search of the way that leads to God, came, at last, upon an oasis, a place at once of peace and of intensive training, of vital restoration and transformation.

And what was this inspiring, sustaining vision that I came to see—an exalted vision, manifesting in real life? It was a community guided and inspired by the light of Allah (*subhana wa ta 'ala*) and His Messenger (saw).

I had arrived in a station in which I could see the stained glass window of my life become complete, and I could see that the light I had been arduously seeking was shining through my very being. Finally all the understandings bestowed upon me along the way, were integrated into the illuminated picture, all as signs of the existence of the Eternal Guide, the One Most Loving and Kind.

Thus, it was to such an oasis of divinely inspired life, that the Most Merciful ultimately guided me—a manifest vision of light and hope shining in the middle of a world shaken, to its core, by the forces of destruction, which threaten to imperil its very existence.

Appearing in the midst of this world of confusion, this endless desert of the world disconnected from its source, what kind of oasis is this? What is the nature of the water flowing from this wellspring, the restoration, inspiration, illumination, guidance, and peace that I found here?

And what relevance or significance does this have to you, dear reader, who have traveled with me through all the pages, states and stations of the journey manifested in this book?

The water flowing in this oasis is Divine Love and Knowledge, from which all thirsty travelers are invited to drink. In the midst of the world shaken and shattered by war fueled by constant conflict between worldly powers, with their unholy agendas and ideologies, it is an oasis filled with divine guidance, inspiration, and peace.

In the midst of the world bitterly scarred by the brutal wounds of racism and slavery, it is a flower garden filled and made more beautiful by the different colors of the flowers growing together, a place in which all colors, all races, are united, in one humanity, as the Creator willed it to be.

In a world in which so many children are tragically "left behind" with no real education and training for their life's journey, it is a place where children are given real knowledge, abundant love and deep training, from the moment that they begin to see. And when each child begins to walk, he or she is walking on the path to God. When he or she begins to speak, it is with the words of God's remembrance.

These children, brought up by the light of God on His path become ambassadors of peace and illumination, ambassadors without borders, and teachers of divine knowledge for the world so much in need of peace and light.

In the midst of a world in which women are often discounted, abused, and debased, it is a place in which women and men, as well as children, are appreciated for who they truly are, and equally guided directly and profoundly on the path to liberation and fulfillment, as the Creator, in His Mercy, has willed it.

In the midst of a world in which the elderly, ailing, and disabled are so often cast away and locked up in homes or simply abandoned in the streets, a world in which the poor have no chance to better their condition, no advocacy at all, I found a gathering of beings specifically, intentionally caring for the needs of everyone, especially concerned with the needs of those who are helpless to care for themselves.

In the midst of a world filled with music, dance, and entertainment specifically aimed to distract, and seduce, I arrived in the presence of a circle of souls immersed day and night in *zikr*, the profound remembrance and continual invocation of God.

In the midst of a world in which the majority of people passionately seek the *freedom* to do whatever they want, it is a community (*ummah*) profoundly pursuing the path towards the liberation that comes, from doing what the Creator, Most Merciful and Wise, wants us to do.

What kind of *oasis* was this that appeared in the course of the deep journey? And what made it such a beautiful vision for the eyes of the soul to behold? It was a community based inherently upon the pattern of living established by the Messenger of Allah (saw), guided by the Grace and Wisdom of the Creator (*subhana wa ta'ala*).

To understand this *pattern of living,* this deeply humane and compassionate mode of operation, to truly believe that it can and does exist, and to be guided in the direction it is going, we need to know with ever deepening knowledge who the Prophet Muhammad, the Messenger of Allah (saw) truly was, contemplating the profound meaning of the passage in the Qur'an, in which Allah (*subhanawata'ala*) says to the Prophet (saw):

> *We have sent you not except as a mercy for all the worlds.*
> The Holy Qur'an 21:107

It is crucially important for us, the creations of the one God, to realize this: that Muhammad (saw), the last of the line of prophets (as), was sent not to bring terror, but to bring *mercy* to the worlds. The realization of this divine truth will heal, exalt and transform our lives and our world.

For those who have been brought up to fear Islam and Muhammad as the *enemy*, the great threat, fear, of what we were told Muhammad was, will be replaced by *knowledge* that he was created and sent, to all the worlds, as a mercy, light, and healing for us all.

For those who have been brought up in a world of intense struggle, conflict, and war, tragically, to become terrorists, even as children, how great would be the impact upon their lives, their destinies, and their practice of Islam, if they could learn and begin to experience the real meaning of these words: *Muhammad was not sent but as a mercy to all the worlds.*

What is needed for those growing up in Islam is the opposite of training in terrorist camps; it is training in the curriculum of the compassion and love of Allah and all of His beautiful qualities, including justice and wisdom. These are the qualities, the tools, most necessary for fighting the war against oppression and injustice, as well as against terror and terrorism.

It is the *Islam,* which is the manifestation of divine mercy, justice, knowledge and peace that these children need to learn about and be nurtured by. This grace is what will save and exalt all our lives, in this world and the next.

The Prophet Muhammad (saw), in contrast to what we may have been led to believe, was the kindest, most charitable, most loving, and most just of human beings that have ever lived.

He loved the children and would shorten the prayer if even one child was crying, so caring was he for both the child and its mother. He cared so deeply for the poor that he fed everyone before himself, and so often went to bed hungry. His love and care for all extended to animals and trees. He guided those who followed him to be kind to all living beings.

He was sent to this world specifically to right the wrongs: to free those bound by slavery and grant them equal rights and status with their former masters, to protect the rights of orphans, the elderly, and the needy, and to create a community within the human family in which every member is called upon to care for every other.

Islam, from its inception, spread as a result of such qualities of the Prophet (saw), his great kindness and forgiveness, as well as his profound piety and inspired diplomacy, as the Holy Qur'an describes:

> *It was by the Mercy of Allah that you dealt gently with them. And had you been harsh or hard of heart, they would have scattered away from you. Pardon them and seek forgiveness for them. And consult with them on the conduct of affairs. And when you are resolved, then put your (whole) trust in Allah. Surely Allah loves those who put their trust in Him.*

The Holy Qur'an 3:159

The divine beauty and grace manifesting through the Prophet (saw) were so overwhelming to the people around him, that, just by being in his presence, they were utterly transformed. Khalid Ibn Walid (ra), one of the worst and most skillful and dangerous enemies of the new Muslims, after a battle in which he bitterly attacked the Muslim army, entered the tent of the Prophet (saw) and was enabled, by the grace of Allah, to really see the Prophet (saw) for the first time.

Khalid (ra) was so overwhelmed by the light, the power, the beauty, kindness and grace pouring through the Holy Prophet (saw) that he immediately surrendered to that grace, embraced the reality of Islam, and, from that moment on, became one of Islam's greatest and most courageous supporters.

This beauty and grace, power and light that manifested through the Prophet (saw) radically transforming the lives of the people who encountered him, is not something we learned about as we were growing up in America.

His divinely inspired being, which not only transformed the lives of those who lived with him, but has continued to transform the lives of billions of people who have remembered him and invoked his presence ever since, is a divine mystery that has been very much hidden to many of us growing up in the non-Islamic world. And we have been led to believe things about him that are greatly contrary to the truth. And that is why the *discovery and experience* of the mercy he was sent to bring so much transforms the life and understanding of all those who finally receive it.

The stories of the kindness, compassion, and love as they were shown in the life of the Prophet (saw) as well as the great wisdom and diplomacy that he manifested and taught his Companions (ra) to manifest fill vast volumes. But they are seldom read with deep (*life-transforming*) sincerity and less often comprehended and implemented with wisdom. And that is why the light of true Islam is obscured like a brilliant sun that is hidden behind dark clouds.

Many of the things being done in the *name* of Islam like much of what have been done in the name of *religion* throughout the ages present to those who have not penetrated the veils, a perception of Islam and all religions that is absolutely contrary to the teachings sent by the Creator through the prophets and messengers (as) to humankind, revealing to us the way that the One Most Merciful wishes us to live and interact with other living beings.

To begin to clarify this deep misrepresentation, misinterpretation and misunderstanding, let us replace the word *hate* with *love*, and then experience the way that love illuminates the teachings and makes these teachings come to life.

For the pure teachings coming from the Merciful Source to be truly comprehended and put into action is what is so greatly needed today to end the wars, heal the wounds, and guide the souls, wandering and lost in darkness, to the clarity and light of the path, taught by all the prophets and messengers (as) leading most directly to the Merciful Lord.

It was this divinely inspired way of living that I discovered unfolding in the small town of Monck's Corner, South Carolina as in the holy land of Senegal, West Africa. After the Prophet Muhammad (saw), there will be no more prophets (as). He was the last and the Seal of the prophets (as).

But there are the heirs—the custodians—of the wealth of knowledge he received from the Source of illumination and bequeathed to humankind. They are the real Sufis.

This distribution of wealth coming from the divine treasury is what drew my soul, ultimately to unite with the *Tariqat Mustafawiyya*, a pure and beautiful manifestation of the *Way of Muhammad* (saw).

What does this mean? How does this work manifest? What do we see and how do we experience what is taking place?

What I saw was that the teachings of the Qur'an and *ahadith* that I had read and loved so much were manifesting in life. Beautiful passages that had so much inspired me were emerging, from the page, into life.

> And the believing men and the believing women, they are protecting friends one of another; they enjoin the right and forbid the wrong, and they establish regular prayers and they pay the poor-due, and they obey Allah and His Messenger. As for these, Allah will have mercy on them. Undoubtedly, Allah is Mighty, Wise.

The Holy Qur'an 9:71

And when they hear what has been revealed to the Messenger, you will see their eyes overflowing with tears because of their recognition of the truth. They say: "Our Lord, we believe, then, inscribe us as among the witnesses (of truth)."

The Holy Qur'an 5:83

And the Prophet Muhammad (saw) said:

"What actions are most excellent?
To gladden the heart of a human being,
To feed the hungry,
To help the afflicted,
To lighten the sorrow of the sorrowful,
To remove the wrongs of the injured.
That person is the most beloved of God
who does the most good to God's creatures."

Such were the qualities and actions, the states of being, understanding, realization, and love that I saw manifesting in many different ways within the assembly of souls, that assembly of the *ummah* to which I had ultimately been guided.

What I perceived on the outside was, as it always is, a mirror reflecting what was coalescing within me. I had thus arrived in the realm, or station, in which I saw the beautiful teachings of the Qur'an, the teachings sent to us by our Creator Most Loving, Most Kind, manifesting before and within me.

Every step I had taken in the journey led finally to this unfolding state of awareness. In what place or station had Allah willed the traveler to arrive? It is a station in which, one by one, the words and teachings of the Holy Qur'an and other Scriptures become alive. It was this awareness arising within me that made realize the special nature of the place to which I had come.

This teaching was being transmitted by Sheikh Harun both internally, specifically as he led me through a series of deeply guided retreats, referred to as *khalwah*, and externally, in the sense that I was able to perceive these living truths in the actions and activities of the Sheikh, and the ever-expanding circle of those that he was training.

Shortly after I met him, I saw the Sheikh in a dream. He was standing in the center of a brilliant swirling vortex of light. I was able to see, fading in and out of that vortex of light, the forms of his students—his companions, all the lives that he was inspiring and empowering.

Later I saw Sheikh Harun standing in a parking lot surrounded by the *fuqara*, his circle of students. He was wearing a white robe and a red *kufi* (prayer hat), whereas in the dream, he had been wearing a white robe and a red turban. From this moment on, I saw, powerfully manifesting in life what I had seen in the epiphany of the dream.

I witnessed the Sheikh as the *catalyst*, galvanizing the circle, by the power of Allah and the blessings of the Prophet (saw) manifesting through him, igniting the souls of all those surrounding him, so that each one of his students was inspired and energized to make the real journey and, station by station, proceed to accomplish what he or she was created to do.

I could see that the Sheikh was not appearing as a figure-head, an idol to be worshipped by those following him, or a distant venerated figure that the disciples were lucky even, rarely, to see. He was manifesting as light of guidance within them, an extremely vital element in their lives and spiritual journey, a powerful catalyst activating their transformation and elevation.

Such a noble, humble, and empowered teacher, one authorized by the Divine to teach the deepest truths, is not looking for disciples, but for companions. He does not want to imprison his companions for life, but to set everyone free. The disciples are not to remain disciples for life, but every capable person is trained to become a Sheikh or Sheikha, teacher or friend, who will then continue to catalyze and transform others.

The amazing tool that the Sheikh wields by the power of Allah, the instrument of transformation, is divine knowledge made manifest in action. The Sheikh teaches by example, and the example that he, himself, embodies, is one that profoundly follows the example set by the Messenger of Allah (saw).

To study with and be guided by such a person, who is the living heir of the transmission of all the prophets (as), is to witness the teachings of the Holy Qur'an and all Divine Scriptures continuously manifesting in everything that is taking place in our lives.

Much of the Qur'an was revealed in the context of what exactly was taking place in the lives of the Prophet (saw) and his Companions (as). From this we learn that the wisdom revealed to us by our Creator is not abstract, but can and should be applied to all the dimensions of our life in this world.

This is the kind of profound practical teaching we gain as we travel inwardly and outwardly with such a Sheikh. Living and studying with such a teacher is a deep and dynamic way of coming to understand the real meaning of the Message of God and how it impacts upon human beings who are truly open and surrendered to it.

Shortly after I made the *bayat* (affirmed allegiance to the Creator, by the light of the Prophet (saw) through allegiance to the Sheikh).

> *Verily, those who give thee their allegiance, they give it but to Allah Himself.*
>
> The Holy Qur'an 48:10

I was standing in line with the Sheikh at Rite Aid. Behind us was a young woman in a wheel chair, handicapped, both physically and mentally. His first impulse was to put her before us, then he paid her bill, and then he put money in her hand. I came to see, as time went on, that this is how he *always* acts.

William Penn spoke, in a beautiful statement about this inclination to goodness and the importance of utilizing every opportunity to express it, when he said,

> *"If there is any kindness I can show, or any good thing I can do to any fellow being, let me do it now, and do not deter or neglect it, as I shall not pass this way again."*

To be profoundly inclined to goodness, kindness and charity for the sake of God, Who is Most Loving and Kind, is the *sunnah* of the Prophet (saw), divine knowledge manifested continuously in action. It is the way that, in any situation, the prophets (as)—those who are representatives of God on earth—would have acted; it is the way that most purely and directly manifests the Divine Qualities. It is the way that the Creator, Most Merciful, wills and guides His servants to be.

Such a person, a true Sheikh who, following the example of the prophets (as), is an agent for the manifestation of God's mercy on earth, will go out in search of those who are hungry and needy if they have not already lined up at his door, seeking food and help. He (or she) will spend sleepless nights praying and seeking divine guidance for everyone that is linked to him in any way, everyone he will ever know, as well as those that he does not know. He will be continuously engaged in serving others, taking care of their needs on every level, never waiting to be, himself, served. This is the way a true Sheikh functions, and all those who follow him sincerely, all those who are being trained by him, become like this also.

Wherever such a Sheikh is, that house, that mosque, that corner (*zawiyyah*) of the universe will become a refuge for all, a place of profound healing in the remembrance (*zikr*) and supplication of Allah, open twenty-four hours a day, every day.

In this contemporary world, in which most mosques, churches, and synagogues are closed most of the time, this example of a place of refuge, healing, solace, nourishment, and continuous guidance precisely follows the pattern of the mosque built by the Prophet (saw) and his Companions (ra) in Medina, which was a sanctuary, clinic, and place of continual teaching and illumination for the believers.

The Prophet Muhammad (saw), except when he retired to a cave for periods of profound isolation and prayer, was always in the presence of his Companions (ra), always teaching them, always sharing with them. The proof of this is in the vast number of *ahadith* (records of what he said and did) that were written down by those who lived with him day and night.

A true Sheikh, who profoundly adheres to the *sunnah* established by the Prophet (saw), will, following his example, live and interact in deep spiritual intimacy with his companions, always aware of what they are going through and how to help them progress on the journey.

The true Sheikh, one who is carrying an unbroken chain of transmission, which he is empowered to give to the sincere disciple, perceives every disciple with x-ray vision. He sees what no one sees and feels what no one feels, and his love, which is divinely inspired, is thus powerfully transformative.

What may appear, to others, to be an abandoned lot, filled with weeds and even piles of trash, is, to him who sees its potential (what it can become), a fertile, bounteous garden filled with rare and beautiful flowers full of fragrance.

He sees the potential in every seed, which is lying dormant in the ground. And he has been entrusted with the life-giving water, which he pours upon the seeds, so that, one by one, they push through the soil, and, moment to moment, reveal the inherent beauty and fragrance, which each one possesses.

No ordinary love is this, but love, which knows about us what we know not, loving, and thus bringing to life, ever-deeper dimensions of our being—our spiritual potential—of which we were not even aware.

These are the seeds planted within us by our Creator when He created us.

He placed within us secrets and mysteries, which only a person of wisdom can see and make us know. These are the Divine Names which link us to our Lord, and when we know them, show us the way that He has decreed for us to return to Him as directly as possible. May every soul that is filled with longing to realize its true purpose be guided on a path that unlocks and activates these divine mysteries.

Connected to the physical body, but not limited by it, is our spiritual being that only a person of God can see. And this is what the Sheikh enables us, ourselves, to see on the inner journey, as veil after veil is penetrated. As we are purified and illuminated, we draw closer to our Lord, less and less obscured by the veils of the world and all that it contains, closer to realizing and fulfilling the purpose for which God created us.

In one after another of the inner journeys we are blessed to make, the Sheikh is inspired to know what words of the Holy Qur'an we are ready to read, behold, and understand. It is a feast that he is serving us in the depth of our solitude, of divine knowledge, that we assimilate and absorb.

No food that we have ever eaten is like this food. This food is the light of Allah, and by eating it we become light. Every divine word, every teaching that we assimilate illuminates our journey within.

And thus, on the inner journey, we come to realize that we, in our true nature, are composed of these beautiful words, the messages of our Lord, which are, one by one, being revealed to us and also bringing us back to Him.

Such is the medicine given to us in perfect doses to heal and transform everything within us, which has throughout our journey, blocked our progress and caused us to be separated from the pure Love, the Majesty and Bounty of our Beloved Lord.

This is the *divine therapy*. The Sheikh is the vehicle, the agent for the grace of Allah (*subhana wa ta'ala*) and His Messenger (saw). So *he* does not give, but the Most Merciful God, in His infinite generosity and love gives, through the agency of the Sheikh's guidance, whatever are the secrets of the knowledge that we are blessed to receive at every stage of our journey.

No journey in the outer world can compare to the journey that leads us to our Lord within us. Everything that we have gone through is only a preparation for this ultimate journey.

After all the conveyances, all the trains and planes, boats, buses and cars, I had traveled in on the journey in search of the Creator and the path that leads to Him, now I was being transported by His Words, His Revelations coming to life within me.

The inner journey is a journey of doorways within doorways and openings within openings. To arrive at each new level of realization, we have to go through a doorway, a process of transformation.

Just as we do in the outer journey, as we are traveling inward, we must deal with roadblocks, hardships and tests, yet deeper and more intense than what we have experienced in our outer journeys, because we are now encountering the very essence of everything within us that we need to truly understand and overcome.

But as we penetrate through each difficulty, and go through the door, we are blessed to enter the next radiant space, the next dimension of the knowledge and love that bring us closer and closer to the Presence our Lord.

We have to profoundly face our fears, pains, and all other negative attributes, and accept and understand them, in order to access that grace that has the power to overcome them utterly.

In one of the retreats, I went into the inner space, seeking the grace, the peace and light of my Lord. But what I saw within my heart, filling it, was a mass of bristling, electrified fibers intertwined with each other, vibrating intensely, filling the wide open space, with intensity. I understood: *This is what is blocking my heart. This is what is standing in my way.*

This configuration that I watched, fiercely burning and bristling, was somehow the embodiment of all the anxiety, fear and pain I had been carrying along with me throughout my life.

It was in a sense so terrifying to behold that I wished to *run out of the room*, but I did not move from my spot, continuing to focus intensely upon the prayer. I sensed that Satan had his hand on that mass. The satanic force was controlling that energy, and I had to summon the inner strength, the power of unshakable faith to overcome that force and send it out of the room.

I beseeched the One of Infinite Mercy and Grace to come and take this heart out of my body, wash it, purify it, liberate it and then put it back again, totally purified and renewed. I prayed and prayed, supplicating profoundly. No one came. No resplendent vision appeared. No words. No message....

But, at a certain moment, in the midst of the deep prayer, I realized—the space was entirely clear. That burning, bristling mass was completely gone. With what profound subtlety had the Most Subtle One (*Al-Latif*) cleansed and restored my heart?

The One of Infinite Mercy, Compassion, and Kindness is Formless. And so all that was obstructing and oppressing me was dispelled, outside of time, by One that I could not see.

Such is the miracle of the Kindness (*Al-Karim*) of our Creator, which, when we surrender to it, becomes the means by which we travel to Him. When we realize the depth of our powerlessness to make it through even the next step of our journey, His Power (*Al-Qawiy*) is the means by which we travel to Him.

When we are battling with the illusory force of our pain and fear, it is His Peace (*As-Salam*) flowing through our faithful heart that can easily dispel all this illusory pain and stress.

When our hearts or minds are closed, may we travel back to Him through His Attribute, the Opener (*Al-Fattah*). When we are broken and in need of restoration, may we travel by means of His Attribute, the Restorer (*Al-Mu'id*). When we seek protection and divine friendship—*Al-Wali*, the Protecting Friend. When we are in darkness, may we return to our Beloved Lord through His Attribute, *An-Nur*, the Light, and whatever may be our difficulty or need, we may travel to Him through His Attribute, *As-Samad*, the Satisfier of all needs.

The beautiful 99 Names of Allah are secret ways and means by which we can return to our Lord, leading us to the One that is Unfathomable and Un-nameable. The beautiful Names and the teachings that He has sent to us, are the very means by which we can make the journey back to Him.

Did we think like the builders of the Tower of Babel, that *we* could build a tower or create a means or method to reach Him? It is only by God's Grace and His Power and His Will that we can discover and follow the path that leads to Him. We have no ability on our own to make this journey. But only if we bow down and give all that we have to that Source of Infinite Bounty, can that One of Infinite Love give to us all that He has for us.

I saw this in the depth of my solitude where I went to draw closer to the Lord. But I know that it is the truth at all times and in all situations. Allah *subhana wa ta'ala* created us to worship Him, so that the infinite Treasure of His Existence could be known. At every moment that we accept what He is giving us, that gift is the power to dispel everything else. At every single moment of our life we can make this exchange... It is to bow down and give Him all that we have. In exchange for what we have given, and what we have given up, we receive what He has to give us—what a great exchange!

I also perceived in the inner journey, in the center of the courtyard of the space within, the fountain of *al kauthar*, abundant grace, ever overflowing with compassion. And I felt the wind of grace pass through my heart like a current, establishing a channel of peace flowing toward everyone I have ever known as well as to innumerable beings that I have never met.

I felt the love and forgiveness of God passing through my heart and moving in all directions. And I very sincerely hope that it has come through the pages of this book, to you!

This was the level of therapy that the Sheikh was teaching me as he guided me again and again to take refuge and do the necessary work in a series of spiritual retreats.

In one of the many inner journeys, I was sitting in the deep solitude of my room, meditating upon the dimensions and aspects of Allah, the Creator, the Fashioner, the One who brings forth all out of nothing, infinitely Glorious and full of Grace is He. I sat in my room meditating deeply upon the absolute power of the creativity of the Creator.

While contemplating this, the realization came to me that, everything surrounding me was man-made, the walls, the floor, the windows. Here, within the sacred space of the sanctuary of my room, the only thing that appeared to me as made by the Creator, that which was vitally alive, filled with the divine secrets, was the human being—the body and all that it contained. This was the

form fashioned by the great Creator in which He placed His treasures and His mysteries, such as His Divine Attributes, the *Asma'ul
Husna*, His Beautiful Names. Realizing this—how filled with His
grace was the creation that was my being—I was carried into the
zikr, the state of remembrance.

Entering deep into the recitation and remembrance of the
Names of Allah, (*subhana wa ta'ala*) I saw and felt them spinning
in all the cells and organs, in all the vital fluids circulating, in the
breath, in the heartbeat, in all the various systems which were
enabling this form to be sustained. This form, although vulnerable
and impermanent, subject to disease and inevitably to death, was,
in the moment, a theater in which the divine mysteries were manifesting, a living temple created by God as the place in which He
should be worshipped and known.

And the center of this mysterious creation is the heart. As the
Holy Prophet (saw) told us,

> *"There is a piece of flesh in the human body; if it is sound and well,
> then the entire body is sound and well and this is the heart."*

This is what the journey of transformation, the alchemical process was leading to. The purified heart, that heart freed of negativity
and cleansed of the worship and praise of anything other than the
One Eternal Lord was becoming a true sanctuary, the wide open
space, filled only with His Love.

That Love, which I found at last most clearly manifested, and
which was, most certainly, with me all along, is not specifically or
uniquely for me, but for us all. If only we could turn, with open
hearts, towards our Creator, who is the unlimited Plenitude of Mercy
and Love and receive the sustenance and grace, guidance and knowledge that He, in His Infinite Generosity, wills to bestow upon us.
Whoever and wherever we are, whatever we have to undergo of trials
in this earthly existence, may we be open to receive this gift of His
Love, and may we travel by means of this, back to our Beloved Lord!

As our eyes are opened, we can see these signs manifesting, both in everything that happens around us and in everything that happens within us. May we be the living witnesses who behold and acknowledge these signs!

Although this is an account of one person's travel, I truly believe that my story is linked with the spiritual journey of all beings. We all come from one Source and to that Source do we return. As I write, I write for every journeyer, every seeker of Truth, just as every step of the way, I walked with everyone; all seekers were walking within me. When I set out on the path in quest of Truth, I had no idea at all where I was going, where the quest would lead me. Only Allah knew. Only He, the All-Seeing, All-Knowing, saw and knew where the traveler was, in what state and station, every moment of this journey.

Once we have set out consciously on His path, we come to see that it is He who is our constant Companion, Witness, Healer, Helper, and Friend. It is to Him who has bestowed upon us all the infinite bounties and treasures discovered in the journey, that we offer our deepest gratitude, submission, and praise. And in this endless journey, leading us into the eternity of His Being, may we never cease to beseech our Beneficent Guide for the ever-unfolding gift of His Guidance.

> *"Allah unveils, unveiling with light.*
> *As You are the remover of coverings, remove my veil.*
> *Allah expands things, extending His benefits.*
> *As You are the Expander, expand my contentment.*
> *Allah heals imperceptibly, restoring to health.*
> *As You are the Healer, heal my debility.*
> *Allah gives prolifically, providing sustenance abundantly.*
> *As You give profusely, let my satisfaction overflow.*
> *Allah is acknowledged as the Sovereign,*
> *With open hands, to accept oaths.*
> *As You are the One Who accepts oaths of loyalty,*
> *Let every atom of my being be loyal to You."*

Sheikh Mustapha Haydar Gueye
The Remover of Coverings